THE TITANIC FILES (VOL. 1)

By the same author

Titanic: Psychic Forewarnings of a Tragedy (Patrick Stephens, 1988)

Lost at Sea: Ghost Ships and Other Mysteries, with Michael Goss (Prometheus Books, 1994)

Titanic: Safety, Speed and Sacrifice (Transportation Trails, 1997)

'Archie': The Life of Major Archibald Butt from Georgia to the Titanic (Lulu.com Press, 2010)

On Board RMS Titanic: Memories of the Maiden Voyage (Lulu.com Press, 2011)

A Death on the Titanic: The Loss of Major Archibald Butt (Lulu.com Press, 2011)

Voices from the Carpathia (Lulu.com Press, 2015)

Titanic Memoirs (three volumes, Lulu.com Press, 2015)

The Titanic Files: A Paranormal Sourcebook (Lulu.com Press, 2015)

Titanic: The Return Voyage (Lulu.com Press, 2019)

'Those Brave Fellows': The Last Hours of the Titanic's Band (Lulu.com Press, 2019)

The Titanic Disaster: A Medical Dossier (Lulu.com Press, 2021)

'There's Talk of an Iceberg': A Titanic Investigation (Lulu.com Press, 2021)

Fate Deals a Hand: The Titanic's Professional Gamblers (The History Press, 2023)

Titanic Collections, Volume 1 (The History Press, 2023)

Titanic Collections, Volume 2 (The History Press, 2024)

The Triumvirate (The History Press, 2024)

Titanic: Her Books and Bibliophiles (Lulu.com Press, 2024)

Titanic: A Disaster Foreseen? (Lulu Press, 2024)

COLLECTED WRITINGS ON RMS TITANIC

THE TITANIC FILES

(VOL. 1)

GEORGE BEHE

Cover illustrations
Front (left to right): Anna, Wiljo and John Hämäläinen (Author's collection); Sun Yat Sen the Pekingese, who was saved from the *Titanic* (Courtesy Randy Bigham); Captain Smith and Ben the Borzoi (Author's collection); Major Archibald Butt (Author's collection).
Back: A rare woven-in-silk postcard of the *Titanic*, pre-tragedy (Author's collection).

First published 2025
The History Press
97 St George's Place, Cheltenham,
Gloucestershire, GL50 3QB
www.thehistorypress.co.uk

British Library Cataloguing in Publication Data.
A catalogue record for this book is available from the British Library.

ISBN 978 1 80399 726 1

Typesetting and origination by The History Press
Printed and bound in Great Britain by TJ Books Limited, Padstow, Cornwall

Trees for Life

Table of Contents

Acknowledgements

I'd like to offer my sincere thanks to Don Lynch, Dr Paul Lee, Randy Bigham, Mike Poirier, Bill Sauder, Phil Gowan, Bruno Piola, Mike Herbold, John Lamoreau, Susanne Störmer and Hermann Söldner for their friendship and for their unfailing generosity in sharing their own research with me.

Thank you, everyone!

Introduction

For many years I have made a habit of filing away little titbits of information about *Titanic*-related topics that happened to catch my interest. I've used some of that information to write articles for the *Commutator* (the quarterly journal of the Titanic Historical Society) and for my own *Titanic* website, but many of my other files have gathered dust waiting for me to take a closer look at their contents. I've finally done something with that information, and the book you now hold in your hands is the result, a first volume presenting my own interpretation of some of these various topics connected with the disaster.

Some of the subject matter I've chosen to write about in this and future volumes is controversial, three examples being whether or not a haze existed around the *Titanic* on the night of the disaster, whether First Officer William Murdoch fired shots in anger before taking his own life, and whether or not Captain Smith attempted to save the life of a child when his ship went down. The Murdoch suicide question is especially contentious, since many 'officer groupies' (to coin a term) refuse to believe that Murdoch could ever have considered doing such a thing.

At any rate, this present volume contains the present author's own thinking on a wide variety of *Titanic*-related subjects, and it presents every scrap of information I'm aware of that pertains to the subject matter at hand. This way the reader can see the information upon which I've based my own conclusions and can decide for him/herself whether I've shed new light on the *Titanic* disaster or whether I'm unable to see the forest for the trees.

I hope readers will enjoy perusing the information I've presented here for their consideration and that I've illuminated a few *Titanic* topics that many researchers have long thought were chiseled in stone.

George Behe
Grand Rapids, Michigan

1

Titanic and the Animal World

In addition to transporting passengers and crewmen, RMS *Titanic* was carrying a number of animals of different species (authorised as well as unauthorised). Let's take a look at these various creatures.

Animals Transported on Board the *Titanic*

Canaries

In 2011 a newly published book by Frankie McElroy made the undocumented claim that Hugh McElroy, the *Titanic*'s purser, was personally caring for a caged canary that was being transported from Southampton to Cherbourg:

> Hugh had taken to canary minding, the canary sailed on the *Titanic* and survived. It was owned by a Mr Meanwell, who lived in [Cerentan], France, and wanted to get his prize-winning precious canary to Cherbourg from England. He asked the Chief Purser to carry it on RMS *Titanic*, and to have the bird in his office, the canary disembarked when the *Titanic* arrived in Cherbourg …[1]

A 31 March 2012 posting by 'Joseph' on the Encyclopedia Titanica bulletin board mentioned the price that 'Mr Meanwell' supposedly paid for the transport of his canary. However, Joseph failed to document his claim about the transport price and seems to have based his overall statement on the McElroy book's undocumented claim that *Titanic*'s purser was caring for a canary in his office:

> The canary in a cage never went down with the *Titanic*, it was carried by Chief Purser Hugh McElroy from Southampton to Cherbourg and recovered after the ship docked in France on April 10th, by the owner who had paid 15 shillings for the fare.[2]

Despite these undocumented claims, there's little doubt that a canary was still on board the *Titanic* when the vessel left Cherbourg and headed towards Queenstown. In fact, in recent years an actual receipt for the bird was discovered by a salvage expedition at the wreck site.

> Last year, Premier exhibited a selection of artifacts in Las Vegas, among them a pair of blue and white striped men's pajamas, a travelling receipt for 'one canary in a cage' and a pair of never-worn white gloves.[3]

Did a 'Mr Meanwell' really pay 15 shillings for Purser McElroy to keep a caged canary in his office and transport it from Southampton to Cherbourg on the *Titanic*? The answer to this question is 'probably not', since no survivor ever reported seeing such a canary housed there. In fact, the supposed identification of 'Mr Meanwell' seems to be a mistake as well.

Marian Meanwell

Mrs Marian Meanwell was a 63-year-old milliner who was born in England and lived there until 1912, at which time she booked a third-class passage on the *Titanic* in order to travel from Southampton to New York to be with her daughter. The contract ticket list also shows that Mrs Meanwell paid an extra fee for the transportation of a canary.[4]

Since Mrs Meanwell was travelling all the way from Southampton to New York, why did her name reportedly appear on the *Titanic*'s roster of cross-Channel passengers who were scheduled to disembark at Cherbourg? The answer is very simple – it didn't.

In truth, the names of twelve *Titanic* cross-Channel passengers are listed at the top of that particular page of the contract ticket list, but at that point a *blank space* separates those twelve names from the beginning of a *second* list of names – a *separate* list of five passengers (Mr Noel, Mrs Meanwell, Mr West, Mr Dulles and Mrs Harper, of whom only Noel was a cross-Channel passenger), who were all transporting *listed items of cargo*. In addition to Mr Noel's '2 cycles', and Edwy West's '8 cases' and '1 crated cycle', a notation shows that Mrs Meanwell paid 5 shillings (not 15 shillings) for the transport of '1 canary', and that William Dulles and Myra Harper each paid £1 19*s* 4*d* for the transportation of one dog apiece. (Obviously the freight charge for a tiny caged canary was much less than the charge for carrying larger, heavier, uncaged canines; interestingly, Mrs Meanwell's 5-shilling canary expense was the same amount of money that Mr West paid for the transport of his '8 cases' all the way to New York, so the superficial impression that Mrs Meanwell's payment was insufficient to ship her canary to New York is clearly mistaken.)

Appearing immediately after the second list of five cargo-carrying passengers is a *third* roster listing three final passengers – Lucian Smith, Eloise Smith and John Baumann – all of whom were travelling to New York and who were apparently the last three purchasers of first-class tickets for the *Titanic*'s maiden voyage. (No serious researcher would ever claim that Baumann and the two Smiths were cross-Channel passengers even though their names appeared on the same sheet of paper as the cross-Channel passengers and the cargo-carrying passengers.)

The reason why the list of five cargo-carrying passengers and the list of three last-minute passengers to New York were recorded on the same page as the cross-Channel passengers is easily explained: it was to avoid wasting the rest of the largely blank ledger page just for the sake of recording those final eight passenger names on a brand-new page. (Instead, the White Star clerk devoted the next page of the contract ticket list solely to 'Rail Fares'.)[5]

It seems clear that the list of five cargo-carrying passengers and the subsequent list of three last-minute ticket-buyers were both completely unconnected with the preceding list of cross-Channel passengers. It seems equally clear that the coincidental inclusion of the Meanwell canary and the Dulles and Harper dogs directly beneath the list of cross-Channel passengers has led several researchers to the mistaken conclusion that Mrs Meanwell's canary disembarked at Cherbourg while for some unexplained reason the Dulles and Harper dogs mysteriously remained on board the *Titanic* and continued onward toward New York. In truth, Mrs Meanwell and her canary were both present on board the ill-fated vessel when she struck an iceberg and went down in the mid-Atlantic.

Elizabeth Nye

In 2009 a curious bit of information appeared in a biography of *Titanic* survivor Elizabeth Nye, who was a member of the Salvation Army. The book quoted an article from a 1912 issue of the Army's publication *The War Cry*:

> The sister has gone through the ordeal in the most wonderful way, and was good enough to give the *War Cry* a fairly connected story of the disaster as she witnessed it. First of all, though, she excused herself as she had left something on board [the *Carpathia*] and wanted to fetch it.
>
> What do you think it was she fetched from the *Carpathia*? Make a guess!
>
> A little yellow canary bird in a brass cage! That was the woman of it! The poor little chap was a little bedraggled; he had been through all the horrors of shipwreck, but not forgotten how to chirp. Mrs Nye had lost money, clothes – everything, but here was a little bit of life she thought should not be forfeited, and she had saved him.[6]

There would seem to be only three possible explanations for this story about a canary that supposedly survived the *Titanic* disaster:

1. Mrs Nye carried her own caged canary into lifeboat #11 even though no survivors ever mentioned seeing a caged bird in that or any other lifeboat.
2. Second-class passenger Nye somehow came into possession of third-class passenger Marian Meanwell's canary on board the *Titanic* and carried it with her into lifeboat #11.
3. A well-meaning *Carpathia* passenger might have given a caged canary to Mrs Nye after the rescue, and the *War Cry* reporter mistakenly assumed the bird had been saved from the *Titanic*.

In a letter she wrote on board the *Carpathia* on 16 April 1912, Mrs Nye said, 'I lost everything I had on board; the only thing I saved was my watch that Dad gave me eleven years ago,'[7] so our first suggestion that she saved the canary in lifeboat #11 is clearly untrue. Likewise, her letter's failure to mention her taking charge of Mrs Meanwell's canary suggests that our second proposed explanation is untrue as well. The present writer is inclined to favour the third explanation, but there's no guarantee that this assumption is correct. In short, we may never know if a canary was one of the few non-human beings fortunate enough to survive the sinking of the *Titanic*.

Cats

Joseph Mulholland

Mr Mulholland served as a stoker on the *Titanic* while she was being transferred from Belfast to Southampton on 2–3April 1912. In 1962 he spoke with a reporter, who transcribed his recollections:

> Big Joe is still fond of cats and perhaps he has reason. He recalls that on his way down to the *Titanic* before she set sail from Belfast with bands playing and crowds cheering, he took pity on a stray cat which was about to have kittens. He brought the cat aboard and put her in a wooden box down in the stokehold.
>
> At Southampton, when he was ruminating whether to take on the job of storekeeper on the trip or sign off, another seaman called him over and said, 'Look Big Joe. There is your cat taking its kittens down the gangplank.'
>
> Joe said, 'That settled it. I went and got my bag and that's the last I saw of the *Titanic*.'[8]

Mulholland also spoke with Irish journalist Paddy Scott, who related his story to fellow journalist Anne Hailes around 1998:

> He [Mulholland] said he was waiting for a stoker's job on a tramp steamer that would bring him work for much of the year when he was offered the job on the *Titanic*.
>
> He took it and immediately made friends with a fellow stoker on board. On the way to Southampton his colleague urged him to complete the voyage to New York and as they got on well working together on the same furnace, the Belfast man told him he would keep an open mind but really he wanted a tramp steamer as that was big money for a long voyage.
>
> Then his mind was made up for him thanks to a cat which came aboard the ship in Belfast and made a home with the stokers.
>
> She had a litter of four kittens and looking after the mother cat and her brood broke the monotony for the stoker.
>
> But when the *Titanic* docked at Southampton the cat made a survey of the place, caught each kitten by the back of its neck and carried them, one at a time, down the gangway onto the quayside.
>
> The New Lodge stoker thought – 'that cat knows something and has decided that the *Titanic* is no place for her or her family to spend their lives.'

> So he took the advice the cat was giving and left the ship, telling Paddy: 'I had reason to give thanks to God for my decision.'[9]

It's curious that our first account has Mulholland being offered a job as *Titanic*'s storekeeper, whereas the second account implies (more realistically) that he was considering serving on the vessel in his then-current capacity of stoker. It should also be pointed out that the first account has Mulholland's cat being kept in the stokehold itself, whereas the second (more likely) account implies that the animal was kept by the stokers in their sleeping quarters. In any case, Joseph Mulholland claimed that he followed his cat's example and signed off the *Titanic* at Southampton on 4 April 1912.

Interestingly, at least one additional account about Mulholland exists that makes no mention of the cat at all. Researcher Bruno Piola has pointed out to the present author that Joe Mulholland once gave a third account that casts an entirely different light on the alleged reason for his departure from the *Titanic*:

> At a late stage in the preparations, one sailor, Joe Mulholland, had a row with one of the Engineer Officers. 'I walked off the ship at Southampton just before she sailed,' he later told Bill Macquitty, maker of the film 'A Night to Remember' (see *Stage & Sound*, 1957).[10]

This, of course, raises questions about whether Mulholland's story about the cat was legitimate or whether it was just a tall tale. Did Joseph Mulholland follow his cat's example and sign off the *Titanic* at Southampton, or did he just have an argument with one of the engineering officers and walk off the ship in a fit of pique? It's unlikely we'll ever know for certain.

Whether or not the Mulholland cat story is true, we have a bit of extra information about other cats that are alleged to have deserted other passenger liners before disaster struck. The *Empress of Ireland*'s own cat is reported to have abandoned that vessel before she was rammed and sunk in the St Lawrence in May 1914, and Dowie, the *Lusitania*'s cat, was likewise said to have deserted that ill-fated vessel before it was torpedoed by the Germans in May 1915.[11] Is Joe Mulholland's story about a cat deserting the *Titanic* true, or did he and other seamen cook up these stories about prescient cats just to add a spine-tingling flavour of the unknown to their stories about these major sea disasters?

Violet Jessop
What might have been a completely different cat from the one owned by Joseph Mulholland was an animal described by Stewardess Violet Jessop, who sailed on the *Titanic*'s maiden voyage:

> Life aboard started off smoothly. Even Jenny, the ship's cat and part of the crew, had immediately picked herself a comfortable corner; she varied her usual Christmas routine on previous ships by presenting *Titanic* with a litter of kittens in April.[12]

Violet Jessop's comment about Jenny's 'usual Christmas routine' suggests that the cat had shared voyages with her in the past, so it seems unlikely that the animal had any connection with the stray cat that was rescued by Joseph Mulholland. If Jenny and her kittens were entirely different animals from Joseph Mulholland's cat and kittens, and if these felines did indeed sail on the *Titanic*'s maiden voyage as Miss Jessop claimed, there is no record of Jenny or her kittens surviving the disaster.

Chickens

Ella White and Marie Young brought poultry (said to be two prize-winning roosters and two hens)[13] on board the *Titanic*. According to one source, the fowl were supposedly purchased from Chasse Ile Rage, Jardin d'Agriculture, and after the disaster Mrs White put in a claim for $250.87 as compensation for her lost live poultry.[14]

Marie Young
In October 1912 Miss Young wrote an account of her experience on the *Titanic*:

> It so happened that I took an unusual interest in some of the men below decks, for I had talked often with the carpenter and the printer, in having extra crates and labels made for the fancy French poultry we were bringing home, and I saw a little of the ship's life, in my daily visits to the gaily crowing roosters, and to the hens, who laid eggs busily, undismayed by the novelty and commotion of their surroundings.
>
> I had seen the cooks before their great cauldrons of porcelain, and the bakers turning out the huge loaves of bread, a hamper of which was later brought on deck to supply the life boats.

> In accepting some gold coins, the ship's carpenter said, 'It is such good luck to receive gold on a first voyage!' Yet he was the first of the *Titanic*'s martyrs, who, in sounding the ship just after the iceberg was struck, sank and was lost in the inward rushing sea that engulfed him.[15]

Miss Young's comments about seeing *Titanic*'s cooks and bakers at work suggest that the chickens might possibly have been kept somewhere near the ship's kitchens on D deck.

Kate Buss

On 13 April Miss Buss, a second-class passenger, wrote the third instalment of her long letter to her parents:

> Saturday, 13/4/12 – Morning; just missed Miss W. on the staircase; there are two to each deck. Just think, all these hundreds of miles from land, and cocks can be heard crowing now at this time of night. Just had a bath, so will write a little of today's doings. Bless those cockerels![16]

August Wennerström

On 19 April 1912 Mr Wennerström, a third-class passenger, wrote an account describing his experiences during the *Titanic*'s maiden voyage:

> But then we lived the life in what could be likened to a small genial city, dancing, playing, singing, and awakening early in the morning to the crowing of the rooster, because we did have such farm animals on board. In addition, we had various country and city accommodations like a jail, an infirmary, midwives, nurses, doctors, ministers, a bakery, a hospital, post offices etc.[17]

Elizabeth Hocking

The evening of 14 April saw Mrs Hocking and her family seated in deck chairs out on the *Titanic*'s chilly second-class promenade deck. They had been sitting there for some time when suddenly they heard a rooster crow. Mrs Hocking was still feeling uneasy about the ship and, being a native of Cornwall, she couldn't help but recall her home area's local tradition that a cock crowing at night was a warning of disaster.

'I don't like that,' Mrs Hocking remarked. 'I think something is going to happen.'[18]

Ellen Mockler

Miss Mockler, a steerage passenger who later became a nun, apparently passed near the chicken coops during the *Titanic*'s evacuation.

One of her former pupils, now a nun herself, remembered Sister Mary Patricia often telling about the *Titanic* disaster in the classroom. She particularly remembered 'hearing chickens and hens' as she headed up to the boat deck, and how, when she reached the boat deck, 'several of her friends, including Martin Gallagher, fell to their knees in prayer and recited the rosary'.[19]

In an interview she granted in later years to a Massachusetts newspaper reporter, Sister Mary Patricia (Miss Mockler) seems to have described seeing the chickens with her own eyes. The reporter wrote:

> She remembers that chickens escaped from the kitchen and began running around on deck.[20]

Cows

Edwina Troutt

Although Miss Troutt said nothing about it in 1912, in later years she told close friends in passing that cows were being kept on board the *Titanic* during the maiden voyage.[21] Although we now know this to be a mistake, Edwina's friend Don Lynch has offered a possible reason for her story:

> [Survivor] Marshall Drew said the third class passengers down on the aft well deck made noises that reminded him of animals, and I always thought perhaps Winnie heard it and thought there were indeed animals down there.[22]

Dogs

On 11 April 1912, while the *Titanic* was bound for Queenstown, artist Frank Millet wrote a letter to his friend Alfred Parsons regarding things he'd seen on board the new White Star liner:

> Queer lot of people on this ship. Looking over the list I only find three or four I know but there are a good many of 'our people' I think and a number of obnoxious ostentatious American women, the scourge of any place they infest and worse on shipboard than anywhere. Many of them carry tiny dogs

> and lead husbands around like pet lambs. I tell you when she starts out the American woman is a buster. She should be put in a harem and kept there.[23]

Frank Millet was destined to die when the *Titanic* went down, but just a few days later American newspapers published an article about the dogs he had noticed during the maiden voyage:

> SAVED DOGS FROM THE *TITANIC*
> There Were About Thirty Aboard and Half Got Away
> New York, April 27 – There were thirty dogs aboard the *Titanic* belonging to first cabin passengers, all of them the best of their sort in the dog line, and a woman survivor and a lover of dogs said yesterday that she thought about half of them had been saved. The dogs were cared for and fed by the ship's butcher and when the crash came he let them loose to shift for themselves.
>
> One of the passengers who had a valuable St Bernard saw it running about on the deck looking for its master and he threw it into one of the departing lifeboats that was not full. He himself managed to get into another boat and when they drew alongside the *Carpathia* one of the first things he heard was the deep toned welcome of the dog which was frantically waving a saved but bedraggled tail over the *Carpathia*'s decks.
>
> The Harpers had their Pomeranian in their stateroom with them and Mrs Harper picked the little fellow up and took it into the lifeboat with her.
>
> There were three other Pomeranians aboard, and all of them were saved.
>
> One of the dogs that was lost was the Airedale that belonged to the Astors and that became familiar to the public last summer when it appeared in pictures of Col. Astor and Miss Force before their wedding.[24]

Unfortunately, only two of the 'facts' presented in the article are *known* to be 100 per cent accurate (the information about the Harper and Astor dogs). One wishes that the unnamed dog-loving female survivor (perhaps Nella Goldenberg?) had been interviewed in more depth so that she could provide specific names, etc. for the owners of those thirty dogs who supposedly lost their lives on board the doomed liner. As things stand, though, we must rely on our own research to shed new light on some of the questions raised by the newspaper article.

Of special interest is a brief newspaper interview with survivor Mrs Walter Douglas, who spoke about a fellow occupant of boat #6 who saved her dog. Mrs Douglas was then asked one additional question by the reporter who was recording her experiences.

'Were there many dogs?' Mrs Douglas was asked.

'There were at least half a dozen saved,' she said.[25]

As will be seen, Mrs Douglas's observation that at least six dogs survived the *Titanic* disaster cannot yet be verified from the evidence currently at our disposal. However, we should at least bear her statement in mind when we come to examine evidence suggesting that more dogs were present on board the *Titanic* than can now be confirmed with certainty.

At any rate, let's begin by examining information about the passengers' dogs that are *known* to have been on board the *Titanic* during her maiden voyage.

Harry Anderson

Dog No. 1: Mr Anderson owned a Chow valued at $50 that was lost in the sinking.[26]

John Jacob Astor

Dog No. 2: Mr Astor owned an Airedale named Kitty that died with her master in the sinking. Kitty was about 14 years old.[27]

In later years Edith Rosenbaum recalled seeing the Astors and their dog on board the tender after the *Titanic* arrived at Cherbourg:

> We sat about on the huge tender, which had been specially built the year before for those new White Star ships, and for three hours shivered and waited. It was cold. It had been raining. I remember sitting next to Colonel and Mrs John Jacob Astor, who were on their wedding trip, playing with their big dog.[28]

A newspaper gave a brief description of the Astors' activities during their honeymoon trip and later on board the *Titanic*:

> The Astor party consisted of Colonel and Mrs Astor, a woman nurse for Mrs Astor and her French maid; the Colonel's valet, Rollins [Victor Robins], who had been with him for fifteen years or more, and the chauffeur. Then there was Kitty, Colonel Astor's favourite Airedale terrier that had travelled all over the world with him. The two had been inseparable companions for years, and they were not to be separated, for Kitty went down on board the *Titanic* with her master.
>
> Pathetically Mrs Astor told of how Kitty got lost in Egypt on the trip up the Nile. She wandered away from Colonel Astor's side one day at a landing and went sightseeing on her own account. Colonel Astor was greatly distressed by the loss of the dog. He spent a great deal of time looking for her,

and when he had to give up and start up the Nile again he employed scores of natives to look for her, promising a handsome reward for her return. Nothing was heard of Kitty until on the return ship she was seen aboard another *dahabeah* [*sic*].

Colonel Astor spied Kitty making herself at home on board. The Astor boat was stopped and Kitty found her master with joyous barks. Kitty wore a collar with her own and Colonel Astor's names and 'No. 840 Fifth avenue, New York City' engraved on it. She went on board the wrong dahabiyeh, evidently looking for her master after being lost for a time, and a party of wealthy Americans who had chartered the boat for a Nile trip quickly knew to whom she belonged and were looking for Colonel Astor's dahabiyeh to return her. After that a closer watch was kept of Kitty. On board the *Titanic* she slept in Colonel Astor's room …

Mrs Astor spent a good deal of the time in her room and was hardly off the one deck until the accident. Colonel Astor and she took frequent walks and he romped with Kitty a great deal …

[After leaving the *Titanic* in lifeboat #4] Mrs Astor watched her husband so long as she could in the darkness and then lost sight of him, but long after she could see him no more she could distinguish persons running up and down the deck. She could follow the terrier's movements easily and watched her as she raced about, evidently having lost her master.

Kitty went down with the *Titanic*.[29]

Another article described the way the Astors spent their days on the *Titanic* and what happened to them during the evacuation:

Owing to ill health, Mrs Astor spent most of her time in her room and did not venture off the one deck from the time the steamship left England until it hit the berg. When she felt strong enough she would take short walks on the deck with Colonel Astor, and with them was always her husband's favourite Airedale terrier, Kitty, which had been his companion for fourteen years …

Mrs Astor denies the story that her husband attempted to get into the boat with her. She says that as he placed her in a seat he said it was only a precautionary measure, and after kissing her goodbye said he would see her in a few hours. Kitty, the terrier, was at Colonel Astor's side all the time, evidently enjoying the excitement of it all …

Before Mrs Astor got into the boat she says her husband put a life belt around her and saw to its adjustment. He then put one on himself. For a time Mrs Astor could see her husband standing on the boat deck and hear

> Kitty's barks as she followed her master as he walked forward. Then as the boat got further away the figures of those left on board became blurred and one could not be identified from another.[30]

In another brief interview Mrs Astor mentioned seeing Kitty on deck as lifeboat #4 pulled away from the ship:

> I noticed the ship was going down as we rowed, and I could see Kitty, my favourite terrier, running across the deck.[31]

Another newspaper article described Mrs Astor's arrival at her home after the *Carpathia* reached New York:

> So that she might be present to be of any service that might be required, Mrs Astor's sister, Miss Katherine Force, spent the night with her. Unnerved by the scenes through which they had passed, little else was told Vincent Astor and Miss Force by Mrs Astor and her attendants than the bare facts of the catastrophe. Young Astor was still in such a highly nervous condition and overwrought, because he was finally prepared to abandon hope that his father might have been saved, that he had no word for anyone.
>
> It was, however, made certain to him before his home was shrouded in darkness that the last seen of Colonel Astor had shown him, accompanied by his valet and by his faithful terrier, Kitty, calmly waiting on the decks of the Titanic for what might come.[32]

Although no eyewitness testimony exists to document it, the following statement appeared in various 1912 newspapers and was reprinted in one of the *Titanic* books published immediately after the sinking:

> In the register of the *Titanic*'s heroes the name of Robbins should appear. He was Colonel Astor's old butler, and like the Colonel's valet, always travelled with him. He is numbered among the *Titanic*'s dead.
>
> Faithful unto death was Kitty, Colonel Astor's Airedale terrier and constant companion on land or sea. Kitty was never far from her master's heels, and the two were familiar figures on Fifth Avenue.
>
> When the crash came, Robbins went below and brought Kitty up on deck. There, the most faithful of friends, she stood beside her master, while the sea embraced them, and she now shares his grave.[33]

Despite the apparent straightforwardness of the above newspaper statements, and Kitty's unquestionable presence on board the *Titanic*, it is unknown if Victor Robins actually went below decks to retrieve Kitty or if the dog was already accompanying the Astors when they left their cabin and went to the boat deck.

Since no known first-hand interviews exist in which Mrs Astor described Kitty being alongside her and her husband during the evacuation, it has occasionally been suggested that the Airedale Mrs Astor saw running around on the *Titanic*'s deck might actually have belonged to passenger William Carter. This unlikely scenario will be discussed in the section devoted to the Carter dogs.

It has also been claimed that John Jacob Astor was the person who released the dogs from *Titanic*'s kennels,[34] but there is absolutely no evidence to support that allegation; no survivors ever mentioned seeing Astor freeing dogs from the kennels, and any such story would have *had* to come from a survivor due to the fact that Astor himself perished in the sinking.

Helen Bishop

Dog No. 3: Mrs Bishop owned a 'small dog' named Frou Frou (breed unknown) that died in the sinking. She reportedly purchased the dog in the city of Florence:[35]

Mr and Mrs Astor and Kitty. (Author's collection)

> It broke my heart to leave my little dog 'Frou Frou' in my stateroom. I had purchased her in Florence, Italy and she was the pet of the ship. The steward wouldn't let me take her to the butler [butcher?]. He said she was too pretty, and she was the only one allowed to stay in the cabin. I made a little den for her in our room behind two of my suitcases, but when I started to leave her she tore my dress to bits, tugging at it. I realized, however, that there would be little sympathy for a woman carrying a dog in her arms, when there were lives of women and children to be saved.[36]

Mrs Bishop later expressed great regret at leaving her dog:

> I feel the loss of my dog more than anything ... She really wanted to go with me.[37]

William Carter

Dog No. 4: The Carter family had two dogs, the first being a Pekingese named Hee Too that Mrs Carter picked up in Europe (probably the United Kingdom) and was bringing back to the States.[38] Hee Too died in the sinking. The two dogs were valued at $100 and $200 each.[39] (In the past, these two dogs were presumed to be either two Airedales or else one Airedale and one King Charles spaniel, but – as will be seen – the evidence does not support the claim about the Airedale breed.)

Stewardess Jane Gold recalled seeing the two Carter dogs during the days of the maiden voyage and referred to them as 'handsome'.[40]

Stewardess Annie Martin and her fellow stewardesses were berthed on B deck near the Carter family in B96 & B98, and she later recalled seeing one of the family's pets before, during and after the sinking:

> I saw one of Mrs Carter's beautiful dogs running about on the deck of the *Titanic* and afterwards swimming in the water. We had got fond of him on board. He used to come into our cabin and say 'How do you do' to us each morning.[41]

Slightly more than a year after the sinking Mrs Carter acquired a second Pekingese that she also named Hee Too:

> There is a certain sentiment surrounding the poodle, too. Mrs Carter made a trip to England especially to get Hee Too. She had a dog just like Hee Too, and she thought a lot of it. With her husband she was bringing the original Hee Too back from Europe on the *Titanic*, when that steamship struck an

iceberg and went to the bottom. Hee Too the First went down with the ship. Mr and Mrs Carter managed to get into a lifeboat with their children and were saved. But poor Hee Too the First, with half a dozen canine companions, was swallowed up in the waters.

The first Hee Too was a great favourite with Mrs Carter, and there was much ado about his sudden and early demise. The Carters heard of another Hee Too in London, who looked for all the world like a twin brother of Hee Too the First. So Mrs Carter got aboard ship, took a trip to England and brought back with her the Hee Too which is now prostrated at Newport.[42]

Dog No. 5: The Carter family's second dog was apparently named Mogul, his breed apparently being a King Charles spaniel. Mogul died in the sinking on 15 April, but on 12 April young Lucile Carter made the following entry in her diary:

> **April 11** [*sic*] – Swimming bath very rough Mother watches me Mogul dog howls William watches.[43]

After the *Carpathia* arrived in New York, a newspaper article published passenger complaints about 'Mrs John Jacob Astor'. The complaints were almost certainly made about Mrs William Carter while she was still on board the *Titanic*, even though the newspaper mistakenly assumed her questionable behaviour took place on board the *Carpathia*:

> A pet St Charles dog was the only apparent concern of Mrs John Jacob Astor [Mrs Carter], according to the members of the crew and passengers aboard the rescue steamer *Carpathia*. According to many of the passengers, she did not concern herself about others who were sick or inquire about lost ones.
>
> The dog, which Mrs Astor carried about at all times, received her entire attention. The dog companion was with her at all times, and even in her lap or on a chair beside her at meals. Passengers who were able to partake sparingly of food were annoyed at times at the special attention she wished conferred on the animal.
>
> On one occasion a waiter unfortunately came near her and disturbed his own equilibrium. She reported the mishap to the steward, who in turn notified the waiter that his conduct had been complained of by Mrs John Jacob Astor.
>
> Mrs Astor had special provisions prepared for her dog companion, which were served to him as though he were a sick passenger. Many complained that the dining room was no place for animals.

> No attention was paid to the inconvenience that passengers suffered by the presence of the pet dog.[44]

Just like her Pekingese Hee Too, Mrs Carter's King Charles spaniel Mogul never lived to reach the *Carpathia*.

Regarding the claim that the Carters had an Airedale with them on the *Titanic*, this (posted on the Encyclopedia Titanica website's bulletin board) originated with a researcher who discussed the subject with 'Henry', a Bryn Mawr resident and Philadelphia antique shop owner who got the story directly from William Carter Jr.[45] According to a message posted by the researcher in an online forum:

> On occasion, William Carter 2d did speak to family and friends about the sinking. He would only comment that he remembered having to tearfully abandon his beloved Airedale when he entered boat #4. The dog was not allowed to enter the boat. He said that John Jacob Astor took the dog's leash and promised young Carter that he would take care of it.[46]

On the face of it, this account seems believable, but a second public statement by the same researcher throws its accuracy into serious question:

> The Ellis Island records indicate that the Carter family arrived in New York City on the *Olympic* on 3 April 1912. Naturally, this could not have happened. Their names are crossed off on the original manifest, indicating that they must have cancelled their passage on the *Olympic* very late. Their names remained on the passenger list and the records were adjusted when *Olympic* reached New York.
>
> The Carters apparently delayed their stay in England for another two weeks in late March/early April, 1912, and decided to take the *Titanic* back. Somehow I think that voyage on the *Olympic* two weeks earlier might have saved the Carter marriage (but certainly their manservant, Alexander Cairns, the two beloved Airedales, and the legendary Renault!)[47]

The key point in this second posting is the researcher's mistaken belief that the Carters brought two Airedales with them on board the *Titanic* – a claim that period documentation shows to be mistaken. We therefore suspect that 'Henry' probably failed to mention the specific breed of young Billy Carter's dog and that the extra detail about the 'beloved Airedale' was added later in the researcher's mistaken belief that the dog *had* to be one of the Carters' two (supposed) Airedales. The third-hand story about Mr Astor caring for a Carter Airedale on the *Titanic*'s deck is therefore unreliable, since the Carters didn't have two Airedales with them on the *Titanic* as the researcher believed.

It is interesting to note that in 1912 Billy Carter never mentioned having his dog on deck with him when he was leaving the *Titanic*; on 16 April Washington Dodge wrote the following account for *Carpathia* passenger Dr Frank Blackmarr while the rescue ship was still at sea:

> One lad of 10, Master [William] Carter, told me that after his mother and sister were in the boat, he was refused permission to enter the boat, and Col Astor, who knew the lad, a moment later picked up a girl's hat and placed it on the lad's head, lifted him up and said to the officer as he was lowering the boat, 'Could you let this little girl go with her mother?' As the lad expressed it, 'They did not stop to examine me, so I got in with mother.'[48]

In short, at the time of this writing the William Carter family is known to have had two dogs with them on board the *Titanic* – a Pekingese named Hee Too and a King Charles spaniel named Mogul.

Robert Daniel

Dog No. 6: Mr Daniel owned a brindle French bulldog named Gamin de Pycombe that was valued at $750. The dog was lost in the sinking.[49]

Gamin was born in January 1910 and was just 2 years old when he died. His breeder was Gwendoline Romilly of what would later be the Taplow Kennel. He was sired by C.H. Charlemagne of Amersham, a French import to Britain who became Britain's first pied champion Frenchie, and who later was the first Frenchie to be a champion in both the UK and the USA. Mr Daniel had bought the dog in the United Kingdom for a very high price of £150 (about £11,000 or $17,000 in today's prices).[50]

During the maiden voyage, 7-year-old Eva Hart regularly saw a crew member taking the *Titanic*'s dogs on daily walks around the fantail of the ship, and she soon befriended Robert Daniel's show dog:

> In the course of our explorations I made friends with a little dog and spent a great deal of time playing with it. I loved this animal so much that I would hurry through my breakfast each morning and then rush off to find him, as by then I hadn't seen him for more than twelve hours. At the age of seven that length of time is an eternity. I was completely fascinated by him and hated being separated for very long. My father saw how fond I had become

> of this small, flat-faced, endearing dog and promised me, 'When we get to Canada I will buy you one.' It was, in fact, another 43 years before I saw that breed of dog again. The animal with which I fell in love was the champion French bulldog which had been purchased in England by Robert W. Daniel, the banker from Philadelphia ...[51]

> I was about all day with my father because as I say my mother was sleeping, and to my great joy, I found there were some dogs on board. They weren't roaming about, they were all in a row of kennels and cages and things at the end of the ship and there was one little French bulldog that I took a great fancy to and my father was quite friendly with I think one of the crew who looked after them and everyday he used to let me go down and play with this little dog, and from that day to this, they have been my favourite dogs, the French bulldogs.[52]

According to Edith Rosenbaum, Robert Daniel's bulldog was not in the ship's kennels on the night of the disaster but instead was in his master's cabin, which was near Rosenbaum's own cabin on A Deck. After *Titanic* struck the iceberg, Miss Rosenbaum was walking along a corridor when she approached Mr Daniel's cabin:

> In going to the lounge I passed the open door of the friend's room, who had told me to put on a lifebelt, who said, 'Do you think we shall have to leave the boat?' I said, 'Certainly not!' This friend had just purchased a beautiful bulldog in France, and it was whining and moaning. I remember taking it and tucking it under the bed-covers and patting its head, and then we went to the lounge on 'A' deck ...[53]

> In going down the corridor I passed the open door of a friend who had purchased a beautiful dog in France. The dog was whining, and I remember tucking it under the bed cover, patting it and then closing the door.[54]

> The dog was scared so I pet him and laid him down in his bed. He was very obedient and sat there and looked at me sweetly as I closed the door. I did not know then that we were in any great danger or else I would have taken him with me.[55]

After he was taken on board the *Carpathia*, survivor Richard Williams spoke with a fellow survivor, who told him something about the *Titanic*'s dogs:

> One man told me that some half hour or so before the end he suddenly thought of a dog that he was bringing home with him. He went up to the top deck and opened up all the kennels. This relieved my mind quite a bit, for as I was in the water swimming towards the collapsible lifeboat I thought I saw the small black face of a French bulldog which was evidently swimming in my general direction. At the time I thought I must be seeing things but as I had more important matters on my mind at the moment I promptly forgot about it. This man, however, told me that there was a black-faced French bull, so that the poor little fellow was evidently doing all that he could to get out of this unexpected situation, just like all the rest of us.[56]

The unidentified male survivor in Williams' account was apparently Robert Daniel himself, who told his daughter in later years that he tried to save the dogs from going down to certain death in their cages.[57]

In later years Eva Hart had vivid memories of Daniel's French bulldog:

> After the ship had sunk and we had returned to England, I longed and longed for a little dog like that, but when I described it to people I couldn't find anyone who knew what type of dog it was. As a result, it wasn't until 1955 that I discovered the breed. A year later I was given one as a present and at long last had the pleasure of owning such an affectionate animal. The beautiful French bulldog I eventually owned was the image of the one I had played with many years previously on the *Titanic*.[58]

William Dulles

Dog No. 7: Mr Dulles brought a dog with him on to the *Titanic*. Dulles paid £1 19*s* 4*d* for the dog's transport,[59] and he and his pet both died in the sinking.[60]

William Dulles owned Tophill Farm in Goshen, New York, and was a breeder and owner of show dogs. Although Dulles might have been returning from France on the *Titanic* with a brand-new canine purchase, it's also possible he might have been bringing his Scottish terrier, EMS Chevalier, back from a breeding trip there.

W.L. McClandish, the owner of EMS Kennels, specialised in Scottish terriers and produced eight champions of that breed between 1905 and 1912. By 1908 Chevalier was being used for breeding purposes at the kennels, and William C. Dulles appears to have purchased the dog early in 1910, as was recorded in the American Kennel Club Stud Book:

EMS Chevalier. (Author's collection)

> **EMS Chevalier** (135,150) – William C. Dulles, Goshen, N.Y. Breeder, J. Love, England. Whelped, June 6, 1904. Brindle. By Camowen's Laddie out of Carter Jean, by Kempoch King out of Bess, by Hardy out of Bessie; Kempoch King by Kempoch Cairn out of Kempoch Cora; Camowen Laddie by Seafield out of Seafield Annie, by St Clair Chief out of St Clair Judy; Seafield by Jock out of St Clair Betsy.[61]

On 11 February 1910 it was announced that Chevalier had been entered in the Westminster Kennel Club dog show in Madison Square Garden and acquitted himself admirably there:

> (Class 492 (Scottish Terriers); open; dogs) – First, Tickle 'Em Jock. Andrew Albright, jr.; second, Ch. Walescott Invader. Walescott Kennels; third, Em's Chevalier, William C.[62]

On 24 February Chevalier was entered in the New England Kennel Show in Boston, and the results of the judging were announced that same day:

Scottish Terriers, Dogs – William C. Dulles' EM's Chevalier. Bitches – N.H. Mulford's Gevyned Lassie; reserve, William C. Dulles' Laindon Lovelock.[63]

By spring 1911 William Dulles was using Chevalier for breeding purposes in the States, and the Newcastle Kennels produced Bodkin, Clipper, Greyrock, Keyway, Puff, Relish, Specialist and a number of other puppies courtesy of EMS Chevalier.[64] However, all new records of Chevalier's breeding activities seem to have ceased after 1911, and the only subsequent reference to the dog (published in 1917) mentions that Albourne Bombardier (born in 1912) was a descendant of Chevalier (stemming from one of the dog's pre-1912 liaisons).[65]

All that is known of Dulles's travels in 1912 is that he sailed with his mother for Paris on 20 January. From Paris they went to Rome and met friends, with whom they toured the Continent, at which point Mr Dulles left his mother in Paris and boarded the *Titanic* at Cherbourg.[66]

Did William Dulles and his mother bring a dog with them when they sailed from the United States to France in January 1912? If so, was that dog EMS Chevalier? Did Chevalier and Dulles die together on the *Titanic*, or did Dulles purchase a brand-new dog in Europe and have it with him on board the ill-fated ship? We may never know for certain.

Myra Harper

Dog No. 8: Mrs Harper owned Sun Yat Sen, a red Pekingese with black mask.[67] She and her husband paid £1 19*s* 4*d* for the transport of their pet on the *Titanic*.[68]

In later years, stewardess Violet Jessop claimed to have seen a woman (whose name she disguised with a pseudonym) who brought a Pekingese on board the *Titanic*. (However, it seems likely that Jessop was remembering another woman from a different ocean voyage.)

> My daydreaming ended with the further arrival of passengers. My heart sank as Mrs Cyrus Klapton, clutching her pet Pekingese, bore down towards my section followed by a downcast maid. She had invariably reduced each successive maid to submission ere she boarded the ship. Their spirits would finally be broken by a combination of Mrs Klapton and the rough sea voyage.[69]

After the collision, Henry Harper carried his dog with him when he and his wife Myra took their places in lifeboat #3:

> I stepped in and sat down among the stokers. There was no one in sight on the decks. I had on my arm a little brown Pekingese spaniel we had picked

> up in Paris and named Sun Yat Sen in honour of his country's first President. The little dog kept very quiet. I found out, after boarding the *Carpathia*, that several dogs had been rescued in the same way in the early boats. There seemed to be lots of room, and nobody made any objection.[70]

Sun Yat Sen arrived safely in the United States and took up his abode in the Harper kennels in New York City. Later that year, a newspaper mentioned the dog's entry in a Pekingese Club of America dog show on 17 December in the grand ballroom of the Plaza Hotel.

'The entries include many interesting and well known Pekingese,' the *New York Herald* reported, 'and the one that will undoubtedly attract the most attention outside of the judging ring is Sun-Yat-Sen, who, with its mistress, Mrs Henry S. Harper, was saved from the *Titanic*.' The dog was entered in the Class 5 division – animals of 8lb and under:

> When visitors to the Pekingese show come to the entry in the catalogue which reads, 'Sun Yat Sen, date of birth, breeder and pedigree unknown,' they probably will want to interview little Sun.
>
> Sun will tell them that it is because all trace of his origin was lost when the *Titanic* sank and he just escaped finding a watery grave himself.

Sun Yat Sen. (Courtesy Randy Bigham)

He was traveling with Mrs H.S. Harper, who had just purchased him in London, and his mistress remembered him all through the awful time and carried him with her in the lifeboat.

Mrs Harper has several other exceedingly good specimens, but Sun Yat Sen is her favorite.[71]

During the months after the disaster, Sun Yat Sen was mated to a Pekingese named Ai-Gee Eureka, of the famous 'Weaver' strain, a massive red belonging to Mrs A. Goodson of New York City.[72]

In June 1913 a newspaper article described Sun Yat Sen's living arrangements in the kennels on the second floor of Mrs Harper's brownstone house in Gramercy Park:

Overlooking Gramercy Park and in a luxurious and polished parquet floored chamber are quartered the expensive and recently imported Pekingese dogs, the property of Mrs Henry S. Harper, wife of one of the brothers of the well-known publishing firm of this city. Although Peter of Braywick, Yuan-Shi-Kai of Braywick, Sun-Yat-Sen of Braywick and their wives and cousins may have had a happy time of it at Hatchford Park, Cobham, England, the seat of Sir Henry and Lady Samuelson, they surely could not have been better looked after than where they are now in the stately residence of their new mistress.

Mrs Harper is fond of dogs, but she doesn't desire to lock up her breed so that it can be of no service or delight to any one save herself. The Pekingese blood that Mrs Harper has in her kennels is available to every person who desires to embrace the opportunity of breeding from these valuable animals. There are about twenty Pekingese at 131 East Twenty-First Street, and these are under the superintendence of Miss Le Doux, an English woman well versed in all that is required in this extremely valuable variety of dogs, which really command greater prices in Europe than they do here. Miss Le Doux was with Lady Samuelson for six years, and when the Hatchford Park kennel of Pekingese was distributed and Mrs Harper acquired the best of them the New York enthusiast prevailed on Miss Le Doux to voyage with her.

Mrs Harper has gone in for Pekingese for about eighteen months, and, like all owners of these quaint little dogs of the Imperial Palace of Pekin and of the temples, she loves them because of their affectionate ways. On entering the picture-hung room, Sun-Yat-Sen of Braywick was the first to rush forward and bark. The sire of this little fellow, Champion Chu-erh of Aldebourne, is reckoned the best Peke that ever lived and his good looks have been handed down to his stock.[73]

A supplementary article gave additional details about the living arrangements of Sun Yat Sen and his brethren:

> Mrs Harper certainly keeps her dogs in splendid shape. They are looked after by Miss Le Doux, an English woman of great experience. There is a kennel maid under her. The dogs are fed on the choicest of foods and kept robust in every way. In a large room, on the walls of which hang several oil paintings, is a capacious exercising ring. In this the dogs are turned to romp and play. If there be a quarrelsome one among them he is left to himself in some other run or placed with a mate disinclined to take any dog insult, which dog, in time, masters the bully, and then all is peace in Gramercy Park.
>
> On all sides these little dogs are carefully looked after. This attention to their needs is due not alone to affection, but is also a means to a profitable end, for a first class puppy is worth $200 or perhaps more when it is three months old. It must not be expected that every puppy in a litter of four or five is worth so much; but a good short faced, square muzzled, big eyed and short bodied specimen will command that figure …
>
> Mrs Harper certainly looks after her dogs carefully, and always has them as her faithful companions both in New York and at her country residence at Long Lakes, NY. Very often the dogs may be seen at exercise, on leashes, in Gramercy Park. Their outlook from their kennels is also upon that strictly reserved piece of ground and the Players Club. There are several international prize winners in Mrs Harper's kennels and many home-breds which will be seen at forthcoming canine events.[74]

On 21 May 1913 the *Olympic* arrived in New York carrying fifteen prize-winning Pekingese, among whom was a dog named Sun-Yat-Sen. (This dog was from a British kennel, however, and was making his first trip to America.)[75]

In July 1913 Mrs Harper began running newspaper advertisements describing Sun Yat Sen's distinguished ancestry ('By Ch. Chu-Erk of Alderbourne') and promoting his stud fee of $25.[76]

Late the following year, a New York newspaper extolled the virtues of this tiny survivor of the *Titanic* disaster.

> Sun Yat Sen is a red dog, the red being a dark shade usually associated with the collies … [The dog] is currently in great shape. He would be the ideal dog to cross because of his excellent blood and his Pekingese temperament.[77]

Margaret Hays

Dog No. 9: Miss Hays owned a Pomeranian puppy named Bebe that was given to her by a friend in Paris.[78] The dog, which had a 'silken brown coat and snappy brown eyes',[79] was carried by Miss Hays into lifeboat #7 and survived the disaster:

> The night of the terrible disaster, when the *Titanic* struck the mammoth iceberg and went down, 'Bebe' was in the stateroom with Miss Hays, and 'Bebe' was one of the first things picked up by Miss Hays when she started to find her way to the deck to be taken off in one of the few vessels that successfully got away from the ill-fated trans-Atlantic vessel.[80]

According to one article, Miss Hays wrapped Bebe in a blanket before carrying him up on deck.[81]

Miss Hays held her Pomeranian in her arms while she stood on the *Titanic*'s deck waiting to board her lifeboat. When James Clinch Smith passed by, he jokingly commented, 'Oh, I suppose we ought to put a life preserver on the little doggie, too.'[82]

> When she climbed into the lifeboat, Miss Hays had 'Bebe' tightly under her arm and she held him there until taken out of the lifeboat onto the good ship *Carpathia*.
>
> But, strange to say, Miss Hays declares she did not know that she had the pretty little brown canine under her arm until she tripped on her skirt in getting out of the lifeboat. It was then that she released her hold on 'Bebe' and the little brown bundle of silken hair fell to the deck of the vessel [lifeboat] and began to whine. Then Miss Hays realized that she had carried her pet Pomeranian with her through the horrors of that awful night and the puppy never so much as whined, seeming to realize that he was safe from harm so long as Miss Hays held him closely to her bosom.[83]

Miss Hays was expecting resistance from the officers when she entered boat #7 with her dog in her arms, but she was surprised when she received none. (Apparently, the officers didn't notice the dog or else thought it was an infant swaddled in the blanket.)[84]

After the *Titanic* went down, Washington Dodge Jr and his mother were apparently transferred from lifeboat #5 to lifeboat #7 by Third Officer Herbert Pitman.[85] In later years Dodge remembered something that happened while he was waiting to exit lifeboat #7 and board the rescue ship:

> A mail sack was lowered for me as I could not climb the rope ladder. Some woman handed a dog to the sailor the same time he was lifting me. He refused to take the dog.[86]

On board the *Carpathia*, Margaret Hays continued to care for her dog and also for the two small Navratil children who had been placed into her care. Miss Hays was said to have covered the two boys, almost naked, with the same blanket she used to cover Bebe in the lifeboat.[87]

> The little brown fellow and the two little French children, whom she so tenderly mothered, became fast friends and were inseparable up to the time the mother of the two children came to claim them and take them back to Paris.[88]

> A little black Pomeranian, which Miss Hays was taking from Paris to her house, attracted the children's attention. They played with the puppy and Miss Hays became attached to them. When *Carpathia* came in on Thursday night [18 April] with the *Titanic* survivors, Miss Hays came down with the two children.[89]

> The two little curly-heads did not understand it all. Had not their pretty 19-year-old foster mother provided them with pretty suits and little white shoes and playthings a-plenty? Then, too, Miss Hays had a Pom dog that she brought with her from Paris and which she carried in her arms when she left the *Titanic* and held to her bosom through the long night in the life-boat, and to which the children became warmly attached. All three became aliens on an alien shore.[90]

Miss Hays was married in 1913, and instead of taking Bebe with her on her honeymoon trip she made arrangements for the dog to live with her bridesmaid, Miss Stewart. This arrangement lasted until 1914, at which time Miss Stewart's sister, Mrs Ernest Stauffen, entered the picture.[91]

> When Miss Stewart recently left California for the east she gave 'Bebe' into Mrs Stauffen's keeping and just at present Mrs Stauffen's little daughter and the sole canine survivor of the *Titanic* are constantly together.
>
> 'Bebe' dislikes to be alone, Mrs Stauffen says. 'He is not nearly so pretty as he once was,' she said. 'His coat is not so glossy and he has lost much of it. He is almost human. I believe he suffered from the shock of the awful experience. He is very playful, but always he wants to be near someone.'[92]

When Mrs Stauffen was diagnosed with tuberculosis, she and her husband moved to Redlands, California. In 1916 Bebe was entered in a dog show in Redlands, and on 15 April he won first prize in the Toy Pomeranian class.

Mrs Stauffen succumbed to her illness in New York in October 1916,[93] and in June 1917 Ernest Stauffen ran a newspaper ad for a missing Pomeranian:

> LOST – LITTLE POMERANIAN DOG, chestnut brown, on June 4, about 9:30; liberal reward if returned to Mr E. Stauffen, 4 North Washington Square, city.[94]

At the present time it is unknown if Bebe was ever found and returned to Mr Stauffen.[95]

In recent years, a mistaken notion has arisen in regard to Margaret Hays, her dog Bebe, and Michel and Edmund Navratil, the two small children of victim Michel Navratil. Although Miss Hays definitely cared for the two children while they were on board the *Carpathia* and afterwards, an interview given by Michel Navratil decades later mistakenly suggested that he and his brother Edmund were saved in lifeboat #7 right beside Miss Hays and her dog:

> I don't recall being afraid, I remember the pleasure, really, of going plop! into the life-boat. We ended up next to the daughter of an American banker who managed to save her dog – no one objected. We had our back to *Titanic* and went to sleep.[96]

Margaret's father, Frank Hays, cleared up this misunderstanding a few days after his daughter, her dog and the two French children arrived in New York:

> The published story that the children were in the same boat with my daughter and clung to her instinctively, is a misstatement. My daughter left in the first lifeboat and the two children followed on later boats … The survivors of the *Titanic* on board [the *Carpathia*] formed a ladies' committee, and as my daughter was the only one among them who had not suffered some personal loss through the disaster she was asked to care for the two children, and gladly did so.[97]

Elizabeth Rothschild

Dog No. 10: Mrs Rothschild owned a Pomeranian that she carried with her into lifeboat #6 and which survived the disaster.

According to Rothschild researcher John Pulos, Mrs Rothschild's husband Martin covered the dog (which was in Elizabeth's lap) with his overcoat.

Researcher Bruno Piola suggests this might explain why nobody noticed the dog until later, and he comments further:

> The article adds that, when boat 6 reached the rescue vessel, the ship's crew at first refused to rescue the Pomeranian. Then Elizabeth decided not to leave the boat without the dog, so that the two of them finally boarded the rescue boat. Pulos, in a conversation with this author on Facebook, said that his sources for the events on board boat #6 (Martin hiding the dog and Mrs Rothschild's refusal to board the *Carpathia*) were Elizabeth's niece and son-in-law, who, in their own words, 'were old enough to remember.' The godson, in particular, spent a lot of time with Elizabeth.[98]

After arriving in New York an unnamed *Carpathia* steward told a New York reporter:

> One of the earlier boats to arrive was seen to contain a woman clasping a pet Pomeranian. When assisted to the rope ladder and while the rope was being fastened around her she emphatically refused to give up for a second the dog which was evidently so much to her. He is now receiving as careful and tender attention as his mistress.[99]

According to Bruno Piola, researcher Daniel Klistorner once quoted an interview (with no mention of the newspaper's name or date) with survivor Mary Hélène Douglas, who was with Mrs Rothschild in boat #6:

> She [Mrs Rothschild] had a dog in her muff, and she absolutely refused to climb [on to the *Carpathia*] until the dog was hoisted and the only thing that made her rise was the cries of the sailors … and the insistence of other women that they would climb if she did not want to.[100]

Piola adds that, although Mrs Douglas did not name the passenger in question, she could only be referring to Elizabeth Rothschild, who was saved in the same boat.[101]

It's possible that survivor Philip Zenni might have been saved in boat #6 as well, because after the disaster a couple of different reporters described his experiences as follows:

> The love of a woman for her pet dog was manifested as the *Carpathia* came alongside their rowboat, said Zenni Thursday, when the woman turned

> to one of the men in the little boat and said, 'Oh, take my little dog up the ladder with you. I must save him.' The man had his hands full, said Zenni, and was looking after the safety of another woman, not after that of the dog, but when all were aboard the *Carpathia* Zenni said he saw the woman again, and she was holding tight to her pet, about the only thing except the clothes on her back which she had managed to save.[102]
>
> An incident that tends to prove the utter selfishness of shallow-minded people is related by the young man. When the survivors were being raised into the *Carpathia* a woman who was in his lifeboat pleaded with him to save her dog, which she had clasped tightly in her arms since leaving the *Titanic*. Zanni [*sic*] informed her politely that human beings came first, and she clung desperately to the little animal until someone lifted her to the deck of the boat.[103]

Dr Alice Leader was saved in lifeboat #8 but may have witnessed Mrs Rothschild's exit from lifeboat #6 after her own boat was picked up by the *Carpathia*. A reporter described Dr Leader's statement as follows:

> In one of the boats a woman was seen tenderly clasping a pet Pomeranian, and when she was assisted up the rope ladder of the *Carpathia*, and even while the rope was being fastened around her, she emphatically refused to give up the dog for a second.[104]

Carpathia passenger William David told a reporter, 'Mrs Rothschild carried a little Pomeranian when taken on board.'[105]

As fate would have it, less than a week after arriving in New York Mrs Rothschild's dog was killed by a larger dog on her brother's estate in East Orange, N.J.[106] According to researcher Ron Vertone:

> Charles Barrett, Mrs Rothschild's nephew, told me that his aunt's Pom didn't last long after the rescue, and was possibly the first fatality among the survivors. Mrs Rothschild went to recuperate with her brother and his family at their home in, I believe, West Orange, New Jersey. Little Charles was playing with his aunt's Pom on the front porch one day not long after Mrs R's arrival when the neighbor's German Shepherd came charging over, attacked the Pom viciously, and finished what the *Titanic* had been unable to do.[107]

According to researcher Bruno Piola, historian Don Lynch was told by Rothschild family members that the scene of the attack on the Pomeranian was New York's Central Park instead of New Jersey.[108]

On the other hand, another version of the dog's demise has it that the animal was killed under the wheels of a carriage amid the dockside confusion after the *Carpathia* arrived in New York.[109] This version of the story seems to be corroborated by friends and family members:

> [John] Pulos interviewed Marian Littell, a niece of 92-year-old Elizabeth's seamstress. The elderly lady reinforced the thesis of the trampling. 'Marian remembered Elizabeth talking about her dog that was killed by the wheels of a carriage in New York after it came from the disaster at sea,' says Pulos. John, in conversation with this Facebook author, explained that Mrs Rothschild's relatives are 'pretty sure' that the dog was run over. Despite the conflicting information (something very common when studying the *Titanic*), the thesis that the dog was run over seems to be more consistent, being supported by authors of books, family and acquaintances of Elizabeth.[110]

Additional Dogs on the *Titanic*

We have just listed the ten dogs that are *known* to have been on board the *Titanic* and whose presence there has been well documented. Most of these dogs seem to have been quartered in their masters' first-class staterooms, but we don't know how many other dogs might have been on board the vessel or how many of those animals might have been quartered in the ship's kennels instead of in staterooms. (It's not impossible that dogs being transported by second- and third-class passengers would have been required to stay in the kennels instead of in their masters' cabins.) In light of the distinct possibility that our list of ten dogs on the *Titanic* is incomplete (especially considering the anonymous surviving dog fancier's claim that approximately thirty dogs were on board), let's examine reports of additional dogs whose presence on board the ship is uncertain.

Dog No. 11? The *Carpathia*'s Second Officer James Bisset later recalled a woman survivor (he believed she was in boat #2) who carried a dog with her in her lifeboat:

> As we fastened one of the women into a bosun's chair, I noticed that she was wearing a nightdress and slippers, with a fur coat. Beneath the coat she was nursing what I supposed was a baby, but it was a small pet dog! 'Be careful of my doggie,' she pleaded, more worried about her pet's safety than her own.[111]

Was Bisset mistaken about this being lifeboat #2? Might the woman in question have been Miss Hays in boat #7 or Mrs Rothschild in boat #6? Researcher Bruno Piola believes Bisset was referring to Mrs Rothschild, since Miss Hayes and Mrs Harper were both well clad that night and were not dressed in night-clothing like the woman the second officer was describing.[112]

Dog No. 12? While on board the *Carpathia*, Vera Dick wrote an account of her experiences on the *Titanic*:

> One woman had a fox terrier in her arms, and the man told her to try a life-saver on the dog.
>
> 'Everybody is wearing them now,' he laughed.[113]

Logan Marshall:

> A moment before the men had been joking about the life-belts, according to the story told by Mrs Vera Dick, of Calgary, Canada. 'Try this one,' one man said to her, 'they are the very latest thing this season. Everybody's wearing them now.'
>
> Another man suggested to a woman friend, who had a fox terrier in her arms, that she should put a life-saver on the dog. 'It won't fit,' the woman replied, laughing.
>
> 'Make him carry it in his mouth,' said the friend.[114]

This story is reminiscent of James Clinch Smith's comment to Margaret Hays about putting a lifebelt on her Pomeranian, but Mrs Dick specifies that the dog she was talking about was a fox terrier.

Dog No. 13? Three months after the sinking of the *Titanic*, Ida Hippach seems to have spoken with a reporter about an incident that supposedly took place in lifeboat #4:

> That some of the men who were rescued from the *Titanic* were less heroic than those who went down with the ship is a moderate way of putting

> the unpleasant truth. Mrs Hippach of Chicago, one of the women survivors, said that the boat in which she and her daughter was saved contained 31 women and two men, one of the latter being a Spaniard who carried a poodle dog in his arms. The women, who were rowing, asked him to take an oar and help, but he said he couldn't as he had to mind his dog.[115]

Ida Hippach was in boat 4, which is not known to have carried any male passengers, and no poodles are *known* to have been on board the *Titanic* at all. Could Mrs Hippach have been relating a hearsay story about the dog, and might the 'Spaniard' in question have been Henry Harper, who was carrying his Pekingese in boat #3?

Dog No. 14? Not long after the disaster, Imanita Shelley recorded her recollection of an incident that occurred at lifeboat #12:

> One woman, after she had been put in our boat, begged a seaman to go down to her cabin and fetch up her pet dog.[116]

Although Mrs Dickinson Bishop is known to have left her dog in her cabin, she and her husband were saved in lifeboat #7 and were not in lifeboat #12 with Mrs Shelley.

Dog No. 15? After arriving in New York, John Snyder described an incident that took place after he and his wife got into lifeboat #7:

> A woman whose name I do not know tried to get in the boat with a dog, but the man in charge stopped her. She started to argue the question with him, and actually wanted him to hold the boat back for her until she could go below and get her pet. We were about to be lowered to the water, when the woman suddenly made up her mind and hastily got in the boat.[117]

This woman might possibly have been Mrs Dickinson Bishop, who left her dog Frou Frou in her cabin and was saved in lifeboat #7. There's no guarantee of this, though, so it's not impossible the unnamed woman might have owned a 'new' dog whose existence is otherwise undocumented. In support of the latter premise, Don Lynch points out that Mrs Bishop was the first person to enter boat #7, whereas the unnamed woman described by Mrs Snyder was one of the very last people to enter #7 before it was lowered away.

Dog No. 16? It's possible that John Jacob Astor owned a second Airedale in addition to his favourite dog Kitty. Survivor Nella Goldenberg, who was 'one of the best-known dog fanciers in this country and Europe',[118] might have been privy to detailed information about the Astor pets that is unknown to us now.

> According to Mrs Goldenberg many dogs were lost on board the *Titanic*, among them two Airedales belonging to Colonel Astor and a bulldog belonging to Robert W. Daniel which was sure to capture ribbons in this country. Mrs Goldenberg said so many fine dogs were on board the *Titanic* that a show was being arranged for the last day of the voyage.[119]

Regarding the possible presence of a second Astor Airedale on the *Titanic*, a newspaper once commented on Mrs Astor's post-disaster attendance at the Westminster Kennel Club's dog show and confirmed the fact that she did indeed own a second Airedale.

> The late Colonel Astor gave his wife an Airedale terrier shortly after their marriage. His constant companion was one of those snappy, intelligent dogs, and when he and Mrs Astor went abroad on their wedding trip his Airedale went along.[120]

It should be pointed out that the newspaper article makes no mention of Mrs Astor's Airedale having accompanied her and her husband abroad in 1912. (A 1913 photograph shows Mrs Astor walking an Airedale on the streets of New York, so that dog might very well have been the dog given to her by her husband after their marriage.) In any case, if the Astors did indeed have two Airedales on board the *Titanic* it's a certainty that neither dog survived the sinking.

Dog No. 17? It's possible that a Great Dane (owner unknown) was on board the *Titanic*, because the same unnamed *Carpathia* steward who mentioned the rescue of Mrs Rothschild's Pomeranian continued with the following report that he gleaned from an unnamed survivor:

> A survivor informs me that there was on the ship a lady who was taking out a huge Great Dane dog. When the boats were rapidly filling she appeared on deck with her canine companion and sadly entreated that he should be taken off with her. It was impossible. Human lives, those of women and children,

> were the first consideration. She was urged to seize the opportunity to save her own life and leave the dog. She refused to desert him and has, I understand, sacrificed her life with him.[121]

Researcher Bruno Piola has discovered a separate account relating the same information contained in the unnamed steward's description of the Rothschilds' Pomeranian; however, instead of continuing by repeating the anonymous survivor's subsequent story about the woman who refused to leave her dog on the *Titanic*, Piola's article makes a point of *naming* the female eyewitness who supposedly observed the latter incident:

> In one of the boats, a woman [Rothschild] was seen holding her pet Pomeranian affectionately, and when she was helped up the *Carpathia* ladder, and even as the rope was being tied around her, she emphatically refused to let go of the dog for a second. Miss [Alice Farnham] Leader further tells how a woman declined to leave the *Titanic* because they would not take off her pet dog with her.[122]

(Please note that the following entry about Dog #18 is very similar to our entry about Dog #17 except that the dog's breed is different.)

Dog No. 18? *Carpathia* steward J.W. Barker described a St Bernard* that was allegedly on board the *Titanic*:

> Another young woman went down with the *Titanic* rather than desert her dog – a huge St Bernard, and a great favourite on board. When the lifeboats were being launched a seat was prepared for her, but she demanded that the dog be taken also. This was impossible, human lives being the first consideration, and she was urged to sacrifice the dog and save herself. She refused, and was last seen on the deck of the vessel, clasping her pet to her bosom. Her dead body was afterwards found floating by the side of her dog.[123]

The bodies mentioned by Steward Barker were seen by passenger Johanne Steinke when the liner *Bremen* passed through a field of floating wreckage a few days after the disaster:

---

* As will be discussed presently, novelist Marty Crisp decided to 'pair up' this lost dog with lost *Titanic* passenger Ann Isham while writing her fictional children's book *White Star*.

> 'I saw,' said Miss Steinke, 'a middle-aged woman, well dressed, showing she had been a cabin passenger, clasping in her arms a large St Bernard dog. I suppose that while the ship was sinking she went to the butcher's shop and fetched her dog. I should have done the same.'[124]

> We saw one woman in her night dress, with a baby clasped closely to her breast. Several women passengers screamed and left the rail in a fainting condition. There was another woman, fully dressed, with her arms tight around the body of a shaggy dog.[125]

Dog No. 19? After arriving in New York and repairing to the St Denis Hotel, *Carpathia* passenger Reuben Weidman spoke with reporters about survivor Gilbert Tucker's positive attitude on board the rescue ship and mentioned the fact that Tucker had a dog with him:

> He was full of life and helped to make things as agreeable and lively as possible. And when he was not looking after the comfort of his fellow survivors, he was taking care of his little dog, which he got in Naples and which he proudly held on to throughout the ordeal.[126]

Reuben Weidman also spoke about the circumstances in which Gilbert Tucker left the rescue ship:

> Yes, and the last I saw of Tucker he was going down the gangplank with the dog under one arm and a baby under the other.[127]

Although it is not impossible that Gilbert Tucker purchased a dog in Naples and saved it from the *Titanic*, it's far more likely the dog in question was actually Bebe, the Pomeranian belonging to Margaret Hays. Tucker travelled in company with Miss Hays on the *Titanic* and was saved in her lifeboat as well, so it seems likely he remained in close contact with her on the *Carpathia* and that he was carrying her dog and one of the two Navratil children in his arms when Mr Weidman saw him walking down the gangplank in New York.

And yet there's a curious story that was written down by *Carpathia* passenger Howard Chapin, who heard it while he was on board the rescue ship; the tale described the way in which an unnamed male *Titanic* survivor reportedly saved his own dog from a watery death:

> One man saw a boat pass his window [as it was being lowered from the boat deck] and threw his dog through the porthole into the lifeboat. He was saved by another lifeboat and so got his dog again on the *Carpathia*.[128]

Could the unnamed man who allegedly pushed his dog out of a porthole into a lifeboat have been Gilbert Tucker? No survivors are known to have recorded witnessing such an incident, and the fact that Tucker left the ship in the *very first* lifeboat (#7) eliminates him as a candidate for having pushed a dog through a porthole into another lowering lifeboat. (Besides, Tucker himself never mentioned having a dog of his own on board the *Titanic*.)

Dog No. 20? In recent years, researcher Geoff Whitfield spoke with relatives of Edith Nile Peacock, who perished on the *Titanic* along with her daughter 'Treasteall' and infant son Alfred. Whitfield reports the following:

> Yes, when I was first in touch with the Nile family, they gave me a photo to copy of Treasteall (which was not her name!) with, if I recall, some sort of spaniel. During the conversation, the old lady was saying she remembers playing with Aunt Edith's daughter (alas, she couldn't recall her name!) and the lovely little dog the family had. She said, 'Of course, the poor dog shared their fate I believe.'
>
> Personally, I think it more likely that the dog was given away before they sailed – I've never seen or heard any evidence that any third class passengers had animals aboard – but that appears to be the family lore.[129]

General Mentions of *Titanic*'s Dogs

Anonymous Newspaper Story

After the *Carpathia* reached New York, a newspaper published an unlikely story that presumably was based on a survivor account:

> One man who had a Pomeranian dog leaped overboard with it and striking a piece of wreckage was badly stunned. He recovered after a few minutes and swam toward one of the lifeboats and was taken aboard. Most of the men who were aboard the *Carpathia*, barring the members of the crew who had manned the boats, had jumped into the sea as the *Titanic* was settling.[130]

Perhaps it's worth pointing out that the article doesn't claim the Pomeranian survived; instead, it just says the man had the dog in his arms when he jumped into the water.

Fred Beachler

Mr Beachler, a *Carpathia* passenger, granted an interview to reporters after the rescue ship reached New York:

> Among the rescued was a Japanese and four Chinese. Two small dogs, one being a handsome chow chow, were also saved and taken care of.[131]

Sallie Beckwith

Mrs Beckwith discussed the sinking with her brother, Peris Moneypenny, who later spoke with reporters:

> Six dogs were saved in the *Titanic* disaster, according to a story told by Peris N. Moneypenny, of this city, who returned from New York, where he met his sister, Mrs Richard Beckwith, and her husband, who were rescued by the *Carpathia*. One of the women who saved her dog wrapped it in a blanket, it is said, and the other passengers thought it was a baby, the error in identity not being discovered until shortly before the *Carpathia* made the rescue.[132]

May Birkhead

Carpathia passenger May Birkhead wrote the following account while the rescue ship was still at sea.

> Five women saved their pet dogs, carrying them in their arms. Another woman saved a little pig, which she said was her mascot. Though her husband is an Englishman and she lives in England, she is an American and was on her way to visit her folk here. How she cared for the pig aboard ship I do not know, but she carried it up the side of the ship in a big bag. I did not mind the dogs so much, but it seemed to me to be too much when a pig was saved and human beings went to death.[133]

Her account was based on interviews she conducted with survivors, but she mistakenly believed that Edith Rosenbaum saved a live pig. In actuality, it was a small pig-shaped music box.

Edith Brown

In 1985 second-class passenger Edith Brown Haisman described her experiences on the *Titanic* while she was touring the vessel's first-class areas:

Q. And there was a nursery for the children?
A. Yes, nice nursery, big nursery too.
Q. Did you go and see it then?
A. No, just looked around and that. They had some beautiful dogs there too.
Q. Did they?
A. Because a lot of the people in the first class brought a lot of dogs and they used to take them up on decks sometimes.[134]

Howard Chapin

Carpathia passenger Howard Chapin wrote an account of the *Titanic* disaster while the rescue ship was still at sea. The account was based on interviews he conducted with the survivors:

> Five dogs, mostly Pomeranians, were saved.[135]

Howard Chapin and May Birkhead both interviewed *Titanic* survivors while the rescue ship was still at sea, and both agreed that five dogs were saved. At the present time, only three dogs are *known* to have been carried on to the *Carpathia* on the morning of 15 April.

May Futrelle

After arriving in the United States, Mrs Futrelle wrote an account of her *Titanic* experience and some of the things she was apparently told by other survivors:

> Many of the women knew better how to handle the boat than the men who were put in charge. On one of the boats a man refused to take an oar. He was a coward. He shivered so with fright that he said that he could not hold an oar.
>
> Another man held a small poodle dog in his arms and spoke to it as if it were a child. This was the kind of a man who would rather save a dog than a child. There are so many men and women who give more attention to dogs than human beings.[136]

Was this man Henry Harper, who was holding his wife's Pekingese Sun Yat Sen, or – less likely – was it Gilbert Tucker holding Margaret Hays' Pomeranian Bebe? Or was this 'poodle' the same one Mrs Hippach supposedly saw a 'Spaniard' holding in boat #4? Who can say?

Mary Glynn

Miss Glynn told reporters about some of her experiences on the *Titanic*:

> Mary said she saw Martin [Gallagher] fingering his rosary beads in prayer as the boat was lowered. She also heard barking dogs, 'neighing horses' and the sweet strains of the orchestra rising above an overpowering soundscape.[137]

William Greenfield

In later years, a relative of Mr Greenfield and his mother Blanche wrote a brief account of Greenfield's *Titanic* experience:

> Blanche avoided talking about the *Titanic* in later life and William only talked about it once with Nell and commented he was more disturbed by the barks and cries from the dogs than the cries of the people.[138]

Mrs Charles M. Hutchison

Mrs Hutchison, a *Carpathia* passenger, wrote the following account while she was on board the rescue ship:

> Two pet dogs came aboard safely, both small long-haired curs. I have an insane desire to kick them.[139]

Charles Joughin

Mr Joughin reportedly saw one of *Titanic*'s dogs during the sinking:

> Walter Lord had recorded that in one of his phone conversations with Charles Joughin, this unsung hero of the *Titanic* was startled to see a dog swimming past him, after the ship had gone down and before he reached the overturned Boat B.[140]

Edith Rosenbaum

In later years Miss Rosenbaum recorded the following memories of her time on the *Titanic*:

> Mr Benjamin Guggenheim and Mr and Mrs S. Goldenberg were also aboard the ship. Mr Goldenberg was a very well-known importer of New York and a keen dog fancier.
>
> He had on board some 35 of the finest bull dogs which he had shown in England, where he had won a number of prizes. As a dog lover I was deeply in sympathy with his concern for his dogs.
>
> At the time of the accident he immediately went to the kennels to be with his dogs and he perished with them.[141]

Samuel Goldenberg did not die in the sinking as Miss Rosenbaum believed, nor did he ever mention having lost thirty-five bulldogs in the disaster. However, perhaps this account should be compared with that of the anonymous female dog fancier (Goldenberg's mother?), who also claimed that approximately thirty dogs were lost on the *Titanic.*

Maude Slocombe

In July 1955 Mrs Slocombe was interviewed by Walter Lord, who took notes while she reminisced:

> The bump of the collision woke her up. She heard scuffling outside room, looked out, saw Steward George Dodd, eyes bulging, who told her to go up on deck.
>
> On the boat deck, a steward offered her a little dog, she refused it but took a baby offered to her. As the confusion grew, First Officer Murdoch called 'Be British'.[142]

Mr Smith

In late April 1912 Mr Smith, the manager of a New York club for merchant mariners, spoke with survivors before writing a letter to his brother Hugh Smith in Portrush, County Antrim, Ireland:

> One woman, while the boat was being loaded, was loud in her demand that a steward should find her little dog for her. The steward picked the dog off the deck, and dropping it over the side, said: 'To blazes with your dog. Wouldn't you rather find your husband?'[143]

Elizabeth Tarkington

After the *Carpathia*'s arrival in New York, passenger Elizabeth Tarkington granted an interview to reporters:

> There were thirty pet dogs on the *Titanic*, and three of those were saved. The women just clung to them like babies. I think it would have been better if they had found babies to cling to.[144]

Fictitious Dogs and Alleged Owners on Board the *Titanic*

Ann Isham and the St Bernard

In online sources it is often claimed that *Titanic* victim Ann Isham owned a St Bernard or Great Dane and that this dog was on board the ill-fated liner with her. Although one or both of these dogs might very well have existed (see 'Dog#17?' and 'Dog #18?), the claim that Miss Isham owned such a dog is untrue and originated in the fictional book *White Star*, a novel for young people written by author Marty Crisp in 2004. The present author knows this to be a fact, because he was serving as a historical consultant to Ms Crisp while she was fleshing out her novel's plot by 'assigning' a specific owner to each supposed '*Titanic* dog' whose true owner was unknown.

Before she 'paired' Ann Isham with the St Bernard whose floating body was seen clutched in the arms of a female victim (see our discussion of 'Dog #18?'), Marty Crisp was originally planning to pair that animal with William Dulles, the actual breed of whose dog is unknown. The present writer therefore sent Ms Crisp an email offering a bit of advice:

> It occurs to me that you should write an introduction (or an afterword) to your book in which you detail exactly which of your dog–human 'partnerships' are fictionalised. That is, you should make it clear that nobody knows if Frou Frou was a miniature poodle or not, that nobody knows if Mr Dulles' dog was a St Bernard, etc. Otherwise the fictionalised portions of your book will be indistinguishable from the factually documented portions and will confuse future readers – who'll think that *all* of your book's details are based on documented fact.

Marty Crisp eventually decided to pair the dead St Bernard with Ann Isham instead of William Dulles, and she also included a caveat about her decision to do so in a supplement that appeared at the end of the novel. Unfortunately, few people bothered to read beyond the text of the novel itself, and the present author's fears subsequently came true: Crisp's fictional pairing of Ann Isham and the St Bernard was soon accepted as fact by the general public, and internet discussions of the *Titanic*'s dogs are now filled with claims that Isham's body was seen clutching the floating body of her beloved St Bernard.

Although the floating body of a St Bernard apparently *was* seen by a passenger on the *Bremen*, and although there's no particular reason why the female victim floating beside that dead dog couldn't have been Ann Isham, there's no reason why that victim couldn't have been any other female *Titanic* passenger who just happened to clutch on to the swimming dog while both were dying of hypothermia. In short, no evidence exists that would connect Ann Isham with any dog that was travelling on board the *Titanic*.

First Officer William Murdoch and Rigel

The story of Rigel, a Newfoundland dog supposedly owned by First Officer Murdoch, originated in a 1912 New York newspaper article and was soon reprinted in the *Titanic* books that came out right after the disaster:

> THE DOG HERO
>
> Not the least among the heroes of the *Titanic* disaster was Rigel, a big black Newfoundland dog, belonging to the first officer, who went down with the ship. But for Rigel the fourth boat picked up might have been run down by the *Carpathia*. For three hours he swam in the icy water where the *Titanic* went down, evidently looking for his master, and was instrumental in guiding the boatload of survivors to the gangway of the *Carpathia*.
>
> Jonas Briggs, a seaman abroad the *Carpathia*, now has Rigel and told the story of the dog's heroism. The *Carpathia* was moving slowly about, looking for boats, rafts or anything which might be afloat. Exhausted with their efforts, weak from lack of food and exposure to the cutting wind and terror-stricken, the men and women in the fourth boat had drifted under the *Carpathia*'s starboard bow. They were dangerously close to the steamship, but too weak to shout a warning loud enough to reach the bridge.
>
> The boat might not have been seen were it not for the sharp barking of Rigel, who was swimming ahead of the craft, and valiantly announcing his position. The barks attracted the attention of Captain Rostron; and he went to the starboard end of the bridge to see where they came from and saw the boat. He immediately ordered the engines stopped, and the boat came alongside the starboard gangway.
>
> Care was taken to get Rigel aboard, but he appeared little affected by his long trip through the ice-cold water. He stood by the rail and barked until Captain Rostron called Briggs and had him take the dog below.[145]

The only problem with this dramatic story is that it wasn't true. Just like the hundreds of imposter *Titanic* survivors who first began appearing in public right after the disaster, occasional *Carpathia* imposters began surfacing as well. Jonas Briggs was one of those imposters; Briggs was not a genuine member of *Carpathia*'s crew and did not appear on her crew roster, and his story about the fictional Rigel was just an example of his own imaginativeness and desire for publicity.

Captain Edward J. Smith and Ben

Titanic enthusiasts are well aware of a photograph showing Captain Smith holding the leash of a large Borzoi dog, and enthusiastic internet postings claim the dog belonged to Smith and that the photograph was snapped on board the *Titanic*. Extra details sometimes claim that the dog's name was Ben and that the animal was given to Smith by Benjamin Guggenheim, who later perished with Smith on the *Titanic*.[146]

Once again, no evidence exists to support any of these claims. Although it is obvious the photo in question was snapped on board a ship, there isn't the slightest bit of evidence to suggest that it was taken on board the *Titanic*. (Ship

Captain Smith and Ben. (Author's collection)

expert Jonathan Smith is certain the photo was snapped on board the *Adriatic* around 1907.)[147]

Although Captain Smith is thought to have owned a dog (breed unknown), there is no period documentation to support the claim that the animal was named Ben or that it was given to Smith by Benjamin Guggenheim. The only reliable information about Captain Smith's dog that has ever come to light was provided by survivor Edith Brown, who spoke with Smith on the subject when he visited *Titanic*'s second-class area during the maiden voyage. When Edith asked him if he had a dog, Smith replied, 'Yes. Not on board the ship, I hasten to add. He's back home in Southampton where he should be. When I get back to Southampton after this voyage I shall have much more time to spend with him.'[148]

Perhaps a fitting conclusion to our discussion of the *Titanic*'s dogs would be a brief mention of third-class victim Patrick O'Connell and the odd experience he had while saying goodbye to his family and his dog in Ireland and heading to Queenstown to board the *Titanic*:

> Patie's first bit of growing up came when he had to part with his dog. It was an emotional wrench, but he managed the leave-taking. The canine howled and mourned all night – and then repeated the anguish four days later, on the night when the *Titanic* was sinking.[149]

Before we leave the subject of dogs, we'll quote the text of a post-disaster letter sent to the *Daily Mirror* along with a contribution to that newspaper's relief fund for *Titanic*'s survivors:

> May I, a fox-terrier, following the example of the little chocolate Pom, ask you to accept the enclosed 10s., which is a contribution from my own money-box and collected by me entirely from eleven other little dog friends.
>
> With our hearts sad at the remembrance of the lady who was seen in the water 'clasping the body of a shaggy dog m her arms,' we dog friends feel that our humble efforts will not be despised.
>
> — 'A Fox Terrier'[150]

Unintentional Animal Passengers

Lice and Insects

Although the present author is unaware of specific references to insects and other arthropod pests on board the *Titanic*, their presence there was an inevitable fact of life.

It is quite possible that occasional infestations of head, crab and other species of lice could have existed undetected among passengers travelling in *Titanic*'s steerage. (These pests could have been present to a much lesser extent in the other two classes as well.)

As for insect problems, fleas could easily have been brought aboard the ship by occasional passengers (most likely in steerage) as well as by some of the dogs that were being transported in first class. (Since fleas prefer feeding on the blood of hair-covered mammals, their presence can often go unnoticed by pet owners until the insects are forced by necessity to switch over to human hosts after the death or departure of a pet.)

It is inevitable that microscopic eggs of insect pests like weevils, meal moths etc. were present in cereal, flour and grain foodstuffs that were brought aboard the *Titanic* and then served to her passengers and crew. This is still the case with flour and grain foodstuffs today, since the tiny eggs of these pantry pests always begin to hatch out of any grain product that sits in storage for a sufficient length of time. (Normally we eat these unhatched eggs without realising it – an unavoidable fact of life that would upset many people if they knew about it.)

Rats

Two survivor accounts exist that document the fact that the brand-new *Titanic* hosted a healthy population of rats that undoubtedly came aboard via mooring ropes and unattended gangways.

John Podesta

In later years Fireman Podesta wrote an account of his *Titanic* experiences in which he mentioned the presence of rats on board the vessel:

> After mails and passengers were on board, we set off for New York. All went pretty well until Saturday … On this very same morning my chum and I

> had just gone across [after] firing our boilers and we were standing against a watertight door – just talking – when all of a sudden, on looking through the forward end on her starboard side we saw about six or maybe more rats running toward us. They passed by our feet; in fact, we both kicked out at them and they ran aft somewhere.
>
> They must have come from the bow end, about where the crash came. We did not take much notice at the time because we see rats on most ships, but I think it is true that they can smell danger.[151]

Mary Katherine Gilnagh
In later years Miss Gilnagh spoke with historian Walter Lord, who made notes recording her *Titanic* experiences on the evening of 14 April:

> The trip over was a delight. Sunday evening a gay dance, enlivened by a strolling bagpipe player [Eugene Daly] the girls all loved. During the evening a rat scurried across the room, and the boys gave chase while the girls squealed with excitement. She remembered thinking that this must be a safe ship – the rats don't like to leave it.[152]

Sightings of Wild Animals

Occasional stories have come to light describing non-domestic animals that were seen in the vicinity of both the *Titanic* and the *Carpathia*. These sightings commenced while *Titanic* was still being built in Belfast and ended while *Carpathia* was returning to New York with *Titanic*'s survivors.

Bears

Elmer Taylor
While the *Carpathia* was steaming toward New York with *Titanic*'s survivors, Mr Taylor began noticing wildlife in the vicinity of the rescue ship:

> A little farther on we passed a big floe of ice on which there was a big white polar bear prowling around.[153]

There's no reason for us to disbelieve Taylor's account, since polar bears have been seen swimming in the open ocean as far as 60 miles from land after having been carried there by ice floes that subsequently melted.[154] It's likely that Elmer Taylor's polar bear eventually drowned in the open ocean after the ice floes on which it was taking shelter melted.

Charles Joughin

In 1999 a message was posted in an online *Titanic* forum raising the remote possibility that Mr Joughin might have seen polar bears shortly after the ship went down. The person who posted the online message reportedly spoke with members of Joughin's family:

> They described him as being a very friendly person but not the most handsome. He was short and stocky and had great big hands. He loved to tell stories of the sea to his family and friends but rarely mentioned the *Titanic*. One of the grandchildren asked him why he was certain the *Titanic* had struck an iceberg if he didn't actually see the collision. His reply was simply, 'because, my dear, when I was in the water, I saw polar bears walking on the ice'.[155]

Might Joughin's granddaughter have misremembered the exact time period when he reportedly saw his polar bear? Might Joughin have actually seen the bear after daylight instead of while he was fighting for his life in the ocean that night? Or is it possible the granddaughter didn't realise that Joughin was gently joking with her? Who can say?

Unnamed Seamen

After the *Carpathia* arrived in New York, a newspaper article reported on the fact that bears had recently been sighted in the icefield:

> There is much conflict between official and unofficial statements, but it seems that the *Titanic* struck an iceberg at 10.25pm on Sunday night and foundered at 2.20am … one of the captains of the Allan liners which run between Glasgow and New York recently passed a berg fully 200ft high and nearly a quarter of a mile long … the proximity of the bergs is usually indicated by a sudden lowering of temperature of the air and water. Now and then a ship's crew, passing close have seen a polar bear stranded on the floe … the largest recorded berg is estimated to have been nearly 900ft high; this would mean that there would be over 8000ft that could not be seen …[156]

Birds

W.J. Nolan

W.J. Nolan worked as a painter for the shipbuilder Harland and Wolff, and while working on the *Titanic* he was assigned to stain, polish and grain the chart tables, chart drawers and various instrument cabinets in 'officers' country' (the bridge, chartrooms, wheelhouse and captain's day quarters).

On the night in question only a small overtime workforce was on board the vessel, and Mr Nolan was working alone while several other men were labouring in the vicinity. Suddenly, Nolan became aware that his mates were standing on the main bridge looking forward at something that was taking place on the forecastle deck. Nolan stopped his task and stepped outside to see what his friends were looking at, and although the night was dark and overcast, the ship's foredeck was well-lit by floodlights. There, according to Nolan's son Joe:

> There was a small derrick for the anchor and chain with winches and chain plates aft of this. He observed that every inch of this whole area, the winches, the derrick and even the jackpole cap was a seething mass of birds of a type unknown to him. More birds arrived each second.

To Nolan and his mates it looked like the birds were landing on one side of the ship and crossing over to the other side before they once again took wing. Although it was too dark near the ship to be certain, the men felt that the birds were circling around and landing again on the side of the extreme forward end of the forecastle deck where they originally appeared.

After five minutes or so, a member of the ship's crew joined the workmen on the bridge and put away a piece of equipment while keeping a close eye on the birds on the foredeck. The man took out his pipe and chewed on it while continuing to watch the birds, and Nolan's son Joe later wrote, 'The birds were continuing to apparently circle, and all the time produced a cheeping noise, but there were so many that the noise was a continuous note rising and falling.' W.J. Nolan himself thought the birds made a sound like the one made by old women when they 'keened' at a wake, and his son Joe recorded that the whole scene had a 'hair-tingling' quality to it that increased the longer the men watched. Finally the old sailor shook his head gravely and in a quiet voice said, 'I don't like the look of this at all …'[157]

Sarah Freeman

In 2005 a woman named Sarah Freeman recalled being told about an odd maritime superstition stemming from *Titanic*'s maiden voyage in 1912:

> My friend's mum told me her aunt was a little girl watching the launch [maiden voyage] of the *Titanic* in Southampton. An old sailor on the quay next to her said 'That ship is doomed. There are no seagulls following.'[158]

Interestingly, we will presently be examining another tradition involving seagulls that was the complete opposite of this one.

Roberta Maioni

Roberta Maioni boarded the *Titanic* at Southampton as the maid of the Countess of Rothes. As the ship was moving along the pier toward open water the suction created by her vast bulk broke the cables of the moored liner *New York* and pulled that vessel out into the channel. Miss Maioni was on deck at the time, and her attention was drawn to the crisis by the sudden silence of her fellow passengers. She later described what happened next:

> Tugs soon took the *New York* back to her place and the majority of us went on our way without giving further thought to this incident, but some passengers took it as a bad omen of ill-fortune and were further discomforted by the fact that large numbers of seagulls followed the ship to the sea. This, they said, was a sign of impending disaster. I had no time for such forebodings, for I had entered a fairy city and spent the first few days of the voyage in exploration and in making friends.[159]

Lawrence Beesley

After the disaster Mr Beesley described something he observed from the deck of the *Titanic* after the vessel left Queenstown:

> In our wake soared and screamed hundreds of gulls, which had quarrelled and fought over the remnants of lunch pouring out of the waste pipes as we lay-to in the harbour entrance; and now they followed us in the expectation of further spoil. I watched them for a long time and was astonished at the ease with which they soared and kept up with the ship with hardly a motion of their wings: picking out a particular gull, I would keep him under observation for minutes at a time and see no motion of his wings downwards or

upwards to aid his flight. He would tilt all of a piece to one side or another as the gusts of wind caught him: rigidly unbendable, as an aeroplane tilts sideways in a puff of wind.

And yet with graceful ease he kept pace with the *Titanic* forging through the water at twenty knots: as the wind met him he would rise upwards and obliquely forwards, and come down slantingly again, his wings curved in a beautiful arch and his tail feathers outspread as a fan. It was plain that he was possessed of a secret we are only just beginning to learn – that of utilizing air-currents as escalators up and down which he can glide at will with the expenditure of the minimum amount of energy, or of using them as a ship does when it sails within one or two points of a head wind. Aviators, of course, are imitating the gull, and soon perhaps we may see an aeroplane or a glider dipping gracefully up and down in the face of an opposing wind and all the time forging ahead across the Atlantic Ocean. The gulls were still behind us when night fell, and still they screamed and dipped down into the broad wake of foam which we left behind; but in the morning they were gone: perhaps they had seen in the night a steamer bound for their Queenstown home and had escorted her back.[160]

Johan Cervin Svensson

On the third day of the *Titanic*'s maiden voyage, steerage passenger Cervin Svensson noted some peculiarities in the behaviour of the people around him:

> About three days out I noticed the sailors acting strangely. At the time I didn't pay much attention, but I heard later that the sea gulls had deserted our ship. When they do that it means a ship is doomed according to an old sailor legend. The air was getting cooler because [the next day] we were heading for the ice fields on the afternoon and evening of April 14, 1912.[161]

Annie Martin

After the *Titanic* went down, Stewardess Martin was seated in a lifeboat with her fellow survivors:

> We hardly spoke in our boat all night. In the early morning a bird rose off the water near us with a cry, and one of the sailors said, 'I like a bird that sings in the morning.' We all laughed. It was the only laugh we had.[162]

Helen Candee

On the morning after the sinking, Mrs Candee noticed the activity of wildlife in the area:

> At the earliest signs of twilight, rapacious gulls are screaming around us.[163]
>
> The icepacks lay for miles, dazzling in the sun, peaks rising proudly here and there ... gulls flew and cried – active white against silent white.[164]

The seagulls continued their activity after the lifeboats were picked up by the *Carpathia*:

> It was then that those in the boats who had been picked up from the water gave up the spirit. It was then that the mother of the fine son began to call for him in the unmeaning repetition of the mind which has snapped.
>
> It was then that the emigrant woman of the many babes sent screams for them ringing to the stars in maniac baby-talk. It was then that the ghostly gulls swung and cried in the icy air.[165]

Frederick Hamilton

In the days following the disaster Mr Hamilton, who was a cable engineer on the cable ship *Mackay-Bennett*, kept a diary describing his vessel's voyage from Halifax to recover the floating bodies of the *Titanic*'s victims. By the time his vessel arrived at the scene, avian activity in the area had decreased considerably:

> **April 21st** – ... With the exception of ourselves, the bosun bird is the only living creature here.[166]

Dolphins

Edwina Troutt

In later years Edwina Troutt MacKenzie spoke with friends about her *Titanic* experiences, and Don Lynch recorded the following observation:

> Edwina Troutt MacKenzie's 1912 account describes seeing both dolphins and whales from the *Carpathia* as they steamed for New York. We saw plenty of both on Jim Cameron's 2001 expedition. The dolphins came right up to the *Keldysh*.[167]

Seals

Helen Candee

While seated in her lifeboat, Mrs Candee began to take note of her surroundings as dawn began to break:

> At the earliest signs of twilight, rapacious gulls are screaming around us. A sleek seal takes a look and slips his round head under water. An unpleasant dawn wind is rising.[168]
>
> The icepacks lay for miles, dazzling in the sun, peaks rising proudly here and there. Seals, black and shiny, showed in the waters, gulls flew and cried – active white against silent white.[169]

Elmer Taylor

After being rescued by the *Carpathia*, survivor Elmer Taylor saw living things in the vicinity that he later described for a reporter:

> The small boats and the ship picked up a few survivors, who had been floating in the water until daylight, but we did not see any people floating on the ice.
>
> While we were on the *Carpathia* … later on we passed a seal that was floating on a cake of ice.[170]

Charles Groves

In April 1957 Mr Groves wrote an account describing *Californian*'s presence at the scene of the disaster:

> The sea was covered by a large number of deck chairs, planks and light wreckage. *Californian* steamed close alongside all the lifeboats which *Carpathia* had left floating and it was particularly noted that they were empty. Scanning the sea with his binoculars the third officer noticed a large ice floe a mile or so distant on which he saw figures moving, and drawing Captain Lord's attention to it, remarked that they might be human beings [but] was told that they were seals …
>
> And what of those figures on the ice floe? Were they only seals, as the captain asserted? It has already been stated that all the *Titanic*'s lifeboats which were left afloat were closely examined and found to contain no occupants. A month later in almost the same spot the White Star liner the *Majestic* picked

up one of these boats, and in it were found the bodies of passengers who had evidently died of starvation, for the ship's doctor who examined them reported the men's mouths contained fragments of cork from the lifebelts. Had these passengers escaped from the sea on to the ice floe and then eventually got into the boat as it drifted past?[171]

Even though Groves' speculation about passengers sheltering on an iceberg before starving to death on Collapsible A was mistaken, his question about the true nature of the moving figures he saw on that nearby ice floe was completely valid – especially in light of the fact that the *Prinzess Irene* later picked up a wireless message from an unnamed vessel that described seeing the bodies of a number of *Titanic* victims huddled at the base of a floating iceberg.[172] Although the moving figures Groves saw on the morning of 15 April were probably seals like Captain Lord said, we can never be *completely* certain that his identification of those dark figures was correct.

Captain Keith

Captain Keith of the British steamship *Aborlon*, from Narvik, with Swedish ore, reported encountering a vast area of drifting ice on which rode hundreds of seals. The vessel struck the floes when some distance east of the Grand Banks of Newfoundland and was forced to steam through it for 50 miles before the course could be shifted to southward so as to return to open sea:

> More than a thousand seals disported themselves on the drifting masses of ice. Several were quite near the ship, while to the southward they were so numerous that one of the sailors remarked that they resembled the notes on a piece of ragtime music.
>
> Captain Keith said it was the first time he had ever seen Arctic ice floes and herds of seals in the paths of transatlantic shipping. He said the ice was at least six feet thick and covered with snow.[173]

Sharks

Sidney Collett

After arriving in New York, Mr Collett told reporters about his *Titanic* experience:

> After we had floated for an hour or more there came our first real scare for our own safety. All about us we could see the backs of monster fish, their shiny skins or scales glimmering gruesome in the moonlight. They were terrible looking monsters and we feared that they would swim under our boats and upset them, but they did not. It was a time when we were close to our Maker. I prayed constantly from the time our boat struck the iceberg until I reached New York.[174]

> At first I was very much frightened by the presence of what I thought was a school of sharks or sea monsters of some kind. We could see all about us great blue blurs of light shining through the water. A man said they were sharks, and all the women believed him; probably they think so yet.[175]

Mary Glynn

In later years Miss Glynn commented on wildlife she'd seen near the place where the *Titanic* went down. Bizarrely, she claimed in later years to have seen sharks feeding on bodies and deck chair pillows alike.[176]

Margaret Madigan

Miss Madigan later recalled something that had disturbed her while she was on board the *Titanic*:

> Yes, she [*Titanic*] was three days sailing and the sharks never left her in three days. You get a funny feeling with sharks a-following your boat.[177]*

Juliet Tarkington

On 17 April Miss Tarkington, a *Carpathia* passenger, wrote a letter to Mr & Mrs Robert Tarkington of Danville, Kentucky:

> I could write pages, but can't stand to stay in the writing room. It is so close. We have had rough sea, wonderfully smooth sea, a storm, burial at sea, rescued people from this disaster, seen whales, sharks, icebergs – certainly have had a variety.[178]

* It's possible these sharks were feeding on food scraps that were dumped overboard daily from *Titanic*'s kitchens, but Don Lynch wonders if Miss Madigan might possibly have mistaken dolphins for sharks.

It will be recalled that the vessel *Prinzess Irene* received a wireless message from an unnamed vessel that sighted the bodies of *Titanic* victims huddled on the base of a floating iceberg. In light of our present topic of 'sharks', it's a curious coincidence that the mother of *Titanic* victim Olof Osén was later filled with a sense of unease that compounded her grief over the death of her son.

According to the Osén family, Olof's mother reportedly was plagued by nightmares, dreaming of her son's body on an iceberg, surrounded by sharks.[179]

Walrus?

Nelle Snyder

In later years Mrs Snyder spoke with a reporter, who wrote an article about her *Titanic* experiences:

> There were other horrors the night the *Titanic* sank. There were the animals – perhaps they were walruses – resting on the iceberg.
>
> 'They were as big as I am,' Snyder said. 'We saw them when we started moving toward the iceberg so we'd have a place to rest if our boat went over. There must have been eight or ten in a group and they started coming toward us because someone had thrown food overboard. We were frightened that they would come and tip the boat, so we started moving away.'[180]

Even though it was the reporter himself who speculated that the animals might have been walruses, it sounds like Mrs Snyder might have been referring to seals – especially since their size was comparable to her own. Indeed, one can picture a herd of seals taking fright at the approach of man and abandoning the iceberg for the safety of the sea.

Whales

Fred Beachler

Mr Beachler, a *Carpathia* passenger, wrote an account of his experiences on the rescue ship:

We did not clear the last of the icebergs and flows until Monday afternoon, and in the meantime we had sighted a half dozen whales, one very large one close up to our ship and spouting away like a geyser.[181]

May Birkhead

Miss Birkhead, a *Carpathia* passenger, wrote an account of her vessel's rescue of *Titanic*'s survivors:

A number of whales were sighted as the *Carpathia* was clearing the last of the ice, one large one being close by, and all were spouting like geysers.[182]

Lucy Duff Gordon

After arriving in New York, Lady Duff Gordon told a reporter about her experiences in her lifeboat:

At last morning came. On one side of us was the ice floes and the big bergs, and on the other side we were horrified to see a school of tremendous whales. Then, as the mist lifted, we caught sight of the *Carpathia* looming up in the distance and headed straight for us.[183]

Mary Glynn

Miss Glynn later described wildlife she'd seen in the area where the *Titanic* went down, including whales blowing spray in the area where the ship had foundered.[184]

Masabumi Hosono

After being picked up by the *Carpathia*, Mr Hosono wrote an account of the *Titanic* disaster for his wife:

At ten o'clock the *Carpathia* began to move. There were numerous icebergs floating all around and was very much scared that we might strike one again. Did this fear originate from my memory of the first experience? Perhaps so. Far in the distance whales were seen spouting, and the sight was interesting and gave me some distraction.[185]

Marie Jerwan

In May 1912 Miss Jerwan wrote a letter to her sister describing her experiences after being picked up by the *Carpathia*:

> Monday morning we saw two whales. Can you imagine if we had seen them from the life boat![186]

Elmer Taylor

After arriving in New York, Mr Taylor told reporters about his *Titanic* experiences:

> While we were on the *Carpathia* we passed through a school of about a dozen whales and later on we passed a seal that was floating on a cake of ice. A little farther on we passed a big floe of ice on which there was a big white polar bear prowling around.[187]

Edwina Troutt

In a letter she wrote to her parents on 16–17 April, Miss Troutt described her experiences in her lifeboat:

> We were on the North Ocean and surrounded with icebergs, and when we reached this ship we could see nothing but fields of ice. It was a beautiful picture; and then the trails of the whales was another sight. I saw about seven.[188]

In later years Edwina Troutt MacKenzie told several friends about her *Titanic* experiences:

> Edwina MacKenzie told me of seeing a pod a whales surround their lifeboat. The whales were close enough that that Edwina was afraid to boat would be swamped or capsized.[189]
>
> ~
>
> Edwina Troutt MacKenzie's 1912 account describes seeing both dolphins and whales from the Carpathia as they steamed for New York. We saw plenty of both on Jim Cameron's 2001 expedition. The dolphins came right up to the Keldysh.[190]

Unknown Female Carpathia Passenger

After arriving in New York an unnamed *Carpathia* passenger spoke with a local newspaper reporter:

> A number of whales were sighted as the *Carpathia* was clearing the last of the ice, one large one being close by, and all were spouting like geysers.[191]

2

The Kennels

In recent years a controversy has arisen regarding the true location of the *Titanic*'s dog kennels. The General Arrangement plans that were offered into evidence during the US Limitation of Liability hearings have the kennels marked as being down on F Deck, and it has been supposed that this proximity to the third-class galley would have made it easy for one of the cooks to feed the dogs with kitchen scraps. A very few researchers even put forth the uncorroborated claim that John Jacob Astor went down to F deck and released the dogs from the kennels shortly before the *Titanic* sank. What is the truth of these matters?

Bill Sauder, an expert on the *Titanic*'s construction, points out that not everything written on ships' deck plans can be taken at face value. 'I know that there are plans that say the kennels were on F deck in the old butchers shop,' he writes. 'I also know that H&W plans have errors in them. I also know how mistakes get into drawings, I am an architectural draftsman and have had uninformed bosses insist on questionable drawings.'[1]

Sauder points out that *Olympic* was originally slated to have a butcher's shop on F deck but that either during the planning stage or after the maiden voyage's conclusion this was found to be redundant. (The butchering was done in one place in the main galleys on D deck.) This, of course, left a large empty room on F deck situated between the bakery and potato wash room; this empty room is marked 'STORE' on *Olympic* deck plans, but on the Mersey *Titanic* deck plans it is marked 'KENNELS'. Sauder adds:

> It is my belief that when the third-class butcher's shop was removed [from *Olympic*'s F deck], somebody had the clever idea of turning it into kennels [on the *Titanic*] and it got marked that way [on *Titanic*'s deck plans.] When a better-informed authority within H&W, or controlling legal authority

> discovered it, it became a storage room and the kennels on the *Titanic* were transferred to the deck house under the No. 4 funnel. I believe the error was copied on to fresh drawings because the directive to change the drawing was never issued or never performed. Its inclusion on a court-submitted drawing [after the sinking] is not surprising because, frankly, White Star was not on the hot seat over where they kept the dogs.[2]

The *Titanic* deck plan Bill Sauder refers to is presently owned by Stanley Lehrer and is hand dated 'May 2nd' [1912] with inked notations of late changes to the ship's arrangements.[3] However, since Harland and Wolff would not have printed a brand-new *Titanic* plan at that late date just for the purpose of submitting it to the British *Titanic* inquiry, there's no telling how long the plan might have been in existence before it was annotated, which means it can't be regarded as the last word regarding the kennels' supposed location on F deck. As Sauder pointed out, the White Star Line had far more important things to worry about at the British inquiry than specifying where the *Titanic*'s kennels were located, and researcher Roy Mengot agreed with that assessment. 'I believe in that notion of changes-never-rescinded [on the deck plan] from my engineering days,' Mengot wrote. 'Also, the White Star Line was under no mandate to use a space the way Harland & Wolff marked it, after they receive the ship.'[4]

Bill Sauder has provided a brief summary of the reasons why he believes *Titanic*'s kennels were located on the boat deck aft of the fourth funnel instead of down on F deck:

1. ALL ships that I can find documentation for have their kennels on an open deck. This [i.e. *Titanic*'s alleged F deck location] is the only example of a kennel deep inside the vessel.
2. Third-class accommodation was closely regulated by the UK and US governments for health reasons. Room size, porthole size, porthole placement and number, occupancy, outfit and vermin control were all governed by laws and then inspected for conformity. In 1912, disease vectors were well understood and the period had elaborate laws in place regarding the handling of livestock. It is beyond my belief that the health and welfare departments of the time would allow a dog kennel in the middle of a kitchen complex. Hair, noise, faeces, urine, vomit, dog fighting. By the way, the chief engineer's cabin is on the other side of the wall. Do you think he's not going to complain about dogs barking?
3. There is no easy access to an upper deck, you have to go up a complicated series of steps. Many dogs do not climb steps well, if at all.

Whatever convenience you may have had in getting food to the dogs is completely lost by having to manoeuvre those dogs, perhaps one at a time, up those stairs for a walk. How long is that all going to take? How many times a day are you going to walk those dogs? What is all this going to cost in labour?

4. Placing the kennels in third class means that first and second class cannot visit them because of quarantine rules.

Do any survivor accounts support Bill Sauder's contention that *Titanic*'s kennels were not located deep inside the ship on F deck? The answer is yes.

Richard Williams
After Mr. Williams reached the *Carpathia*, a fellow survivor told him something about the *Titanic*'s dogs:

> One man told me that some half hour or so before the end he suddenly thought of a dog that he was bringing home with him. He went up to the top deck and opened up all the kennels.[5]*

Eva Hart
Second-class passenger Eva Hart also mentioned the kennels' location, without knowing that the topic was a subject of controversy:

> I found there were some dogs on board. They … were all in a row of kennels and cages and things *at the end of the ship* [author's emphasis] …[6]

Since the forward end of *Titanic*'s boat deck was where the ship's bridge was located, Eva Hart's comment suggests that the kennels were on a second-class deck at the aft end of the ship (which, as we shall see, agrees with Bill Sauder's analysis).

Edith Brown
Second-class passenger Edith Brown asked Captain Edward J. Smith if it was true there were dogs on board the *Titanic*. Smith replied that the ship had what was known as a 'dog deck' that was situated up by the funnels, adding that there were kennels there where the dogs were looked after by one of the ship's butchers.[7]

---

* In later years, survivor Robert Daniel told his daughter that it was *he* who opened the kennels to release the dogs from their cages.[6]

The authors of the huge reference work *Titanic: the Ship Magnificent* agree with these survivor accounts and believe *Titanic*'s kennels were located in one of two converted storerooms located on the second-class boat deck aft of the No. 4 funnel deckhouse:

> This opinion is given further weight by the fact that *Olympic* would have a dog kennel in this area after 1912. *Britannic* was also to have a kennel very close to this area, but it was removed from the plans at a later stage in her construction … It is possible, and likely, that this boat Deck kennel was an impromptu arrangement that would carry over as a permanent arrangement on *Olympic*.[8]

That the kennels of *Titanic*'s sister ship *Olympic* were located in the boat deck's No. 4 funnel deck house is confirmed by Cyril Codus, who possesses a 1913 *Olympic* deck plan showing the kennels situated aft of the ship's fourth funnel. *Britannic*'s kennels were originally placed there as well, but when the gantry davits were installed, it was moved a few feet to a shed next to the No. 4 funnel.[9] Undoubtedly these upper deck locations on both *Olympic* and *Titanic* were decided upon because of the noise, smell and sanitation problems that would have occurred if the kennels were located below decks.

A typical boat deck kennel arrangement. (Courtesy Bill Sauder)

After undertaking a great deal of research on the subject, Bill Sauder has offered additional thoughts regarding the *Titanic*'s kennels:

> I suspect that a small locker under the port quarter of the No. 4 funnel was converted into kennels with a total of 12 cages, each cage 3 feet wide, 4 feet deep and stacked on top of each other.
>
> The evidence comes from a very careful examination of the *Britannic*'s general arrangement plans. The configuration I am proposing was the same for the pre-1912 *Britannic*, but the entire area was redesigned and heavily drafted over post-disaster.
>
> The kennels were a very last-minute addition to the *Olympic* class. Whether *Olympic* had the kennels in April 1912 is unclear at the moment, but *Titanic*'s consisted of a small compartment under the No. 4 funnel on the port quarter that was originally slated for deck storage.
>
> The door opened on to a small passage that separated the twelve cages, six right, six left and stacked two high. The bottom cages were four feet deep and three feet high. On later ships, the upper tier was smaller but at this point, I doubt the arrangement was that sophisticated. I strongly suspect there was a 6-prism deck light overhead. (One was recovered from the *Titanic* wreck site and it has stumped us all as to where it might be from. Without this deck light, the room has no natural light at all.) A sink and worktable would be highly desirable, but probably not present in this configuration.
>
> This info comes from detailed general arrangement plans of *Britannic*'s boat deck. The plans were drawn in ink on linen. When the boat deck was completely redesigned after *Titanic*, the deckhouse was greatly modified to permit the boats clearance and the kennels removed completely. When the erasure was made, the ink was scraped off the linen, scarring it, and then drafted over for the new configuration. My analysis of the scars on the linen are the basis for this conclusion.
>
> The White Star ships probably had kennels because of their stops in France. As you know, the UK had a strict six-month quarantine on dogs entering the country. Since *Lusitania*, etc. never reached the Continent, the number of dogs that they carried to the UK would have been practically zero. Cunard brochures of the period (1910) specifically warn that permits must be obtained. I have been looking for references in White Star material but have not seen any so far.
>
> As 'dog travel' caught on in the 1920s, the small kennel on *Olympic* was enlarged to double its original dimensions.[10]

It has often been pointed out that the book *Titanic: Triumph and Tragedy*[11] by Jack Eaton and Charles Haas places *Titanic*'s kennels on F deck and that this was supposedly based on the vessel's own Harland and Wolff specification book. However, Bill Sauder makes it clear that the two authors' assignment of the kennels to F deck is based on a mistaken notion:

> Regarding Eaton and Haas' 'F' deck location – they are in fact reporting what the specification book says, but muddle the source and take it at face value.
>
> The original plan was to fit the *Olympic* class with duplicate bakeries and butcher shop for third class, next to their main galley on 'F' deck. The butcher's shop was found to be redundant so it was eliminated creating a few extra rooms that nobody ever found a satisfactory use for (their purpose drifts around a lot during the *Olympic*'s career).
>
> When *Britannic*'s specification book was prepared, somebody recalled those empty rooms and without looking into the matter put the kennels down there as part of the ship's PRELIMINARY specifications.
>
> Haas and Eaton repeat this but make the following mistakes: (1.) they claim the book is for *Titanic*, not *Britannic*. (2.) they do not consider that the placement of a dog pound in the middle of a cooking complex was (probably) illegal at the time (in honesty, I have to qualify it since I haven't looked the regulations up, but it is inconceivable even in 1912 with the American Purity of Foods and Drugs act, plus the British Emigration Acts – not to mention bad publicity). (3.) The 'F' deck location contradicts *Olympic*'s later plans, contradicts reports from the sinking and frankly makes no sense, since dogs don't do well climbing stairs on their way to exercise.[12]

Regarding the sanitary aspects of sheltering dogs below decks in the vicinity of the ship's food-handling areas, period regulations governing these practices are difficult to obtain. However, the British government publication *London Statutes from 1750 to 1907* contains a pertinent entry for the year 1907:

> Chapter 76: An Act to Consolidate and Amend the Laws Relating to Public Health in London
>
> 1. It shall be the duty of every sanitary authority to cause to be made from time to time inspection of their district, with a view to ascertain what *nuisances* [author's emphasis: see below] exist calling for abatement under the powers of this act, and to enforce the provisions of this Act for the purpose

> of abating the same, and otherwise to put in force the power invested in them relating to public health and local government, so as to secure the proper sanitary condition of all premises within their district.
> Nuisances (General)
> 2. - (1.) (c.) Any animal kept in such a place or manner as to be a nuisance or injurious or dangerous to health.[13]

The harbouring of animals near food storage and preparation areas would certainly be regarded as a 'nuisance or injurious or dangerous to health' in the eyes of a public health inspector. Indeed, according to Section 1, Part 1 of the Public Health (Regulations as to Food) Act, 1907, that dealt with 'Food Inspection', such inspections were for the 'prevention of danger arising to public health from the importation, preparation, storage, and distribution of articles of food and drink … intended for sale for human consumption …'[14] Needless to say, the presence of animal hair and faeces near *Titanic*'s food preparation areas on F deck would have constituted a 'danger' to 'public

Madeleine Astor, *Titanic* survivor, in 1913. (Courtesy Randy Bigham)

health' due to possible contamination of areas used for 'preparation, storage, and distribution of articles of food'.

In conclusion, every bit of available evidence points to the likelihood that *Titanic*'s kennels were not located down on F deck as has been claimed in the past. Instead, it's far more likely they were located at the aft end of *Titanic*'s second-class boat deck inside the deckhouse behind the ship's fourth funnel.[15]

3

A Mystery Solved: Identifying *Titanic*'s Officers

Immediately after the *Titanic* disaster, a 1912 memorial postcard was issued picturing nine White Star officers dressed in the line's dark winter uniform. The caption on this postcard stated: 'Captain Smith and officers S.S. *Titanic*'. Three of the men in the photo (Captain Edward Smith, First Officer William

CAPTAIN SMITH AND OFFICERS S.S. TITANIC.
Lost on 15th April, 1912, after collision with Iceberg in North Atlantic.
PHOTO BY KENNEDY. 50 YORK ST.

This 1912 postcard was long believed to picture the officers who sailed on *Titanic*'s maiden voyage. (Author's collection)

Murdoch and Purser Hugh McElroy) were readily identifiable as genuine *Titanic* officers, and ever since 1912 it has been assumed that the remaining six officers were the other officers whose names we have become familiar with during our studies about the *Titanic* disaster.

In recent years a number of *Titanic* books have included this 'nine-officer photograph' among their illustrations, and the authors of some of these books (most notably Peter Thresh) attempted to put names to the faces of the lesser-known men. Thresh did this by matching the visible rank markings on the officers' uniforms with the known ranks of the officers who served on the *Titanic*; the officers whose rank markings were not visible in the photo were necessarily 'identified' by matching their facial resemblance to actual *Titanic* crewmen pictured in other photos of unquestionable authenticity. The identifications that Thresh arrived at by these methods were, from left to right, as follows:

Standing: Hugh McElroy, Charles Lightoller, Herbert Pitman, Joseph Boxhall, Harold Lowe.
Seated: James Moody, Henry Wilde, Captain Smith, William Murdoch.

Several researchers were uncomfortable with these purported identifications, because several officers in the photo did not resemble likenesses of *Titanic*'s officers that were taken at other times and under other circumstances. This

First Officer Murdoch, Joseph Evans, Alexander and Captain Smith. (*Fort Wayne Daily News*)

uncertainty led to our continued efforts to determine if the alleged identifications arrived at by Peter Thresh were indeed accurate.

In 1996 a new piece to the puzzle came to light during a research trip the present author made to Indiana. While perusing the 17 April 1912 issue of the *Fort Wayne Daily News* I came upon a photograph of four White Star officers, all of whom were identified in the photo's caption (see previous page). The men in the photo were identified as Captain Smith, First Officer Murdoch, J. Evans and an officer named Alexander. I immediately sat up and took notice of this caption, because Evans and Alexander were clearly and recognisably two of the officers who appeared in the 'nine-officer photo' that Peter Thresh believed was a photo of *Titanic*'s full complement of officers.

The fact that two of the men in the 'nine-officer photo' were not *Titanic* officers at all suggested that the photo had nothing to do with *Titanic*'s maiden voyage, but how could we be sure about that? Four officers in the photo were still unidentified, and there was at least a slim chance that one or more of them might truly be genuine *Titanic* officers.

Our next step in the identification process occurred when relatives of a former White Star officer contacted Titanic Historical Society (THS) historian Don Lynch and told him that the officer standing on the far right side of the photo was their relative, Maurice Parkhouse.[1] Even though this identification turned out to be incorrect, it still suggested that the men in the photo were not all *Titanic* officers as had formerly been claimed.

Meanwhile, German researcher Hermann Söldner was conducting his own study of the 'nine-officer photo'. Söldner knew that the photo had been snapped on the boat deck of a liner, so in April 1999 he tried to determine the name of the ship upon which the photograph had been taken.

Unfortunately, the background of the 'nine-officer photo' was a bit overexposed, and it was difficult to make out many background features that would otherwise be visible. However, Söldner examined a slightly different version of the photo that was taken at the same time. (This second photo depicts the same men but in slightly different poses.) The second is a much darker exposure than the first, and its background features are more clearly visible; it showed enough of the ship's background details (air shafts, davits, compass platform, railings, etc.) to enable Söldner to determine that both photos were taken on board the *Olympic*, that the camera was facing aft and that the officers were seated on the boat deck beside the raised roof of the reading and writing room. He knew that the photo depicted the *Olympic* (and not the *Titanic*) because of the distinctive placement of certain ventilators that are visible in other photographs of both ships.

After becoming fairly certain that all nine officers in the photo were probably *Olympic* officers instead of *Titanic* officers, Söldner contacted the Public Record Office and obtained copies of some of *Olympic*'s early crew sign-on sheets. Upon receiving these documents he discovered that Joseph Evans was indeed *Olympic*'s chief officer during the period prior to the completion of *Olympic*'s 14 June 1911 maiden voyage. Moreover, David W. Alexander was listed as *Olympic*'s fourth officer throughout that same time period.

Without additional information upon which to base further identifications, Söldner looked at *Olympic*'s sign-on sheets and noted the ages of the officers who served on board the vessel on her maiden voyage; he then speculated (incorrectly, as it turned out) about the probable identities of the remaining unidentified officers based upon their apparent ages. Söldner published all of his findings in the June 1999 issue of *The Navigator*, journal of the German *Titanic* Society.

After the publication of his article, Söldner's next challenge was to determine the *Olympic*'s location when the 'nine-officer photo' was taken. Söldner knew that Joseph Evans was Chief Officer until the conclusion of *Olympic*'s maiden voyage, so three important pre-maiden voyage opportunities for taking photographs immediately suggested themselves: *Olympic*'s departure from Belfast on 31 May 1911, her arrival at the intermediate waypoint of Liverpool on 1 June, or her arrival at the port of Southampton prior to the commencement of her maiden voyage on 14 June 1911.

The only way to resolve this question was to discover the ship's exact location when the 'nine-officer photo' was taken. Söldner did this by searching for recognisable terrain features in the background, and he found one object he thought might be possible to identify – a 'shadow' (resembling a tower or chimney) that is faintly visible behind the head of First Officer Murdoch.

Söldner knew that a chimney like that existed in Southampton, but he realised its shape didn't quite match the shape in the photo; furthermore, the Southampton chimney would not have been visible in the photo because of the direction in which *Olympic* was pointed while sitting at the dock. The photo could not have been taken at Liverpool, either, because when *Olympic* arrived there she remained far outside the docks on the Mersey.

That left only Belfast. Söldner knew that *Olympic*'s construction was completed at Harland and Wolff's outfitting wharf located right beside the Thompson dry dock. The dry dock was dominated by two towers or chimneys; one of these, the smaller, belonged to the pumping house, and Söldner saw that it was shaped astonishingly like the rectangular shadow situated behind Murdoch's head in the photo. This satisfied Söldner that the 'nine-officer photo' was very likely taken while *Olympic* was still in the Harland & Wolff shipyard.

One nagging problem complicated this conclusion: the location of the Thompson dock chimney was wrong when Söldner took into consideration the place on *Olympic*'s boat deck where the photo was taken. However, Söldner then discovered that the *Olympic* had been turned around in the outfitting wharf on 28 May 1911 prior to undertaking her trials; *Olympic*'s orientation on 28 May would therefore have put the chimney in exactly the right place to show up in the photograph.

After determining that the photo was taken at H&W in Belfast, Söldner next tried to determine exactly *when* it was taken. He knew that *Olympic* was in Belfast a number of times: first, during her initial construction; next on 6 October 1911 for repairs after her collision with the *Hawke*; and lastly, following her loss of a propeller blade on 24 February 1912. Which of these was the occasion upon which the nine officers gathered to have their photo taken?

Söldner realised that the two keys to the puzzle were Joseph Evans and Henry Wilde, the two chief officers of the *Olympic*. According to the ship's sign-on sheets, Wilde did not replace Evans as chief officer until after the conclusion of *Olympic*'s maiden voyage. This meant that the 'nine-officer photo' must have been taken in Belfast prior to Wilde's assignment as *Olympic*'s chief officer.

Söldner saw that *Olympic*'s maiden voyage crew agreements contained the names of the following White Star officers: Chief Officer: Jos. Evans; First Officer: William M. Murdoch; Second Officer: R. Hume; Third Officer: Henry O. Cater; Fourth Officer: David W. Alexander; Fifth Officer: A. Tulloch; Sixth Officer: Harold H. Holehouse.

The fact that the 'nine-officer photo' shows Joseph Evans wearing the rank of chief officer means that the photo was probably taken while Evans held that rank prior to *Olympic*'s initial departure from Belfast on 31 May 1911. From analysis of the shadows seen in various photos, it is Söldner's belief that the 'nine-officer photo' was taken shortly after noon on 31 May 1911, just prior to *Olympic*'s departure for Liverpool, Southampton and the commencement of her maiden voyage. Söldner published all of this supplementary research in the December 1999 issue of *The Navigator*.

To recap, by this point, definite identifications had been made for two of the unidentified men in the 'nine-officer photo': Chief Officer Joseph Evans and Fourth Officer David W. Alexander. A third identification, that of 'Maurice Parkhouse', had been rendered uncertain by the discovery that Harold H. Holehouse was *Olympic*'s sixth officer on her voyage from Belfast to Liverpool/Southampton. And that is where matters stood for the next few months – until a crucial piece of information came to light that put the subject to rest once and for all.

As it turned out, the information in question had actually been available to researchers since 1993 when Onslows auction house published its catalogue of *Titanic* memorabilia to be auctioned in April of that year. Several items scheduled to go under the hammer in that action had originally belonged to the *Titanic*'s Third Officer, Herbert Pitman.

The key item that finally clinched the identities of the men in the 'nine-officer photo' was Pitman's copy of a photograph of thirteen White Star officers dressed in summer white uniforms. Without ever realising the importance of his having done so, Mr Pitman labelled his photograph with the names of twelve of the thirteen officers who were pictured in the photograph. The present author had glanced at this photo in 1993 and then set it aside without examining it with the care it deserved. It was only in late February

Olympic's officers (miscaptioned above as *Titanic*'s). Standing: Purser Hugh McElroy, Third Officer Henry O. Cater, Second Officer Robert Hume, Fourth Officer David W. Alexander, Sixth Officer Harold H. Holehouse. Seated: Fifth Officer Adolphus Tulloch, Chief Officer Joseph Evans, Captain Edward Smith and First Officer William Murdoch. (Author's collection)

of the year 2000 that I took another look and realised the importance of the information it contained; all of the officers pictured in the 'nine-officer photo' were also present in Pitman's photo of thirteen officers in summer whites – and all were identified by notations in Pitman's own hand.

At that point I posted a message on Mark Taylor's internet *Titanic* Discuss List and publicly identified every man depicted in the 'nine-officer photo'. My posting indicated that Pitman's annotated photograph was the key item that finally unravelled the mystery, since it permitted the matching of specific names to specific faces. German researcher Susanne Störmer saw my posting and kindly made me aware of Hermann Söldner's independent research on this subject. The rest, as they say, is history.

All of the men pictured in the 'nine-officer photo' at the top of this page were officers on board the *Olympic* during her voyage from Belfast to Liverpool/Southampton.

A long-standing *Titanic* mystery solved at last.

4

'Archie': The Life of Major Archibald Butt

Major Butt's entire life story is described in detail in my 2,400-page trilogy Archie *(available from Lulu.com). The last hundred days of Archie's life (including his* Titanic *experiences) are described in my shorter book,* A Death on the Titanic.[1]

It can honestly be said that the relative to whom Archie Butt felt closest during his lifetime was his mother, Pamela. Pamela Boggs was born in Augusta, Georgia, in 1836, and in 1858 she married Joshua Butt, a 30-year-old slave owner who operated a local mercantile establishment in partnership with his brother. The couple eventually had four sons (Edward, John, Archibald and Lewis) and one daughter (Mary Ann).

Archibald Willingham Butt was born on 26 September 1865 in the aftermath of the Civil War. Archie's early schooling took place in Augusta, but life was hard during Reconstruction and made it necessary for the family to do without many of the comforts that it had enjoyed in pre-war Georgia. Joshua Butt and his brother opened and closed several incarnations of their mercantile establishment, but in 1876 they were finally forced to declare bankruptcy. Joshua opened his own mercantile firm the following year, but in 1878 he passed away unexpectedly and left his family in dire financial straits.

When his father passed away, 13-year-old Archie Butt, who was attending Augusta's Summerville Academy at the time, was forced to drop out of school and get a job in order to keep the wolf from his family's door. Archie obtained his first employment as a telegraph messenger in Augusta, and from 1880 to 1882 he worked for his brother Edward in Columbia, South Carolina.

In 1882, with the aid of a generous family friend, Pamela Butt was able to enrol Archie in the preparatory school of the University of the South at Sewanee, Tennessee, and Pamela moved to Sewanee with Archie, his brother Lewis and (perhaps) his sister Mary Ann in order to be near her younger children while they obtained their education. Tragedy struck the family in 1883 when Archie's elder brother John was killed in a railway accident, but Archie continued his education and became a gownsman at the university in 1884. When his sister Mary Ann passed away in 1885, Archie moved into the small apartment in the university library where his mother Pamela and brother Lewis were living.

While attending the university, Archie joined the Delta Tau Delta fraternity, participated in dramatics, debating and journalism, was associate editor of the school paper and received some military training in the school's cadet corps. He received diplomas in Latin, chemistry and moral science in 1886 and graduated in 1888 with a certificate in political science and a Bachelor of Arts degree in English. Archie was well aware of the many sacrifices that his mother had made in order to ensure he received a good education, and that

Major Archibald Butt. (Author's collection)

fact merely served to increase the intense devotion to Pamela's happiness and welfare that he felt for the remainder of his life.

Upon graduating from college, Archie returned to Augusta and obtained a job at a life insurance company. He was not particularly cut out for a life in business, though, and around 1 January 1890 he travelled to Louisville, Kentucky, with the idea of becoming a newspaper man. When Archie applied for work at the *Louisville Courier-Journal*, General John Castleman brought him to the city room and asked city editor Thomas Watkins to put the young man on his staff. Archie Butt became the youngest reporter on the *Courier-Journal's* staff and was assigned to police work. While working for the paper he became attracted to General Castleman's beautiful daughter, Alice, even though no real romantic feelings ever blossomed between them.

In March 1890 a cyclone struck Louisville, and the *Courier-Journal*'s editor sent Archie Butt to the Falls City Hall, where a large number of people had been killed when the building collapsed. A fellow reporter was sent to relieve him at 2 a.m. and the two reporters were comparing notes on the disaster when the pile of bricks upon which they were standing suddenly began to move underneath their feet. A faint sob was heard, and Archie exclaimed, 'There is a woman under here, and we are standing upon her.' The two reporters began to dig and found a woman lying trapped underneath a beam, a circumstance that saved her from being crushed to death. Archie picked up the injured woman and carried her across the street; her injuries proved to be not very serious, so Archie proceeded to the newspaper offices to finish writing his story.

Archie Butt remained at the *Courier-Journal* until 1893, at which point he moved back to Georgia and went to work for the *Macon Telegraph*. He stayed at the *Telegraph* for slightly more than a year, after which he went to Washington, D.C. and served as a local correspondent for several Southern newspapers.

Archie's outstanding newspaper work in the nation's capital enabled him to make the acquaintance of many important men, and in 1895 Major Matt Ransom chose him to be his secretary and attaché when President Cleveland sent Ransom to Mexico City as Ambassador. In June of that same year Archie accompanied Mexican President Porfirio Diaz on a rail inspection trip to some of Mexico's rural mountain areas, and after returning to Washington in late 1895 he wrote a critique of the Mexican silver-based economy and several other magazine articles that described the architecture of some ancient Mexican buildings in which he had taken an interest. In 1896 Archie's critique of Mexico's silver currency was published in pamphlet form and was used in the political campaign to elect William McKinley as President of the United States.

In February of 1897 Archie submitted a short story called 'Behind the Lines' to *Lippincott's* magazine, and in October 1898 his brother Edward, sister-in-law Savannah and niece Arrington sailed for the United Kingdom, where Edward was to work as a cotton broker for the next two decades.

In 1899 Archie was lodging with a relative in Washington, but when he contracted blood poisoning in his foot the infection became so serious that it was feared amputation might be necessary. He was bedridden for seven weeks, but he was finally nursed back to good health by the constant ministrations of the family's Black cook Fannie. He never forgot the debt of gratitude he owed to her, and in later years he secured a good position for her nephew as a messenger in one of the government departments; not long before his death, Archie wrote a letter to Fannie and offered her a permanent position in his own service.

It was during this period that Archie gave up all hope of marrying Alice Connally, a girl he'd been courting for some time and loved very deeply. Miss Connally's mother did not want to see her daughter wedded to an impecunious newspaperman, though, and she applied so much pressure on Alice to marry into the Vanderbilt family that Archie finally saw the hopelessness of his situation and quietly withdrew from the fray.

In 1898 hostilities commenced at the outbreak of the Spanish–American War, and Archie wrote newspaper stories about the conflict from the viewpoint of the generals and politicians who were running the affair from the nation's capital. He had always had an interest in military life, and on 2 January 1900 his friend, Adjutant General Henry Corbin, granted Archie's fondest wish by securing a commission for him as Assistant Quartermaster in the Volunteer Service with the rank of captain. Pamela Butt was very upset that her favourite son had chosen to enter the military, but she nevertheless hastened to Washington to spend time with Archie before he departed for his first duty station. He and his mother returned to Augusta together, and Archie then travelled to Portland, Oregon, to board the army transport *Lennox*, which sailed for the Philippines on 8 March. Archie's success in transporting a shipment of army mules to the islands without the loss of a single animal was the cause of much favourable comment in official circles, and the article he later wrote on the subject influenced the army to revise its outdated procedures regarding the safe shipment of army livestock by sea.

Captain Archie Butt arrived in the Philippines in mid-April, and on the 20th he began his tour of duty by commanding the *Lennox* while she resupplied the far-flung army outposts that were scattered throughout the islands for the purpose of 'pacifying' the insurgents. Several similar voyages followed, and on 3 July he and several unarmed subordinates came under fire from Filipino insurgents after they pulled their small boat away from the transport and were rowing toward the shore.

'It was almost dark, but we could easily be discerned from the beach …,' Archie recalled. 'Several bullets whizzed over the boat, and two spattered in the water near our stern. The men pulled faster, but the bullets came likewise faster as if they were intent upon getting one of us at any rate.'[2] Despite the danger, Captain Butt and his men ultimately succeeded in reaching shore unscathed.

On 2 August Archie learned that he was being withdrawn from transport duty, and by the 17th he received his permanent assignment in Manila as Assistant Quartermaster in charge of the Land Transportation Department, which was responsible for supplying all American troops stationed in the insular possessions. When a typhoon struck Manila, Captain Butt ignored his own safety and spent the night in company with his teamsters keeping a watchful eye on the army's equine property.

It was during this period that Archie Butt became good friends with William Howard Taft, the new Civil Governor of the Philippines, and Taft and his wife Nellie were tremendously impressed with Archie's diligence and efficiency in assisting them at several important social functions. On 7 January 1901 Governor Taft wrote a letter to the Secretary of War recommending Archie for an appointment as captain and assistant quartermaster in the United States regular army. This recommendation was acted upon, and on 2 February 1901 Captain Butt was promoted to quartermaster, his volunteer rank of captain being converted to a full commission in the regular army.

During spring 1901 Archie came down with a bout of malaria, but his spirits rose in mid-April when the transport *Indiana* arrived in Manila carrying his mother Pamela, who had finally yielded to her son's urgings to travel to the islands and enjoy the tropics while he was stationed there. Several months later, Pamela even made a brief excursion by herself when she boarded an army transport and travelled to Shanghai to see that exotic location with her own eyes.

In October 1901 Pamela left the Philippines to return to the United States, but Archie remained in Manila in charge of the Land Transportation Department. In February 1902 one of his civilian Filipino office employees absconded with several thousand dollars from the office safe, and Captain Butt replaced the money out of his own pocket rather than have an official complaint go on his permanent military record. In April of that year Archie experienced a bout of dengue fever, and later in the summer he suffered an injury to his leg in a wagon accident and was also knocked unconscious by a baseball at a company ball game.

Captain Archibald Butt served in the Philippines until 1 May 1903, at which time he and Quartermaster General Charles Humphrey boarded a transport and returned to the United States. After spending his army leave time in Georgia, Archie returned to Washington, D.C. to work in General Humphrey's office, but Humphrey was so impressed with Archie's capabilities that he soon appointed him as Washington's Depot Quartermaster, a billet that was usually granted to officers with greater seniority in the service.

In June 1904 Archie's younger brother, Lewis, married Clara Doughty, and it was to his new sister-in-law that Archie would later write most of his personal letters describing his service in two presidential administrations. The following year *Lippincott's* published a serialisation of Archie's novel *Both Sides of the Shield*, a work that dealt with Southern life and drew the appreciative attention of President Theodore Roosevelt, whose own mother was from Georgia.

Archie continued to serve as Depot Quartermaster until late September 1906, when General Fred Funston sent him to Cuba to establish a base of supplies for the American army of pacification. Captain Butt served as Depot Quartermaster at Havana, and his mother Pamela eventually joined him in Cuba and shared quarters with him there. Archie served in Havana until May 1908, at which time he was recalled to Washington to begin serving as one of President Theodore Roosevelt's military aides.

President Roosevelt utilised Captain Butt's services at a formal reception on his very first day at the White House, and that night Archie went to the Army and Navy Club and told his friend, Lieutenant Victor Blue, 'Old boy, it is mighty tiresome, but I believe I am going to like it.' Pamela Butt accompanied her son to Washington and set up housekeeping in the Gordon Hotel while Archie briefly took up bachelor quarters with a group of young military officers and career diplomats who called themselves 'The Family'. It might have been this group living arrangement that first gave Archie the idea of allowing friends to board with him when he acquired a home of his own, so that their rent money could add to his own financial security.

The year 1908 was a hectic but exciting one for Captain Butt. In addition to advising the President on military and social matters, Archie became part of Roosevelt's so-called 'Tennis Cabinet' and was called upon to accompany him during rock climbing excursions, horse galloping sessions, swimming outings, tennis matches and other physical activities of the outdoors-minded chief executive. Captain Butt's sterling personal qualities very quickly made him a valued friend and trusted confidant of President Roosevelt, and Archie became completely devoted to TR and his wife Edith, who Archie felt was the nicest woman he had ever known.

The year 1908 proved to be a year of mixed blessings for Archie, because his mother Pamela was now seriously ill. Thinking that exposure to sea air might help to improve her health, Archie took his mother to Philadelphia, booked two passages on the American liner *Friesland* and sailed with her to the United Kingdom so that she could visit her son Edward and his family. Archie returned to the States alone, but in October he received a cablegram announcing the tragic news that his ailing mother had passed away at Edward's home. In December, with his own hands, Archie placed his beloved mother's ashes in the ground of her native soil in Augusta, Georgia. (The following February *Uncle Remus's Magazine* posthumously published Pamela's short story 'Aunt Peggy, Lady', a personal reminiscence in which Pamela told the story of the life and death of her beloved ex-slave after the Civil War.)

Now that his mother was gone, Archie felt a need to continue sharing regular news of his presidential activities with a member of his family, so he began writing regular letters to Clara, the wife of his brother Lewis. These letters were filled with behind-the-scenes reports of the personal goings-on inside the White House, and Archie had a vague notion that he might eventually use these letters to write a book during the quiet days that would follow his eventual retirement from the service.

President Roosevelt was a staunch advocate of physical fitness, and in January 1909, in atrocious winter weather, Captain Butt earned Roosevelt's undying respect by accompanying him on a marathon seventeen-hour, 98-mile horseback ride from Washington to Warrenton, Virginia, and back again. In February Archie accompanied President Roosevelt on an official trip to Kentucky to dedicate the Lincoln birthplace memorial, and later he was with the chief executive on board the presidential yacht in New York Harbour when the navy's Great White Fleet returned from its world tour.

Captain Butt served as President Roosevelt's military aide-de-camp until March 1909, and when William Howard Taft assumed the presidency on 4 March he asked his old friend Archie Butt to remain at the White House as his own military ADC. President Taft was quickly reminded of how much value he placed on Captain Butt's friendship, integrity and devotion to duty, and Archie soon became as highly esteemed an advisor to Taft as he had been to Roosevelt.

Although Archie was not required to play tennis or go rock climbing with his new commander in chief, the two men did go horseback riding together, went for long car rides during the evenings and played a lot of golf whenever the President felt like making the rounds at the local course. In addition to making sure Taft's day went smoothly, one unspoken duty that Archie took very seriously was his responsibility for the chief executive's safety, a duty he shared with the Secret Service agents who were assigned to the White House. It was for that reason that Captain Butt took to carrying a small gold-plated pocket pistol in his waistcoat pocket while he was on duty accompanying the chief executive.

'The President seems to excite so little hostility that it [might seem] useless to always keep guarded around him,' Archie wrote to his sister-in-law, 'yet experience shows that [when] one least expects anything such tragedies occur. However, it would be fatal to one's reputation in case of such a contingent to be shown at a later examination that an aide-de-camp was not properly equipped to protect his chief even if he could do nothing at the time.'

Captain Butt's official duties did not end at 5 p.m., because he often accompanied the chief executive to official engagements lasting well into the wee hours. Since he was still required to resume his official duties at the regular time the following morning, Archie's schedule was exhausting but was one that gave him a tremendous feeling of accomplishment and satisfaction.

On 23 March 1909, President Taft sent his aide-de-camp to New York City to bid Theodore Roosevelt a cordial goodbye upon the latter's departure for a post-presidential African safari. In mid-May, however, tragedy struck the Taft household when the President's wife, Nellie, suffered a stroke that half crippled her and left her with a long-term speech impediment. 'I led her, or rather half carried her, into the saloon [of the presidential yacht],' Captain Butt recorded. 'I called the President, and he went deathly pale, and as he entered the room where she lay he closed the door.' Archie helped hide the severity of Mrs Taft's illness from the general public, and the President was deeply touched by his aide's attentiveness to the ailing First Lady.

Beginning in mid-May, Archie began posing for a painted portrait by his friend, artist Frank Millet, and on 14 July he received the finished portrait (which he wound up disliking because Millet kept fiddling with it in an attempt to improve it). 'I confess that [it] … positively nauseates me when I look at it,' Archie wrote to his sister-in-law. 'And so long as Millet lives I will have to keep it out of the fire. My advice is never to let an intimate friend paint your portrait, for you can never destroy it while he lives and the danger is he may outlive you.' During this same time period Archie also commissioned a stained-glass window memorialising his mother Pamela, and he arranged to have it installed in Augusta's Church of the Good Shepherd when it was completed.

By September 1909 Captain Butt was living in a home of his own on I Street, but on 15 September he accompanied President Taft and his staff on a lengthy cross-country rail tour that was dubbed the 'swing around the circle'. In mid-October the presidential party found itself in Texas, where Archie was able to renew his acquaintance with Mexican President Porfirio Diaz during the latter's presidential conference with Mr Taft in El Paso.

In January 1910 Archie was inducted into the Masonic order, and in February he began studying so that he would be prepared to take the upcoming test for his army promotion. By March Archie was sharing a home with President Taft's naval aide, Lieutenant Commander Leigh Palmer, and with Frank Millet, and – in looking to the future – he decided to acquire a burial plot in Arlington National Cemetery where he hoped to be laid to rest after the sands of life finally ran out of his hourglass.

Although he had long got over losing Alice Connally, by 1910 Archie lost his heart to Mathilde Townsend, a beautiful young Washington socialite. ('The only two women I ever really loved were Alice Connally and Mathilde Townsend,' he once confided to his sister-in-law.) Archie wasn't able to hide his feelings very well either, because his friend Beatrice Fairfax wrote that 'everyone knew [Archie] was hopelessly in love with Mathilde Townsend'. Sadly, Miss Townsend did not reciprocate Archie's romantic feelings, and when she announced in April that she would be marrying another suitor named Peter Gerry, the news broke Archie's heart.

By early June Archie owned a new home on H Street, but he was duty bound to leave Washington and accompany the Taft family to the summer White House that had been established the previous year at Beverly, Massachusetts. During that same month, President Taft once again sent Archie to New York to convey presidential greetings to Theodore Roosevelt upon the latter's return from his African safari. Roosevelt visited President Taft at Beverly on 30 June, but it was starkly evident to everyone present that the two old friends had grown apart since TR left office and that the former president did not approve of many of his successor's political policies. This political parting of the ways became even more apparent when Taft and TR met again in New Haven in September.

In November 1910 Captain Butt accompanied President Taft to Panama for an inspection of the Panama Canal, which was still under construction. The presidential party returned to Washington in plenty of time for Christmas, and on 1 January 1911 Archie fulfilled his usual official duty of standing opposite President Taft in a reception line and announcing the names of thousands of visitors who attended the White House New Year's reception.

In March 1911 Captain Butt took the tests that were required for his military promotion, and on the 24th President Taft signed his ADC's army commission as a major. During that same month Major Archibald Butt purchased a new home on G Street and continued to share his domicile with his friend Frank Millet and a couple of other friends.

Perhaps it was the purchase of his new home that caused Archie to start thinking about the joys of family life and made him realise how fond he had become of Marjorie Ide, the daughter of an American diplomat, who he had known since his Philippine days. Archie felt that he and Marjorie could easily fall in love with each other if they could only spend more time together, and Marjorie (who apparently had similar feelings) confided that she didn't want to share Archie with President Taft if her 'plans' for him came to fruition.

Archie wrote to Marjorie:

> I think you are very fond of me and I certainly am very fond of you. We might love one another could we be thrown together enough. We are certainly good pals and you are lovely to look at, and when I take an hour off and put my mind to thinking of you I even feel very sentimental, but you are so far away and at heart I am rather practical, so I manage to keep my imagination in hand before it begins to rear palaces in Spain. Sometimes I think of you in one of them, but it is always with an Hidalgo and not with an American. When it is all over and you come back to American mother earth, who can tell, perhaps we may clasp hands in the mist and wander along seeking the light together.

Unfortunately, later that year Marjorie met another man who was destined to become her husband, and once again Archie was left out in the cold in a romantic sense. By late May Archie was starting to despair of ever finding a girl with whom to share his life, and he confided to his sister-in-law that, despite his loneliness and his longing to have children, he thought he had probably delayed marriage too long and that he thought it was now rather unlikely that he would ever marry.

On the political scene, the relationship between William Howard Taft and Theodore Roosevelt continued to deteriorate, and by the end of July the situation had got so bad that Major Butt despairingly gave up all hope of ever reconciling his two presidential friends.

'What's the use?' Archie lamented. 'If it's to be a fight to the finish between them, nothing I can say now will be of any good. I have done my best, and they simply see things differently, that is all.'

The stress caused by his two friends' political disagreement might have been one underlying reason for Archie's occasional bouts of illness during the previous two months, but it wasn't until he was accompanying the presidential party through Kansas during that autumn's cross-country 'swing around the circle' that Archie's illness prostrated him so badly that he was briefly unable to fulfil his duties to the President. Although he soon rallied, Archie still felt very ill and placed himself under the watchful care of a physician, who determined he was suffering from hives over his entire body and from severe digestive problems that were releasing poisonous toxins into his bloodstream, causing him great discomfort and nausea.

When the travelling presidential party reached Louisville, Kentucky, in late October, Major Butt received the surprise of his life. The friends Archie made throughout his life seem to have remained exceptionally loyal to him through the years, and his old associates at the Louisville Press Club now gave a banquet at which Archie himself was the guest of honour instead of President Taft; Major Butt was flattered when the chief executive approved of the banquet and joined in honouring his most trusted aide-de-camp.

The presidential rail trip finally came to an end on 12 November, but Archie was still feeling tired and weak because of his ongoing illness. Tensions between President Taft and Theodore Roosevelt continued to escalate, too, and it was feared that Roosevelt would eventually express his intention to displace President Taft and secure the Republican Party's nomination for the presidency in 1912. This schism placed Major Butt in an impossible position; Taft and Roosevelt were both his close friends, and he was distressed by his divided loyalties and felt enormous pressure at being caught in the middle of their conflict. Archie's dilemma intensified on 3 December when Roosevelt – through his daughter Alice – urged him to resign his job as Taft's military aide-de-camp. Archie refused to do so, but the strain he was labouring under continued to have an adverse effect on his health; indeed, Archie had lost 15lb during the recent transcontinental trip, and by 18 December he was still tired and feverish.

On the last day of December 1911 Archie wondered how he would ever manage to fulfil his duties and get through the annual New Year's reception that was to be held at the White House the following day. But get through it he did when on 1 January 1912 he presented slightly over 7,000 guests to President Taft before the official reception concluded. At that point Archie hurried home to act as host to 300 personal friends at his own New Year's reception at which he served his famous eggnog along with hot buttered biscuits filled with Smithfield ham. At the conclusion of the reception Archie's physician checked in to see how he was doing, and it was determined that his weight had decreased by 20lb since the day he began travelling with President Taft on the autumn cross-country tour. Archie insisted that he was 'feeling like my old self again', but later that month Theodore Roosevelt's wife Edith opined that Archie still didn't look well.

Archie regularly rented rooms in his spacious Washington home to friends who needed a place to stay while they were in the city, and in February 1912 Major Blanton Winship, artist Frank Millet and diplomats Archibald Kerr and Eustace Percy were all boarding in Archie's home. Later that same month, Millet took special note of his friend's ongoing ill-health and asked President Taft to allow Archie to accompany him on a trip to Italy for rest and recreation. Taft urged his chief military aide to follow Millet's advice, so Archie agreed to do so and applied to the army for sick leave. Three days later Archie had second thoughts and cancelled his travel arrangements

Frank Millet.
(Author's collection)

rather than abandon his commander in chief during this challenging political time, but he finally relented and reinstated his plans after the President urged him to accompany Millet.

On 2 March 1912 Archie and Frank Millet travelled to Hoboken, New Jersey, and sailed for Gibraltar on the liner *Berlin*, and upon reaching the latter destination the two men continued onward to Algiers and finally arrived in Rome on 10 March. Archie spent the next two weeks enjoying the Eternal City coupled with private audiences with Pope Pius X and King Victor Emmanuel, and he was among the huge throng of people who stood beneath the window of the royal residence and cheered when the King showed himself to his subjects following an unsuccessful assassination attempt. 'He kept us waiting over half an hour,' Archie joked later while thinking about his own duties to President Taft, 'but I did not blame him, for I knew he had an aide who was afraid to tell him for the third time that it was time to keep his appointment.' Contrary to newspaper rumours, Major Butt's visits with the King and the Pontiff were of a personal nature and were not part of a secret mission conducted on President Taft's behalf.

On 29 March Archie left Rome and passed through Switzerland while on his way to visit friends in Berlin. After arriving in Paris on 31 March, Archie met his niece, Arrington, and accompanied her across the Channel to England to visit her parents, Edward and Savannah Butt (Archie's brother and sister-in-law). After arriving at their home in Mickle Trafford, Cheshire, on 2 April, Archie spent the next few days visiting his relatives and seeing the sights in London and elsewhere. Around 8 April Archie bade his brother's family farewell for the last time and travelled to London to pay a brief visit to the Baron and Baroness Marcus Rosenkrantz before the time came for him to return to the United States.

The fact that Archie had been travelling abroad for almost a month did not decrease the strange feeling of foreboding he'd been experiencing ever since he first agreed to accompany Frank Millet to Europe. Newspapers later reported Archie had made a specific point of drawing up a new will before he left Washington, and a friend recalled Archie confiding that he 'had the strangest feeling he had ever had in his life that he was to be at the center of some awful calamity'. This feeling of impending doom did not decrease after Archie left the States, and friends and relatives in Europe were deeply troubled by the fact that his normally cheerful personality had disappeared and been replaced by a quiet, thoughtful, resigned frame of mind in which Archie made occasional cryptic comments about his not having long to live. It was in this subdued frame of mind that Major Archibald Willingham Butt bade a final farewell to his friends on 10 April and took the boat train from London to Southampton to board the *Titanic* for his return to the United States …

Eight days passed, and on the evening of 18 April the rescue ship *Carpathia* arrived in New York carrying the 712 people who had survived the sinking of the *Titanic* three days before. The next morning, it was a shaken President William Howard Taft who issued a public statement regarding his chief military aide, Major Archibald Butt, who was among the missing. It read:

> Major Archie Butt was my military aide. He was like a member of my family, and I feel his loss as if he had been a younger brother. The chief trait of his character was loyalty to his ideals, his cloth, and his friends. His character was a simple one in the sense that he was incapable of intrigue or insincerity. He was gentle and considerate to everyone, high or low. He never lost, under any conditions, his sense of proper regard to what he considered the respect due to constituted authority. He was an earnest member of the Episcopal Church, and loved that communion. He was a soldier, every inch of him; a most competent and successful quartermaster, and a devotee of his profession. After I heard that part of the ship's company had gone down, I gave up hope for the rescue of Major Butt, unless by accident. I knew that he would certainly remain on the ship's deck until every duty had been performed and every sacrifice made that properly fell on one charged, as he would feel himself charged, with responsibility, for the rescue of others. He leaves the widest circle of friends, whose memory of him is sweet in every particular.

Some Personal Observations on Major Archibald Butt

As a small child I used to run to my grandmother's bookshelf and pull down her copy of Logan Marshall's *The Sinking of the Titanic and Great Sea Disasters*, a compilation of newspaper accounts that was published in book form during the weeks following the disaster in 1912. This book contained a photograph of a dignified, uniformed man named Major Archibald Willingham Butt, and the text offered a number of accounts that purported to describe the manner in which this uniformed man met his death on the *Titanic*. The fact that some of these accounts differed from each other was something I did not think very deeply about at the time, nor did I wonder about how this military man might have lived his life in the years prior to 1912.

As I grew older and began to do original research into the sinking of the *Titanic*, Archibald Butt's name continued to crop up in the thousands of period newspaper articles that I perused on microfilm. I still did not focus a great deal of attention on Major Butt, because there were approximately 2,200 other *Titanic* passengers and crewmen who I was interested in researching as well. It wasn't until after THS historian Don Lynch gave me a volume of Major Butt's published letters that 'Archie' (as he was known to his friends) suddenly 'stepped out of the crowd' and became a living, breathing human being to me. I was fascinated by the edited versions of the letters I had just read and immediately searched out the two remaining out-of-print volumes of Archie's edited letters, and – by the time I finished reading them – I felt almost as if I had lost a close personal friend in the *Titanic* disaster.

Although the three volumes of Archie Butt's published letters necessarily focused on his official relationship with Presidents Theodore Roosevelt and William Howard Taft, I noticed that the editor of those volumes used plenty of ellipses – the little dots signifying that one or more passages had been deleted from the published versions of the letters. I suspected that many of those omitted passages might contain information that would be of great interest to historians, and a quick examination of Archie's original manuscript letters proved that I was not mistaken: the Archibald Butt papers did indeed contain a great deal of fascinating material dealing with his service at the American legation in Mexico, his military service during the Philippine insurrection and many other subjects that never appeared in the published versions of his letters. As for his experiences during the Roosevelt and Taft administrations, Archie's original letters are filled with comments, asides and observations that the editor of the published versions of those letters felt did not contribute to the political history of the Roosevelt and Taft administrations. Although the editor was probably correct in that respect, his deletions nevertheless hid many details about Taft and Roosevelt that I realised would appeal to historians who are interested in the *personal* lives of both presidents as well as Archie's *own* life. Many of Archie's manuscript letters contain five or six pages of typewritten text that were omitted from the published versions of those same letters, and the knowledge that those manuscript letters still contained so much un-mined biographical material was the stimulus behind my decision to write a full-length biography of Archie Butt using his own words and those of his friends whenever possible.

This task was easier said than done, because the microfilming of Archie's letters that was undertaken in the 1950s was woefully incomplete and was also very poorly executed, with many hundreds of microfilm frames being so badly overexposed photographically that the letters in those frames are completely invisible. I therefore found it necessary to visit the Georgia Department of Archives and History in Atlanta in order to examine the original letters in manuscript. Many hundreds of dollars were spent in obtaining photocopies of Archie's letters from the year 1909 (which were never microfilmed) as well as obtaining photocopies of selected letters from other years in order to remedy the informational gaps caused by the defective microfilms. These documents – plus thousands of printouts made from the pages of the *Washington Post*, *New York Times*, *Augusta Chronicle* and a couple of hundred other period newspapers – enabled me to trace Archie Butt's movements through the years and create a reasonably full picture of his life. Books and memoirs written by Archie's friends and associates have played their own part in adding colour to the overall record of his life, and the papers of Theodore Roosevelt and William Howard Taft were of course a veritable gold mine that added innumerable details to his story and helped me to piece together the last weeks of Archie's life.

The story that emerged from this research makes it clear that Archibald Willingham Butt was a competent, talented and amazingly popular man whose sense of discretion was legendary and whose loyalty, integrity and friendship were valued by more people in more corners of the world than can possibly be counted. Archie's steadfastness and ability to give sensible advice caused two American presidents to come to rely on his judgement, and his sunny personality and sense of humour brightened their lives so much that both men practically adopted him into their own families and regarded him as a beloved younger brother.

Despite the fact that he was loved and admired by family and friends – and even by strangers – Archie Butt was a typical child of his times. Born in Georgia at the close of the Civil War, Archie was a thoughtful, kind-hearted boy who grew up to be a thoughtful, kind-hearted man, who nevertheless was the possessor of one unsurprising personal prejudice – his attitude towards Black Americans. Even though this attitude was not the overriding principle upon which he based his life, and even though his letters mentioned it only rarely, the mere fact that Archie's opinion of Black Americans was unremarked upon by most of his contemporaries makes it deserving of a brief mention here.

It is, of course, natural that Archie was exposed to the beliefs and prejudices of his elders during the years he was growing up in poverty-ridden Augusta. Having been thoroughly steeped in the *zeitgeist* of the post-Civil War South, Archie frankly disapproved of Black people who attempted to 'rise above their station' and become the social equal of the white man. Although he knew and liked individual Black people (and was liked by them in return), Archie could never allow himself to feel it was proper for a white man to invite a Black man into his home or to sit down and fraternise with them at the dinner table. (Archie's mother, Pamela, never forgave Theodore Roosevelt for inviting Black educator Booker T. Washington to dine with him at the White House, and a large proportion of American citizens agreed with her and felt that Roosevelt's egalitarian act had set American race relations back a hundred years.) Indeed, such fraternisation between the races was simply not done in the American South – and Archie's letters make it clear that such things were not often done in the American North, either. In short, Archie was a product of his times, but this shortcoming – important as it is – should perhaps not be compared with the more enlightened standards of the present day. In these contexts, the personal viewpoints and opinions of any human being must be considered in the light of the era in which that person grew up, the place in which he lived and the people from whom he received his set of personal values.

And yet, despite his inability to regard the Black man as the social equal of the white man, Archie Butt was loved and respected by almost everyone who knew him – Black people as well as white. Indeed, Archie is known to have gone out of his way to help many individual Black people to better their lives. 'He was broadly catholic and sympathetic,' William Howard Taft declared. 'No servant was too insignificant, no Negro too humble, to escape his kindly attention.' A Black employee at the White House agreed, saying that Archie was the 'haughtiest to rich folks' but the 'nicest to our folks'.[3]

Robert Heinl, the Washington correspondent of *Leslie's Weekly*, agreed:

> This is borne out by the way his old [Black] employees follow him. Swarms of them trailed the Georgian from the Philippines to Cuba and then back to the United States. He is probably more sought for positions by coloured labourers than any man in the army ... Now that Captain Butt is with the President, his old friends think surely he can help them. They fairly besiege him. A Negro teamster called the other morning and was ushered into the house, hat in hand. He pleaded for something to do. 'I am the only man in the service who has nothing to give,' Captain Butt answered, 'except a few secrets. And they are not worth giving away.'

Even though Archie was a practitioner of the casual racial prejudice of his day, he (unlike many of his contemporaries) was able to sympathise with individual Black people who fell victim to that prejudice. One example of this was the way he was saddened at a White House reception when he saw how the Haitian minister and his wife – both of whom were Black – were shunned by the other ministers and ambassadors of the diplomatic service. In short, while he was brought up to regard racism as being a normal and accepted part of everyday life, and as such felt that Black people could never be regarded as the social equal of the white man, it can honestly be said that Archie's feelings were a fault of the head, not of the heart.

Archie's critical attitude toward the Catholic Church was apparently based on slightly better grounds than his attitude towards Black people. Archie was a religious man who was perfectly content to let other people worship God in their own way, and – despite reservations about the retarding effect that Catholicism had had on the evolution of free thought and religious tolerance – he was definitely not anti-Catholic; indeed, he enumerated to Cardinal Merry del Val the many positive influences that the Catholic Church was exerting on American schoolchildren. Nevertheless, Archie definitely disapproved of the way American Catholic officials tried to exert behind the scenes political pressure for the Church's own benefit. For example, he was keenly aware of the Church's efforts to obtain President Taft's support for a certain politician who was facing expulsion because of his disreputable behaviour; the Church wanted to save this politician without regard for the rightness or wrongness of his cause, but simply because he was a Catholic. What concerned Archie most was that, in public, President Taft gave the impression that he was unduly influenced by the Catholic Church at the expense of the country's Protestant citizens, who – unlike their Catholic brethren – never asked the President to promote strictly Protestant causes. Indeed, it should be pointed out that Archie also disapproved of powerful Jewish lobbyists who pressured the American government to interfere with Russia's internal passport policies regarding Russian-born American Jews, and he likewise disapproved of the 'grafters' of the Grand Army of the Republic who pressed for costly government pensions for their membership, which consisted solely of Civil War veterans. In short, a careful reading of Archie's letters shows that his occasional criticisms of Catholic, Jewish and G.A.R. lobbyists were actually expressions of his disapproval of *any* organisation – religious or civic – that applied secret political pressure in order to further its own private agenda.

In recent years it has become more common for occasional writers to speculate that Archie might have been gay. Richard Davenport-Hines has gone so far as to claim that Archie's friendship with Frank Millet was in truth a 'love story' whose 'enduring partnership' was 'an early case of "Don't ask, don't tell."' The fact that theory was uncorroborated by any meaningful documentation was unsurprising, since my eight years of research into Archie's life failed to produce a single shred of evidence that Hines' interpretation reflected actual events. Quite the opposite, in fact.

The main piece of evidence advanced by Davenport-Hines and other proponents of Archie's alleged homosexuality is the fact that he and Frank Millet (who was bisexual) lived together in Archie's large Washington D.C. home. This bare-bones statement is true as far as it goes, but Hines somehow neglects to tell his readers that three other men (Major Blanton Winship and diplomats Archibald Kerr and Eustace Percy) were likewise renting rooms in Archie's home just as Frank Millet was doing – a fact that puts the supposedly private Archie/Millet living arrangement in a completely platonic light. Needless to say, it would have been difficult for 'dear old Frank Millet' (as Archie once referred to his friend) to creep into Archie's bedroom at night without causing a furore among their friends and fellow tenants. Indeed, Peter Engstrom (Frank Millet's own biographer) never raises the slightest suggestion that Archie and Millet might have been lovers – mainly because most biographers aren't willing to make such huge leaps of judgement based on zero evidence. (Even writer James Gifford does not believe Millet had a sexual relationship with Archie, even though it's still his 'impression' that Archie was gay.)

Proponents of the belief that Archie was gay usually bring up supposedly stereotypical traits like Archie's devotion to his mother, his fondness for his army dress uniform and the fact that his writings occasionally described ladies' dresses and the handsomeness of male friends. Yes, Archie was devoted to his widowed mother, but it was because of the many personal sacrifices she willingly endured in order to raise him and his brothers by herself in the post-Civil War South and ensure that they received a college education. (Escape artist Harry Houdini was devoted to his own mother as well, but we don't see social historians suggesting that Houdini's devotion had any bearing on his sexuality!)

Yes, Archie was a snappy dresser and was very proud of his army uniform, but being a snappy dresser has nothing to do with one's sexuality. (The present writer has a married, heterosexual friend who is so fastidious about his personal appearance that he once went on a rather muddy canoe trip while wearing dress slacks and a dress shirt.)

Yes, Archie did occasionally write to his sister-in-law and mention ladies' dresses and handsome Washington men who attended various presidential gatherings, but Archie wrote enthusiastic descriptions of beautiful Washington ladies as well – and he did it *far* more often than he mentioned handsome gentlemen. (Everyone recognises a good-looking man or woman when they see them, and Archie Butt was no exception to that rule.) In short, Archie's letters were merely painting word pictures for his sister-in-law in Georgia so that she could use her imagination *in absentia* and share in the excitement of attending a presidential function in the nation's capital. Occasional writers, though, have cherry-picked uncommon references to handsome men contained in Archie's many hundreds of letters and have presented those uncommon descriptions in isolation as 'proof' that Archie was gay. (This is similar to a few modern-day writers who claim Abraham Lincoln was gay merely because he indulged in the then-common practice of sharing a bed with other men while spending the night in a small boarding house with limited facilities.)

Instead of providing any evidence that he was gay, all of Archie's surviving writings make clear the fact that he was interested in women instead of men. 'Oh, he's the successful sailor when it comes to women,' a friend of Archie's once exclaimed with a grin. 'He sails right in and sails right out again.' President Taft agreed. 'Doctor,' he once advised an associate, 'I would advise you keep any good-looking girls by that name out of the Captain's reach. He has got more kissing kin than any man I ever knew, and he is not troubled about the remoteness of the relationship if the cousin happens to be pretty.' Taft expressed a similar observation at another time. 'Don't I know that he is kissing kin to every girl south of the Mason and Dixon Line,' the President exclaimed with admiration.

Although she was not the first woman to win Archie's heart, Mathilde Townsend was truly the love of his life – and everyone in Washington knew it. (Beatrice Fairfax once commented that 'everyone knew [Archie] was hopelessly in love with Mathilde Townsend' but that he had been pre-empted by 'a more successful suitor'.) Indeed, after Mathilde told Archie she'd just become engaged to another man, Archie's heartbroken outpourings to his sister-in-law Clara made it clear he was deeply in love with the young woman:

> I, who have grown accustomed to analyze my deepest feelings before you, fail completely here. I had always thought that the announcement of an engagement to anyone else would have been a terrific blow to me, for there is no use to attempt to conceal the fact from you, after all I have said of Mathilde, that she is the only woman who has ever dominated my mind and heart …
>
> We talked all the evening and I marveled at myself that I was able to discuss the matter with her at all, for, Clara, my heart was cold and my throat dry and choked. I went through the night like one in a dream and woke this morning as if someone had died in the night. I shall move on in the same way. It will not make any difference in my daily routine, and I fall back on my belief that I was not intended to be one of the happy people of the world … I have written all this merely because I had set my hand to the task of being frank in everything, even where my own wounds are exposed. I shall not mention her again, save only as one who has passed out of my life into that world of New York and Newport, into which I have peeped but will never enter.

Despite his heartbreak at losing Mathilde Townsend, Archie was unable to completely abandon the idea that he might one day find the woman of his dreams. 'Somehow marriage has never fitted into my scheme of life,' he wrote later. 'Love and [career] ambition seems always to have crowded it to one side until now I am growing accustomed to the thought that I may never marry. Who can tell? Possibly tomorrow I may meet the right person for whom I would be willing to lay down all this trumpery and display.'

Sadly, the *Titanic* disaster prevented that from ever happening.

Writer Richard Davenport-Hines has suggested that the post-disaster memorial fountain erected to Archie Butt and Frank Millet near the White House was built in recognition that 'their affection for each other was undying'. Likewise, James Gifford claims, 'It was said that the idea for the Butt-Millet memorial originated with Taft, who may have known a thing or two about their intimacy.' ('… a memorial to two men – and that fact alone speaks volumes,' Gifford adds.)

The 'volumes' Gifford refers to are not the same volumes he *thinks* they are, though, because neither his nor Hines' claims about the memorial fountain's origin and purpose are true. On 20 April 1912, presidential secretary Charles Hilles wrote a letter regarding subscriptions for the proposed memorial fountain (completed in October 1913) that reveals the fountain's true origin and purpose:

> It has been suggested, and this suggestion has the approval of the President, that an enduring memorial be erected on public grounds in Washington to the memory of Major Archibald W. Butt and Mr Frank D. Millet. It is believed that they were the only officers of the United States who went down with the *Titanic* ... Together they gave up their lives that others might live, and it seems fitting that a memorial be erected to them jointly.

In other words, the joint memorial to Archie Butt and Frank Millet had everything to do with their government service and nothing to do with their sexuality.

It must be admitted that Archie's personal comments in his letters about his daily activities add distinct splashes of colour to his life story, a fact that becomes especially evident when we contrast his letter-writing periods to other periods of his life when he had no need (or no time) to write letters outlining his daily activities. The dearth of recorded personal anecdotes during the latter time periods causes those portions of his story to take on an 'impersonal' quality that contrasts strongly with the periods during which he was recording his colourful personal observations about life around him. (President Taft's cross-country trips in 1909 and 1911 provide two excellent examples of this; Archie had little time to write personal letters during those trips, and his entries in the official presidential diary were merely formal recitations of fact that are completely lacking in the personal observations and anecdotes that make his letters so fascinating to read.) Fortunately, Archie Butt *did* write plenty of letters during the most interesting periods of his life, and we are indebted to him for making sure that those letters would be preserved for posterity. ('... I think they may be of some interest if I can only stop writing about myself so much and more about the President and the public men of this day,' he wrote to his sister-in-law on 23 January 1910. 'But I find I am so bound up in his life, the unofficial part of it, that I must needs put a great deal of myself in to get him in them at all.')

One unexpected discovery stemming from my research on Archie Butt was the fact that the hectic nature of his life often caused him to misdate his letters. Archie also had an occasional tendency to begin writing a letter on a given date and then postpone finishing it until one or two days later – a fact that sometimes made it difficult to determine just what he meant when he used the terms 'today', 'yesterday' and 'tomorrow' in the same letter. (Cross-referencing the contents of Archie's letters with independent newspaper coverage of then-current events has revealed the correct dates for most of Archie's letters as well as the events that he wrote about.)

While working with the texts of Archie Butt's manuscript letters the present author found it strangely touching to discover that Archie consistently misspelled certain words and names that he found occasion to use in his writings. (The name 'Rockefeller', for instance, became 'Rockefellow' in his letters.) Indeed, Archie's consistent misspelling of specific words eventually made it easy for the present author to determine whether Archie typed a letter himself or whether he dictated it to a typist, since the typist always spelled those specific words correctly whereas Archie did not. It was interesting, too, to see that Archie even misspelled the names of people who meant a great deal to him personally. For instance, the name of his second true love Mathilde Townsend was one that he never learned to spell correctly, while his misspelling of the surname of Alice Connally (his first true love) made the determination of the latter's true identity a very difficult mystery to unravel (albeit one that the present author succeeded in solving). Lastly, I was forced to smile at one particular example of Archie's misspellings, since it strongly suggests that he spoke with a very pronounced Southern accent; Archie Butt spelled the word 'orphan' just the way many Southerners pronounce it: 'auphan'.

At any rate, my three-volume biography *Archie* is my best attempt to present an accurate chronological account of the key events in the life of Archibald Willingham Butt. I have tried to present a reasonably complete picture of how he spent his days and have described the many and varied duties that he was required to perform while serving as military aide to two Presidents of the United States. I have also taken pains to provide thorough descriptions of the many social and political gatherings that Archie attended during his lifetime, since these details serve to highlight how drastically American customs have changed since that long-ago time and graphically illustrate the astoundingly extravagant lengths that Washington's millionaires went to when entertaining guests in their private mansions.

In addition to illustrating these 'public' facets of Archie Butt's life, I have deliberately included the *little* things that played an important part in his *personal* life – the books he read, the plays he attended, the music he enjoyed, the Christmas gifts he purchased … These little details are of no earthshaking historical importance, of course, but I hope readers will identify more closely with Archie's *personal* life when they learn that he played the stock market, got sick, had furnace problems, lost his dogs and experienced grief just as human beings have always done in the past and as they will continue to do as long as the human race exists.

Archibald Butt was indeed a human being, and a fascinating one at that.

5

The Two Deaths of John Jacob Astor

John Jacob Astor. (Author's collection)

For many years it has been 'common knowledge' among *Titanic* researchers that Colonel John Jacob Astor lost his life when the *Titanic*'s forward funnel crashed down on top of him as he struggled in the sea next to the sinking liner. This belief is based on the claim that Mr Astor's body was badly crushed and impregnated with soot when it was recovered by the *Mackay Bennett* a few days after the disaster.[1]

But is this claim accurate?

Despite a wide-ranging search for the original report that Mr Astor's body was crushed and blackened by soot from a falling funnel, only one account has come to light that partially supports this contention. Page 31 of Archibald Gracie's *The Truth About the Titanic* contains the following statement:

> From the fact that I never saw Colonel Astor on the Boat Deck later, and also because his body, when found, was crushed (according to the statement of one who saw it at Halifax, Mr Harry K. White, of Boston, Mr Edward A. Kent's brother-in-law, my schoolmate and friend from boyhood), I am of the opinion that he met his fate on the ship when the boilers tore through it, as described later.

The reader will immediately notice that, although the Gracie account claims Colonel Astor's body was indeed recovered in a crushed condition, there is no suggestion at all that the body was blackened by soot as if from a falling funnel. The present author believes that the 'extra' detail about the soot was just an imaginative addition to Gracie's account that was tacked on to it by modern researchers who felt a need to pin down the exact cause of Astor's death.

Despite Archibald Gracie's claim that Colonel Astor's body was crushed, the present author has uncovered several previously unknown eyewitness accounts that cast serious doubt on the claim that Astor's body was badly damaged during the sinking of the *Titanic*.

Let us examine these accounts:

Gerald Ross (an electrician on the *Mackay Bennett*) said: 'I saw the recovery of Col. Astor's body. Like the others it was floating buoyed by a lifebelt. Both arms extended upwards. The face was swollen, one jaw was injured. His body was clothed in a business suit and tan shoes. His watch, a costly thing, studded with diamonds, was dangling from his pocket. It had stopped at 3.20. Practically all the other watches on bodies we recovered had stopped at 2.10. His watch chain was of platinum and so were the settings of the rings he wore.'[2]

John Snow (the undertaker who served on board the *Mackay Bennett*) made the following observation: 'Colonel Astor's body was in an excellent state of preservation. It was clad in full evening dress. Col. Astor's handsome gold watch was dangling from the chain out of one of his pockets as though he had looked at it just before he took the final plunge. There was $2,500 in cash in his pocket.'[3]

Captain Richard Roberts (the commander of the Astor yacht) was the first to view the body of his employer when it was brought to Halifax. The features, he said, were unharmed, the face being only slightly discoloured by water. When the body was recovered it was in ordinary garments, on which were Colonel Astor's initials, and by this means as well as by certain documents in his pockets he was identified. He also carried considerable cash. Colonel Astor was also wearing a belt with a gold buckle that had been in the family for years.[4]

Although these three accounts differ slightly in certain particulars, all three of them seem to confirm the fact that Colonel Astor's body was not crushed, soot-blackened or disfigured in a manner suggesting that he had been killed by either a falling boiler or a falling funnel. Quite the opposite, in fact.

The three interviews we have just reviewed make it very clear that *Titanic* researchers cannot afford to take 'common knowledge' for granted; these interviews prove that serious researchers must regard undocumented secondary sources with a great deal of caution and should instead rely on original 1912 sources as often as possible. If this cautionary advice is not acted upon, it is easy for well-meaning researchers to expend a great deal of time and energy discussing the fine points of historical events that never occurred in the first place.

6

Thomson Beattie's *Titanic* Experience

Thomson Beattie. (*Winnipeg Tribune*)

In 1912 Thomson Beattie resided in Winnipeg, Manitoba, and had ten brothers and sisters living in various parts of Canada. One brother, Fred B. Beattie, lived in Vancouver, while another brother, Charles, was in business somewhere in the west.

At one time Thomson Beattie was connected with the Haslam Land Company in Winnipeg, after which he entered into a real estate business partnership with Richard Waugh, under the firm name of Waugh and Beattie. In 1911 Waugh was elected Mayor of Winnipeg and was deeply involved in municipal affairs, so the management of the business fell solely on Beattie's shoulders.

Beattie and his friend J. Hugo Ross were members of the Manitoba Club, and, along with their friend Thomas McCaffry of Vancouver, they had long been planning a holiday trip to the Continent. In January the three men made the eastward crossing on the *Franconia* and toured the great cities of Europe, and Beattie and Ross stayed in regular contact with friends in Winnipeg by sending postcards as they travelled.

The party arrived in Cairo on about 10 February, and while they were there they visited W.E. Thompson, a friend who was in hospital recovering from pleurisy. Hugo Ross told Thompson that he must start for home soon, as he had important business in Paris. The party then took a side trip up the Nile to Luxor and Assouan (Aswan), and the men left Cairo for good on 23 February and headed for Naples. By March, Ross had fallen ill and Beattie and McCaffry were both exhausted from their travels, so they sent a postcard to a friend in Canada saying, 'We are on the last lap of doing the old lands and ready for Winnipeg and business.' The three friends decided to return home on the *Titanic*, so they crossed the Channel to London and threw themselves a bon voyage party at the Carlton Hotel on Easter Sunday. On that same day Beattie and Ross jointly wrote a postcard to Winnipeg saying, 'We are changing ships and coming home in a new, unsinkable boat.'[1]

On Wednesday, 10 April, Beattie, McCaffry and Ross boarded the *Titanic* at Southampton, although Ross was so weak from dysentery that he was carried aboard on a stretcher. Ross was booked into cabin A-10, and Beattie and Ross shared cabin C-6.[2]

On the night of 14 April Beattie was seated in the first-class smoking room with McCaffry. At about eleven o'clock they were joined by Major Arthur Peuchen, and the three men spent their evening smoking and chatting together.[3] At about 11.20 p.m. Peuchen said goodnight to his two friends and left the smoking room.

Shortly after the *Titanic* struck the iceberg, Peuchen did a little investigating on deck and then went down to Ross's cabin and knocked on his door to tell him the problem wasn't serious.

'What is it?' Ross called through the closed door.

'We have struck an iceberg and you better come out on deck,' Peuchen replied.

'Is that all?' Ross told Peuchen. 'It will take more than an iceberg to get me out of bed.'[4] Peuchen left his friend in his stateroom, and William Sloper likewise stopped by Ross's cabin to reassure him.[5]

Not long afterwards, Peuchen saw a distressed Beattie standing near the grand staircase and went over to him.

'What is the matter?' Peuchen asked his friend.

'Why, the order is for lifebelts and boats,' Beattie replied.

'Will you go tell Mr Ross?' Peuchen asked.

'Yes; I will go and see Mr Ross,' Beattie replied.[6]

Mrs Mark Fortune must have encountered Beattie right after he left Major Peuchen, because Beattie told the Fortunes, 'Things are looking pretty bad. I will go down and help Ross to dress.'[7]

Later Mrs Fortune and her daughters reportedly saw Ross and Beattie on the boat deck helping to load lifeboat #10 with women and children. The two men refused to enter the lifeboat themselves.[8]

When the *Titanic* foundered, Beattie managed to swim to the swamped boat Collapsible A, but the icy water had taken its toll and he died in the bottom of the boat. After the boat's survivors were rescued by Fifth Officer Lowe, Beattie's body was left in the flooded collapsible along with two other bodies and the boat was set adrift.

On 13 May 1912 the *Oceanic* came across the drifting, half-swamped lifeboat still carrying the three bodies. Beattie was identified by his watch and the labels in his clothing, and his body and those of the other two victims were buried at sea.

7

The Boat Train

After the *Titanic* went down, it was reported in British newspapers that on the morning of 10 April the first-class boat train from London to Southampton was unexpectedly delayed in arriving at its destination. The train was scheduled to leave Waterloo station at 9.45 a.m.,[1] but one reporter reported that as the train pulled away from the platform the engine suddenly developed mechanical difficulties and stopped. It was some time before the locomotive could be restarted.[2] According to researcher Jay Roches, the first-class boat train's delay resulted in a three-and-a-half-hour journey time for what should have been a one-and-three-quarter-hour trip,[3] and another source says the first-class train arrived in Southampton at 11.30 a.m.[4]

Problems arose with the second-class boat train as well. One passenger who had first-hand experience with this delay was cross-Channel passenger Stanley May, who began writing a letter on the evening of 10 April while the *Titanic* was heading for Queenstown:

> My dear Em,
> Will start a few lines tonight & finish before we arrive at Queenstown in the morning, or I rather expect it will be the afternoon as we are quite two hours late owing to a mishap as we left Southampton or rather just as we got clear [i.e. *Titanic*'s near-collision with the *New York*]. I will tell you about it later. We left Waterloo at 9.45 & arrived at Southampton a little late owing to the brakes going wrong directly we left Waterloo. Dick & I were first on board from the special train & met Lily, Jack & Miss Odell at once.[5]

After arriving in New York following the disaster, Sidney Collett was another passenger who spoke about the delay incurred by the second-class boat train:

> Well I might say in the beginning that I was just an hour or two late to book on the *St Louis* of the American Line, and was unable to sail on the *Philadelphia* because of the coal strike. Then I transferred to the *Titanic* and so, of course, I came here on the *Carpathia*. We left Waterloo Station and I was accompanied by my uncle Sydney. At the very start there was trouble. The train stopped because somebody had interfered with the brake valve. We reached Southampton and there I met my aunt, so you see I had my aunt on my mother's side and an uncle on the paternal side to see me off.[6]

Another passenger who recalled the problems with the second-class boat train was Elizabeth Dowdell:

> We were delayed on a special train to reach the *Titanic* in the time we had planned, and feared we would miss it. However, we arrived just in time for the gateman to remark, 'You're lucky to have caught it.'[7]

The second-class boat train arrived in Southampton at 11.30 a.m.,[8] but one wonders what would have happened if railway mechanics had been unable to resolve the first- and second-class locomotives' mechanical problems in a timely manner. Would railway officials have provided last-minute substitute locomotives in order to transport *Titanic*'s passengers to Southampton before their scheduled noon sailing time, or would the mechanics have tinkered with the two locomotives so long that a timely arrival in Southampton would have been impossible? Although the former possibility was clearly the most desirable one for the travellers in question, one wonders how many *Titanic* passengers' lives might have been spared if the delayed boat trains had arrived on the White Star pier just in time to see the largest vessel in the world pulling away from the dock to begin her maiden voyage?

Interestingly, on 10 April Edward Parsons, the *Titanic*'s chief storekeeper, wrote a letter on *Titanic* notepaper lamenting the fact that one travel connection failed to reach the ship on time and caused many people to miss the sailing.[9] The present author does not know what connection Mr Parsons was referring to or if it was a rail connection, but I'd definitely like to learn more about it.

8

Attempted Bribes

Emotional movie buffs sometimes complain about James Cameron's film portrayal of First Officer William Murdoch in which the character supposedly actively accepts a bribe from a passenger. (I disagree with this interpretation of the film Murdoch's actions, by the way.) However, now that we have raised the subject of bribes, is there any evidence that real bribery might have been attempted on board the real *Titanic*? The answer is a very tentative and qualified 'yes', because three reports of one such alleged incident made their way into print in 1912.

Charles Judd

After arriving back in the United Kingdom, Mr Judd (who was saved on one of the swamped collapsible lifeboats) spoke with reporters about things he saw and heard while on board the sinking *Titanic*:

> The water was getting higher and higher, and a wave caught her [the collapsible] and flung her up in the davits.
>
> Everybody was wild. It was at the last moment a passenger tossed me a knife. I just managed to cut her free when a big wave swept us all off deck. The boat was full when it started, but scarcely half the people managed to scramble into her in the water. A big wave plunged me aboard as clean as you please. I turned around as soon as I had my breath, but there was the most terrible screaming I've ever heard.
>
> The *Titanic* was nowhere to be seen. Five hours we stayed in that boat, I with my legs in ice-water.

> All the while another man, who held an old lady in his lap, was the same. Just as we were pulling away from the wreck a man shouted: 'Five thousand dollars for a place in the boat,' but he didn't get it.[1]

A couple of unnamed crewmen also mentioned this supposed incident, and (whether correctly or incorrectly) it appears that the name of a specific American passenger had become linked with the stories.

Unnamed Crewman #1

> A large number of the survivors of the *Titanic*'s crew were landed at Plymouth yesterday by the *Lapland*.
>
> Some of them had amazing stories to tell. One spoke of a millionaire who offered $5,000 if he could be saved ...
>
> 'I heard [of] one millionaire who was offering $5,000 if he could be saved,' one man told me. 'I didn't hear him myself, but it was all the talk among our gang. Some of them heard it. Today the American papers are printing the man's name in letters a foot long as a national hero.'[2]

Unnamed Crewman #2

> One fireman was emphatic in affirming that it was by the purest matter of good luck any rescues had been effected ... Our informant added, 'I have also seen in the American papers the overpraise for the millionaires on board. It has been over-done. None thought she was going to sink at first, and the behavior of all was much as it should be, but when she left no sort of doubt that she was settling down, then alarm was felt by many. One particularly well-known magnate was heard to offer 5,000 dollars for a seat in one of the boats. Mind, I do not say that he either attempted to prevent anyone else getting in, or that he actually tried to get in himself.'[3]

Many years after the sinking of the *Titanic*, two additional reports of (apparently) this same incident surfaced in the United States.

Albert Horswill
In 1954 Mr Horswill spoke with an American newspaper reporter and showed that he was aware of the 1912 British reports that a passenger had attempted to bribe his way into a lifeboat. Horswill told the reporter that the evacuation of the *Titanic* had begun calmly:

Later, when the realization came, they became panicky.

The crew got the sixteen lifeboats ready. Passengers ran around the deck, yelling.

One man was running around trying to bribe everybody to save him. He didn't survive. On his body was found $7,000 hidden in a money belt.[4]

Bert Johns (Borak Hannah)

In 1938 a Michigan *Titanic* survivor spoke with a newspaper reporter and seems to have mentioned the same incident that was publicised in the United Kingdom twenty-six years before:

> I saw a woman with a baby in her arms. She was screaming for help – for someone to save her baby. I took it and pushed my way to the rail and help the mother and baby get on a lifeboat.
>
> A rich man was offering large sums of money to get saved. Many people were drinking to make the last moments of their lives easier to bear.[5]

It is unknown where Albert Horswill obtained his details about the passenger's money belt or whether the information is factual. It's also unknown how Bert Johns became aware of the 'bribe accounts' that do not seem to have been published anywhere outside of the UK. (Although Johns might have made up his story for dramatic effect, it seems just as possible that he had personal knowledge of the man who was making the bribe attempts.) However, at this late date it is unlikely we'll ever know the name of the American passenger whose name became associated with these reports or whether or not the stories have any basis in fact.

A different type of bribe was mentioned by another *Titanic* passenger, but this so-called 'bribe' was actually more in the nature of an extortion attempt made by a crewman.

Philip Zenni (Fahīm Rūḥānā al-Za'innī)

Two months after arriving in the United States, Mr Zenni spoke with a reporter about his *Titanic* experiences:

> 'I was in my bunk in the steerage when one of the fellows with whom I was travelling woke me and said the ship had hit something,' said Zenni.
>
> 'The engines were not working right, I could tell that because of the unusual noise from the engine room, and I knew that something was wrong. I had made trips across the water before and I was not scared like

some of the other passengers who had never been on the ocean much. I partly dressed and went up on the deck, when one of the steamship's waiters said the vessel had struck an iceberg. The waiter, like the other passengers, had strapped on the life preservers, and when I saw these I knew it was something serious. I asked for a life preserver, having left mine down in my bunk.

'"How much will you give me for a life preserver?" said the waiter to me, and I told him I had left all my money and my gold watch under my pillow, and that he was welcome to all of it if he would hand me a life preserver. I got the life preserver and never went back to the steerage.'[6]

The 'almighty dollar' was just as important to some people in 1912 as it is to other people today, but it can't always perform miracles. Although we don't know the ultimate fate of the British waiter who traded a lifebelt in exchange for the life savings of Philip Zenni, we do know that the American passenger (if he truly existed) who attempted to buy his way into a lifeboat was unsuccessful in using part of his personal fortune as his chosen means of salvation.

9

William Murdoch and the Question of Suicide

The following essay is a rebuttal to certain information posted online a few years ago that has misled many researchers into disbelieving reports that First Officer Murdoch might have taken his own life.

During the days and weeks following the sinking of the *Titanic*, it was widely rumoured that the ship's first officer, William Murdoch, had taken his own life with a revolver shortly before the vessel foundered. For a long time these rumours were spoken of in almost hushed tones, with very few people wanting to publicly commit themselves to the notion that the stories about Murdoch might be true. As the years went by these suicide rumours slowly began to be out-and-out disbelieved by many *Titanic* researchers, and it eventually became an article of faith that the stories were false and had originated with sensation-hungry newspaper reporters who created them in a misguided attempt to make a good news story better.

In 1997 James Cameron released his blockbuster film *Titanic*, which drew on a number of 1912 sources that support the contention that Murdoch did indeed take his own life. Public furore in certain quarters was immediate, and people with vested interests in Murdoch's reputation (family members, citizens of his home town of Dalbeattie in south-west Scotland, etc.) came out of the woodwork to protest about Cameron's treatment of Murdoch and to insist that the officer had died 'an honourable death' and had not died by suicide. The end result of this hubbub was the creation of a website whose purpose was to defend Murdoch's reputation by 'proving' that the first officer did not take his own life.

This was all well and good, but when attempting to publicly 'prove' a specific historical premise, one must first verify the accuracy of evidence before placing that evidence before the public. If this is not possible, one should point out and discuss the pros and cons of the evidence instead of presenting it as if the authenticity were already established. Sadly, this was not done in this instance and a great deal of misinformation was presented that was inaccurate and misleading, seemingly with the purpose of 'proving' that William Murdoch did not die by suicide. Requests to correct errors were declined despite information being provided by the present author, Dave Billnitzer, Tad Fitch, Bill Wormstedt and a number of other researchers, who were advised there was insufficient time to make such corrections. Nonetheless, additional misinformation about Murdoch was subsequently added to the site, seemingly backing up the clear desire to assert that William Murdoch did not die by suicide.

It is not the present author's purpose to prove that Murdoch did in fact die by suicide, since there is insufficient eyewitness testimony to enable us to identify the officer who was seen by several eyewitnesses to have taken his own life. Instead, the purpose of this essay is to ensure researchers are fully equipped to question the information on the Murdoch website and to correct historical errors presented there as being true. The only way researchers can form an accurate opinion about whether a specific officer did – or did not – die by suicide is if they have access to *accurate* historical information on the subject;

William Murdoch.
(Author's collection)

after that they can make their own informed conclusions rather than be forced to rely on one-sided evidence driven by an agenda.

The intention here is to point out the specific misinformation promoted by the Murdoch website in its effort to prove Murdoch's 'innocence'. This task was rendered difficult because the information purportedly documenting the non-suicide death of *Titanic*'s first officer was scattered far and wide across the website. Indeed, it was this very scattering that made the information so difficult to ferret out, since occasional dubious 'facts' hidden within paragraphs of otherwise reliable information remained unnoticed by most people and were accepted by them as being true. Nevertheless, let's begin our examination of the various claims made on the Murdoch website.

The heart of the Murdoch website's defence of *Titanic*'s first officer was the content of a 1954 interview granted to researcher Ernest Robinson by Harold Bride (the *Titanic*'s junior wireless operator). Although a verbatim transcript of this interview was not made available to researchers, its content was summarised and posted on the Murdoch website. I will now summarise each of the Murdoch website's claims and will then provide critical analysis of those claims.

Website claim: Harold Bride was standing right next to First Officer Murdoch on the starboard side of the ship while Murdoch was working to launch Collapsible A. When the bridge suddenly submerged, a surge of seawater rushed over the deck and threw Bride and Murdoch into the sea together. Bride was therefore an actual *eyewitness* to Murdoch being swept into the sea and could therefore state with authority that the first officer did not shoot himself.

Analysis: This claim was based on Ernest Robinson's 1954 interview with Harold Bride and seems (on the face of it, anyway) to be authoritative. What the webmaster failed to tell his readers, however, is that this interview contradicts every other piece of information we have concerning Bride's movements and activities that night.

The simplest way for us to disprove the claims made in Bride's 1954 interview is for us to examine the official report to the Marconi Company that Bride himself wrote immediately after the disaster. That report states:

> Leaving our cabin, we [Bride and Senior Operator Jack Phillips] climbed on top of the houses comprising the officers' quarters and our own, and here I saw the last of Mr Phillips, for he disappeared walking aft.
>
> I now assisted in pushing off a collapsible lifeboat [i.e. Collapsible B], which was on the *port* [author's emphasis] side of the forward funnel, onto

> the boat deck. Just as the boat fell I noticed Captain Smith dive from the bridge into the sea.
>
> Then followed a general scramble down on[to] the [port] boat deck, but no sooner had we got there than the sea washed over. I managed to catch hold of the boat we had previously fixed up and was swept overboard with her.

The facts Bride gave in his official report to the Marconi Company are confirmed by the testimony he gave at both the Senate and British *Titanic* Inquiries. Despite the claims made by the Murdoch website, Harold Bride was on the opposite side of the ship from First Officer Murdoch when the bridge submerged and had no idea how Murdoch spent the final moments of his life.

The present author asked historian Don Lynch for his opinion of the information that Harold Bride is said to have relayed to Ernest Robinson in 1954, and Lynch replied as follows:

> In the course of my research and writing *Titanic – An Illustrated History* I encountered a number of examples where I had testimony or accounts by survivors from 1912 as well as from years or decades later. It became apparent that the testimony and writings from 1912 were superior. These were obtained when the disaster was still fresh in their memories, and as a result were clearer, usually more detailed, and consistent with what other survivors wrote or recalled at the time.
>
> Whenever I had conflicting accounts by a survivor to deal with, I would use the earlier of the two. As Harold Bride's interview in the *New York Times* and his testimony at both the Senate and British Inquiries were so specific that he assisted in launching Collapsible B from the port side, I would place no value on second-hand information based upon an interview with Bride which had occurred over four decades after the sinking.

The present author has no doubt that Bride probably told Robinson the things he is claimed to have said in 1954. However, the irreconcilable differences between Bride's multiple 1912 accounts and his questionable 1954 account force us to conclude that Bride's memory had begun to play tricks on him by 1954.

Website claim: Harold Bride reportedly insisted in 1954 that First Officer Murdoch would never have died by suicide because he was not that kind of man.
Analysis: Despite Bride's 1954 claims about Murdoch's character, his 1912 testimony to the Senate inquiry makes it clear that Bride was utterly unqualified

to comment on what Murdoch would or would not have done. Senator Smith queried Bride about a message he delivered to the *Titanic*'s bridge and asked the young wireless operator which officer he had delivered the message to:

> **Smith:** Who was the officer on the bridge?
> **Bride:** I could not say, sir; I do not know the officers, sir.
> **Smith:** Was it Mr Lightoller?
> **Bride:** I could not tell you.
> **Smith:** You do not know whether it was the first or second officer?
> **Bride:** I did not know any of the officers there; I did not know which watches they were keeping …
> **Smith:** Was that officer Mr Murdoch?
> **Bride:** I could not tell you, sir.
> **Smith:** Do you know Mr Murdoch?
> **Bride:** No, sir; I know the officers by sight, but I do not know their names.

Harold Bride's 1912 testimony makes it clear he had no idea who Murdoch was and was utterly unqualified (forty-four years after the sinking) to make authoritative pronouncements about Murdoch's propensity to take his own life.

Website claim: In 1954 Harold Bride reportedly claimed to have seen both First Officer Murdoch and Sixth Officer Moody in the water after he was swept overboard with them when the bridge submerged. Murdoch was lying motionless in the water when Bride last saw him, and Moody had apparently suffered a head injury (which prompted Bride to wonder if Moody had been shot).
Analysis: Aside from the fact that Harold Bride was on the opposite side of the ship from Murdoch and Moody when the bridge submerged, the fact that Bride did not know any of *Titanic*'s officers in 1912 proves the above claim to be spurious.

As for the reference to Sixth Officer Moody ('was Moody shot?'), this seems to be an attempt to divert attention away from First Officer Murdoch even though the attempt does not hold up to close scrutiny. We know that *Titanic*'s senior officers – Smith, Wilde, Murdoch and Lightoller – were issued company weapons during the evacuation of the *Titanic*, and we also know that Fifth Officer Lowe carried his own personal weapon that night; however, there's no evidence that *Titanic*'s junior officers (Moody, Boxhall and Pitman) were armed during the sinking of the *Titanic* – which means Sixth Officer Moody could not have taken his own life with a revolver even if he wished to.

Website claim: Second Officer Lightoller claimed that he crossed to the starboard side of the roof of the officers' quarters and saw Murdoch swept away by a surge of water as the bridge submerged.
Analysis: Lightoller made this claim in a letter he wrote to Murdoch's widow after the disaster, and the letter's text was published in the *Dumfries & Galloway Standard and Advertiser* on 11 May 1912; its pertinent statements follow:

> I was practically the last man, and certainly the last officer, to see Mr Murdoch. He was then endeavoring to launch the starboard forward collapsible boat. I had already got mine from off the top of our quarters … Having got my boat down off the top of the house, and there being no time to open it, I left it and ran across to the starboard side, still on top of the quarters. I was then practically looking down on your husband and his men. He was working hard, personally assisting, overhauling the forward boat's fall. At this moment the ship dived, and we were all in the water. Other reports as to the ending are absolutely false. Mr Murdoch died like a man, doing his duty.

Lightoller's testimony at the British *Titanic* inquiry seems to confirm the things he wrote to Mrs Murdoch. Lightoller told of seeing Murdoch working at Collapsible A, and he then said: 'Well, she seemed to take a bit of a dive and I just walked into the water.' This would lead one to believe that Lightoller was actually *watching* Murdoch when the bridge area submerged and that Lightoller actually *saw* Murdoch swept into the sea like his letter to Murdoch's widow implied. If true, this would naturally make Murdoch's suicide an impossibility.

Interestingly, the above inference is not supported by Lightoller's testimony at the Senate inquiry a few weeks previously. Although Lightoller told Senator Smith that he did see Murdoch working below him on the starboard boat deck, Smith then began querying Lightoller about his exact location when the bridge submerged:

> **Lightoller:** … As I say, I was on top of the officers' quarters, and there was nothing more to be done. The ship then took a dive, and I turned face forward and also took a dive.
> **Smith:** From which side?
> **Lightoller:** From on top, practically amidships; a little to the starboard side, where I had got to.

Lightoller makes it clear here that he was practically amidships on the roof of the officers' quarters when the ship made a sudden dip downward and a wave swept over the boat deck. This, of course, suggests that Lightoller was in no position to see Murdoch down on the starboard boat deck when the water rose to where Murdoch was working beside Collapsible A. It therefore follows that Lightoller did not really *know* what happened to Murdoch after leaving the starboard roof of the officers' quarters and moving amidships to where he eventually dived overboard.

Corroboration of this suggestion comes from an interview given by survivor Victor Sunderland. According to Sunderland, the ship trembled and dropped suddenly, at which point Second Officer Lightoller shouted, 'Here she goes!' and jumped over the *port* [author's emphasis] side. Sunderland said he followed Lightoller over the port side and later found refuge on the same overturned lifeboat (Collapsible B, on the port side) that saved the second officer. If this interview is reliable, it shows that the *Titanic*'s second officer was in no position to know what fate had befallen First Officer Murdoch on the starboard side.

What might have caused Lightoller to 'alter' his story between the time he testified at the Senate inquiry and the time he wrote his letter to Mrs Murdoch (which conformed to his British inquiry testimony given a few days after he wrote his letter)? The present author believes Lightoller's motives were humanitarian in nature. It's obvious that Lightoller had seen newspaper reports of Murdoch's suicide, and it is equally obvious that his purpose in writing to Murdoch's widow was to soften the blow of her husband's death by insisting that Murdoch had died 'like a man' and that 'other reports' of his death were 'absolutely false'. However, the fact that Lightoller was in no position to see Murdoch at the very end makes us wonder what Lightoller *really* saw – if anything – from his position amidships on the roof of the officers' quarters.

Interestingly, researcher Susanne Störmer once spoke with a friend of the Lightoller family, and Lightoller – in later years – is said to have admitted that he knew someone on the *Titanic* who had taken his own life.[1] This doesn't prove Lightoller was talking about Murdoch, of course, but it *does* demonstrate that Lightoller did not tell everything he knew about the *Titanic* disaster when the inquiries were taking place in 1912.

Website claim: Lightoller disliked Captain Smith and had an 'abiding hatred' for Henry Wilde due to the fact that Wilde's last-minute importation as *Titanic*'s chief officer caused Lightoller to be demoted from first officer to second officer. Lightoller never spoke much about Wilde, which was because of his dislike for the man or, more ominously, because of a possible unspecified 'unpleasant occurrence'.

Analysis: The claim that Lightoller disliked Smith and hated Wilde is completely without foundation and is based solely on the webmaster's assumption that Lightoller *must* have deeply resented his temporary demotion to second officer and that he blamed Smith and Wilde for that demotion. The truth of the matter is that Lightoller himself never said *anything* that would lead one to believe he even mildly disliked either Smith or Wilde. In fact, Lightoller's autobiography describes Smith thus: 'He was a great favourite, and a man any officer would give his ears to sail under. I had been with him many years, off and on … [he] used to make us fairly flush with pride …'

As for Lightoller's supposed reticence in speaking about Chief Officer Wilde, Lightoller likewise never said much about Sixth Officer Moody, Fourth Officer Boxhall or a host of other people connected with the sinking. The inference about Lightoller's 'ominous silence' seems to be a method employed to paint Wilde in the darkest possible colours so as to encourage 'dark thoughts' about the man and predispose readers to think that Wilde was more likely to take his own life than Murdoch.

The Murdoch website's strong focus on the supposed mental state of Chief Officer Henry Wilde was the result of a predisposition to prove that Wilde is seemingly a more likely candidate for suicide than First Officer Murdoch. Although there is nothing wrong with attempting to establish the likelihood of this possibility, it's nevertheless incumbent on the website to present its readers with a full spectrum of information that bears on the subject. We have already mentioned the apparent propensity for painting Wilde in dark colours, presumably to condition its readers to accept the premise that Wilde was a natural candidate for suicide. Let's look at some of the other claims the website made about Wilde.

Website claim: The question of whether Murdoch, not Wilde, would have been chosen to be the next officer to command the White Star liner *Oceanic* speculates that Wilde's performance was 'so poor' that Murdoch was able to 'pass him up' in the normal chain of promotions, etc. It concludes that Wilde might have been tempted to die by suicide because if he somehow survived the *Titanic* disaster, his future association with the disaster in the public mind might have prevented him from taking command of the *Oceanic*.

Analysis: The speculation (done without documentation) is just that – speculation. Nevertheless, its musings about Wilde's mental state and supposed poor performance were clearly intended to cast the chief officer in a bad light.

Interestingly, a counter-argument to the premise can be found in the unedited version of historian Don Lynch's *Titanic: An Illustrated History*. In commenting on Chief Officer Wilde's importation to the *Titanic* and the resulting demotion of Murdoch to first officer, Lynch says Murdoch was 'a man whom he [Captain Smith] had not trusted enough to keep as his second in command …'

It's worth noting that the Murdoch website speculates that Wilde may have decided to shoot himself because he feared he'd be prevented from assuming command of the *Oceanic* due to his involvement in the *Titanic* disaster. Curiously, though, there is no speculation about whether Murdoch (who was in actual command of the *Titanic* at the time of the collision) might possibly have considered shooting himself while contemplating his own future career at sea. (One suspects Murdoch would not have had very good prospects for advancement in his chosen nautical field had he somehow survived the sinking of the *Titanic*.)

Website claim: The theory on the website was that Henry Wilde was suffering from 'delayed shock' following the death of his wife but that the White Star Line nevertheless placed Wilde, an 'unstable' officer, in a position on the *Titanic* that he was emotionally unfit to handle. (It was mphasised that the White Star Line also provided Wilde with 'the means to shoot himself'.) The claim was that Wilde was passive and ineffectual during the evacuation of the *Titanic* and concluded that it's 'impossible not to pity Wilde', a man who supposedly should not have been on the *Titanic* at all.

Analysis: Strenuous efforts were made to paint Henry Wilde as an emotionally shattered man whose troubled mental state caused him to be overwhelmed by the evacuation of the *Titanic*; this emotional upset supposedly forced Wilde to take 'the easy way out' of his troubles by taking his own life. How accurate is this portrayal, though?

Not very.

Regarding the website's suggestion that Wilde was suffering from a delayed reaction to the death of his wife, it's true Wilde had previously lost his wife and twin sons due to complications of childbirth. It might reasonably be considered that the traumatic events of the night of the sinking could have brought this previous trauma rushing back for him, and it would be no surprise if he was a man still struggling with grief. However, the reader will be interested to learn that these deaths occurred on 24 December 1910 – almost a year and a half before the maiden voyage of the *Titanic*. It seems more likely to the present author that Wilde would have been someone more in control of his grief by then, and less likely he would suddenly fall apart and become suicidal in the middle of a sea disaster. It also seems unlikely that Wilde would deliberately orphan his four surviving children (ages 4 to 12), who were waiting for him to return home to the United Kingdom. No, to the present author, the website's Wilde suicide scenario does not ring true.

As for the claim that Wilde was strangely passive during the evacuation of the *Titanic*, it should be remembered that he was *Titanic*'s senior officer and was acting like any good supervisor – that is, he was quietly circulating among his junior officers and monitoring their methods as they dealt with the launching of the lifeboats. If Wilde approved of what his officers were doing, there was no reason for him to bawl orders and otherwise make himself the centre of attention. This is why many people did not have vivid memories of Wilde that night, but the chief officer was definitely present during the loading or launching of lifeboats #2, #8, #10, #12, #14, Collapsible C and Collapsible D – a level of activity that would hardly be expected from a man who was as emotionally distraught and withdrawn as the Murdoch website tried to make him out to be.

The Supposed 'Eyewitnesses'

We come now to the list of so-called eyewitnesses the Murdoch website quotes in support of its claim that First Officer Murdoch did not die by suicide but that Chief Officer Wilde *did* take his own life. The reader will soon see that the website's selection of 'eyewitness' accounts is curious at best. The website's *modus operandi* is interesting, too – it groups all the most reliable suicide witnesses in a single section devoted to the possible suicide of (surprise!) Henry Wilde, while it reserves its 'Murdoch section' for presenting a group of supposed eyewitnesses who purportedly saw William Murdoch swept away by a wave (which, naturally, would make Murdoch's suicide an impossibility). Let's look at the witnesses the Murdoch website reserved for its 'Wilde Suicide Section'.

Supposed Witnesses to the Death of Wilde

Website claim: Passenger George Rheims was floating in the ocean beside the *Titanic* when he saw an officer die by suicide on board the ship. It was Rheims who started the 'outrageous slur' on the name of William Murdoch.
Analysis: These claims do not stand up. Rheims did indeed see an officer shoot an unarmed passenger before turning his weapon upon himself, but Rheims was not 'floating in the ocean' when he saw the incident take place; instead, he was standing just a few feet from the unnamed officer and heard him bid a quiet farewell to the bystanders around him before using his revolver to end his own life.

Likewise, Rheims was not responsible for the many press stories that told of Murdoch's suicide, because the only two places he ever mentioned the incident were in a 20 April newspaper interview and in a private letter to his wife Mary; in neither document did Rheims ever name the officer who shot himself. The website's claim that Rheims was responsible for all of the press accounts of Murdoch's suicide was simply unwarranted and was the result of a poor understanding of the evidence at hand.

Website claim: Passenger Eugene Daly heard shots fired but did not actually see the event in question. The website says Daly saw three bodies lying on the deck but that his personal reliability is 'not known'.
Analysis: Contrary to the website's claim, Daly did indeed see most of the event in question. Daly watched as an unnamed officer shot two passengers who attempted to rush a lifeboat, and a moment later he heard a third shot; Daly then saw the officer's body lying on the deck and was told he had just shot himself. Daly described this incident during a private interview with Dr Frank Blackmarr on board the *Carpathia*, in a private letter to his family, in a personal interview with New York's Mayor Gaynor and at the 1915 Limitation of Liability hearings (although the only available version of the latter is a paraphrased newspaper account in which a reporter claimed Daly heard two shots and saw two bodies afterwards). In any case, Daly's 1912 accounts are consistent enough that doubts about his reliability seem completely unwarranted.

Website claim: Robert Daniel saw an officer's suicide from 10ft away and later said, 'It must be Murdoch.' (The website kindly cautioned its readers that Daniel 'apparently' didn't know Murdoch personally, though.)
Analysis: The above claim is untrue. Daniel was not on the *Titanic*'s foredeck when the bridge submerged and was nowhere near First Officer Murdoch (or any other officer) at the time of the suicide. Instead, Daniel was seen near the *Titanic*'s stern by Thomas Dillon and subsequently jumped into the sea from that location as the stern rose skyward. Daniel's own account corroborates Dillon's story.

Website claim: Steward Thomas Whiteley was a purveyor of hearsay evidence and that he is 'generally considered unreliable'.
Analysis: Whiteley never claimed to have witnessed an officer's suicide himself – he merely said he learned of this incident from three fellow survivors who *did* witness the event. However, the present author wonders how much research was conducted to reach the conclusion that Whiteley is 'generally

considered unreliable'. Besides, the inclusion of Whiteley in the website's 'Death of Wilde' section is grossly misleading, since the only officer Whiteley ever mentioned in connection with the suicide was *First Officer Murdoch*.

Now that we've examined the witnesses that the Murdoch website claimed are germane to the supposed suicide of Chief Officer Wilde, let's examine the witnesses the website marshalled in its attempt to prove that First Officer Murdoch was swept into the sea and therefore could not have taken his own life. The reader should be warned, though, that the website's so-called 'eyewitnesses' to Murdoch's non-suicide death will evaporate like a delicate mist on a warm summer day when we subject the claims to close scrutiny. Significantly, most of the witnesses themselves *never claimed* to have witnessed Murdoch's death at all – it is the Murdoch website itself that attempted to use these people to bolster its own case.

Supposed Witnesses to Murdoch's Non-Suicide

Website claim: The webmaster claims that Second Officer Charles Lightoller saw Murdoch swept away by a wave when the bridge was submerged.
Analysis: We have already examined Lightoller's testimony and seen how unlikely it is that he actually saw Murdoch swept into the sea as he later claimed.

Website claim: Harold Bride testified at the *Titanic* inquiries (and told Ernest Robinson) that he was working alongside Murdoch at Collapsible A when he and Murdoch were both swept into the sea.
Analysis: Harold Bride said no such thing at either inquiry. Every one of his 1912 accounts specifies that he was on the opposite side of the ship from Murdoch when he was washed overboard. The Murdoch website is mistaken about Bride's supposed adventures with Murdoch on the *Titanic*'s starboard side.

Website claim: Archibald Gracie was working on Collapsible A with Murdoch and saw him swept overboard. The website adds that this is mentioned in Gracie's book *The Truth About the Titanic*.
Analysis: Archibald Gracie never claimed that he saw Murdoch swept into the sea; instead, he clearly says that he walked away from Collapsible A shortly before the bridge submerged and a wave surged over the boat deck. Gracie never claimed to have seen what happened to Murdoch after he walked away from Collapsible A; that claim is made solely by the Murdoch website.

Website claim: Able Seaman George McGough was working beside Murdoch at Collapsible A and testified about Murdoch's non-suicide death at the subsequent inquiry.
Analysis: Contrary to the website's claims, George McGough never testified at either inquiry nor was he present on board the *Titanic* when Murdoch met his death; McGough left the *Titanic* in boat #9 at 1.30 a.m. – nearly an hour before Murdoch lost his life.

James Cameron's Depiction of Murdoch

The reader will recall that it was James Cameron's 1997 film *Titanic* (with its interpretation of William Murdoch's alleged suicide) that was the original cause of the uproar among the present-day citizens of Murdoch's home town and was the genesis of the Murdoch website as well. The website blasted Cameron's credibility by quoting what purported to be the sentiments of Don Lynch (a leading *Titanic* historian who was Cameron's historical advisor on the film) in support of his contention that the film's depiction of Murdoch shooting two passengers (followed immediately by the officer's suicide) had no valid historical basis. The website quoted the BBC's Independent Teletext Borders service for 23 March 1998 as follows:

> An advisor to the film *Titanic* has said he warned the director against inaccurately portraying the Scottish first officer as a cowardly murderer. Historian Don Lynch said the screen character of William Murdoch is not backed by any historical evidence.

Although the Murdoch website might be excused for believing the BBC report to be accurate, the report is nevertheless untrue and does not accurately reflect Lynch's thoughts on the matter.

The present author has long known that James Cameron based his Murdoch shooting/suicide scene on the eyewitness accounts of George Rheims and Eugene Daly plus the multitude of 1912 survivor accounts that allege William Murdoch (by name) was the officer who took his own life during the sinking. The certain knowledge that Don Lynch was likewise familiar with these accounts caused me to wonder why – or *if* – Lynch said anything remotely similar to what the BBC quoted him as saying. It therefore seemed logical to ask Lynch for his personal opinion of Cameron's film portrayal of Murdoch, and the historian was kind enough to reply to my query.

Question: Did you ever warn James Cameron that his film portrayal of William Murdoch's suicide 'is not backed by any historical evidence'?'
Lynch: If you want to do so in your posting you can say, truthfully, that I have continually defended Jim's right to put that scene in the movie since there is no proof that the suicide didn't happen, despite my feelings that it didn't.

Conclusions

Although the Murdoch website undoubtedly contains useful biographical details about First Officer William Murdoch, by now the reader knows that much of the information the website uses to 'document' a supposed non-suicide death for Murdoch is inaccurate at best and downright false at worst. Historians would do well to exercise a great deal of caution when consulting the suicide information presented on the Murdoch website, because such caution will save future researchers from the inevitable difficulties arising from someone else's questionable research.

An Alternative to the Murdoch Website

Now that we've highlighted everything that was *not* said in 1912 about First Officer Murdoch's death (either by suicide or drowning), the reader might like to review survivor statements that *were* made in reference to Murdoch's death. There is no better way to do this than by visiting Bill Wormstedt's *Titanic* website. Wormstedt has presented every available reference to Murdoch's death that he and other researchers have discovered in contemporary 1912 sources, and these statements are presented verbatim with analysis so that readers can decide for themselves just how strong the case for Murdoch's suicide really is: **wormstedt.com/Titanic/shots/shots.htm**

Did William Murdoch Really Take His Own Life?

To repeat a statement made early in this essay, it's not the aim of the present writer to prove that William Murdoch took his own life during the sinking of the *Titanic*; instead, my sole purpose has been to correct misinformation that the Murdoch website has presented to its readers in an attempt to 'prove' that Murdoch did not die by suicide.

In correcting the Murdoch website's factual errors, however, it has been necessary for us to rehash a great deal of that website's speculation about the supposed mental state of Chief Officer Wilde and the reasons why Wilde was allegedly more likely to die by suicide than Murdoch. Even though the website's explanations do not hold up to close scrutiny, it would be unfair to Wilde for us to conclude our discussion without examining reasons why *Murdoch* might have considered taking his own life that night. I will attempt to outline those reasons in the form of a 'mental checklist' as it might have occurred to Murdoch while he was working to evacuate passengers from the sinking *Titanic*:

'Captain Smith entrusted me with command of the *Titanic* when he left the bridge earlier this evening. He knew (as did I and all the other officers) that *Titanic* would reach the outskirts of the icefield at around 11 p.m. Why didn't I consult Captain Smith at that point? After all, the Commander had a right to know when the ship was entering the outer fringes of this icefield, and perhaps his judgement about ice visibility would have been more conservative than mine; maybe he would have ordered a course alteration or a decrease in speed or taken *some* action that I didn't take that might have prevented a collision. As things stand, though, it was *I* who decided not to consult him; it was *I* who decided that the situation did not warrant any alteration of the ship's standard operating procedure; it was *I* who was entrusted with the safety of the ship and her passengers, and it was *I* who "let the side down".

'The Sailing Orders posted on the bulkhead behind me specify that "No thought of making competitive passages must be entertained, and time must be sacrificed or any other temporary inconvenience suffered, rather than the *slightest risk* should be incurred". Even though I thought we could see all icebergs in time to avoid them, and even though this was standard operating procedure, I was nevertheless taking a calculated risk in maintaining the status quo, and – according to the Sailing Order – even calculated risks are not condoned by the company.

'The *Titanic* will sink in a few moments, and two out of three of her passengers and crew will find themselves floundering in the ocean when that happens. Nobody will survive immersion in that icy water for long, which means that roughly fifteen hundred people will die tonight as a direct result of actions that I did – or didn't – take.

'A moment ago I shot two unarmed passengers who disregarded my orders but who, after all, were only trying to save their own lives. How can I live with myself if I should happen to survive tonight's tragedy? In any event, my future career as a ship's officer will be non-existent, because what company would ever hire a man who was responsible for losing two-thirds of the lives that had been entrusted to his care?

'And what about my wife Ada? How could I ask her to live with the shame I'd be certain to bring upon her if I were to survive? I can almost hear the slurs that would be cast in her direction: "There goes Mrs Murdoch; her husband killed fifteen hundred people but was careful to save his *own* life."

'How could I possibly ask her and the rest of my family to endure something like that on my account?

'I couldn't. And I'm holding a Webley revolver in my hand …'

Although the present author does not know if First Officer William Murdoch truly took his own life during the sinking of the *Titanic*, I can at least understand why the thought of doing so might have crossed his mind.

10

Shot in the Jaw

After the *Carpathia* brought *Titanic*'s survivors to New York, seemingly melodramatic stories appeared in the newspapers claiming that, before taking his own life, a *Titanic* officer shot a panic-stricken steward in the jaw because he refused to obey orders and attempted to force his way into one of the lifeboats. (The most reliable stories claim the officer who did the shooting was William Murdoch.) For the time being, we urge the reader to temporarily suspend judgement on these stories and give serious consideration to the possibility that they might have a basis in fact.

The existing accounts describing the shooting of a steward in the jaw fall into several different categories of reliability. Since no true primary sources exist that were written by surviving eyewitnesses themselves, let's begin our discussion by examining newspaper accounts that summarise information purportedly obtained from survivors but which contain 'extra' details whose accuracy is unknown.

Unattributed Paraphrased Descriptions

Since no specific survivors can be named as having provided the information contained in the following excerpts, we won't be using these unattributed accounts as evidence and are presenting them here just to give the reader a general idea of the kind of reports that were circulating on the pier after the *Carpathia* brought the survivors to New York:

> The superiors rushed to the bridge with the shock of the collision, and Murdoch in the discipline of the ship took immediate charge of the

starboard side of the ship, with Second Officer Lightoller on the port side. But Murdoch did not hold himself to his station. So soon as the captain had learned of conditions forward and below Murdoch was everywhere assembling the women and children, calming them and reassuring the men. When the orders came to man the boats he took personal charge of this work and prevented the first impulse of fear on the part of men passengers from rising to a panic. When the rush from the steerage came the leaders found themselves confronted by Murdoch, revolver in hand. There were some English-speaking men in this crowd, and the first officer looked at them silently for a little while.

'Don't forget you are British,' he said quietly, and this turned those men back who understood him. Behind him were men of other races who did not understand or were too frightened to heed. His revolver went up to a level. 'Don't,' he said, 'or I'll bore you through.' Some did not heed this, and he shot twice, quickly but unerringly.

The foremost man dropped, shot through the brain: the second man reeled back, his jaw shot off. A quartermaster's good right fist accounted for a third man, who dropped and lay where he fell.

Murdoch never paused until every one of his boats were filled and away.[1]

'Stand back,' shouted the officers who were manning the boat. 'The women come first.' Shouting curses in various foreign languages, the immigrant men continued their pushing and tugging to climb into the boats. Shots rang out. One big fellow fell over the railing into the water. Another dropped to the deck, moaning. His jaw had been shot away. This was the story told by the bystanders afterwards on the pier. One husky Italian told the writer on the pier that the way in which the men were shot down was horrible. His sympathy was with the men who were shot. 'They were only trying to save their lives,' he said.[2]

This … is the tale told by sailors of the ill-starred *Titanic*, brawny seamen who only lived to tell it because it happened in the line of their duty to help man the boats into which some of the *Titanic*'s passengers were loaded …

For obvious reasons the identity of the sailormen who described the foundering of the *Titanic* cannot be divulged …

The spokesman for the sailors here asserted: 'We want to make it plain that the officers and crew of the *Titanic* did their duty. Not a male passenger got into the lifeboats. During the early excitement men tried to force their

> way into the boats, but the officers shot them down with revolvers. I saw probably a half dozen men shot down as the lifeboat to which I was assigned was being filled. The men shot were left to die and sink on the upper deck of the *Titanic*.'[3]

Now that we've seen these general summaries containing 'extra' details that were undoubtedly added by the newspaper reporters themselves, let's turn our attention in a more serious direction by examining interviews that were attributed to named survivors. After we've finished examining all the different 'classes' of these survivor interviews, we'll summarise the information they contain and will try to determine what we can legitimately conclude from those survivor accounts.

Newspaper Survivor Accounts

Our first group of shooting accounts was recorded by newspaper reporters who spoke with named *Titanic* survivors on the pier. Even though most of these survivors did not claim to have seen the shooting incident with their own eyes, and even though their accounts of the shooting were 'filtered' through reporters, the overall consistency of many of these hearsay accounts is noteworthy.

Edward Beane

After arriving in New York, Mr Beane described his experiences to a newspaper reporter:

> 'The stern of the boat floated for nearly an hour after the bow was submerged,' said Mr Beane, 'and then went down. I heard a report that two steerage passengers were shot by the officers when they started to crowd in the boats.'[4]

William Carter Jr

After he arrived in New York, 10-year-old William Carter apparently spoke with a *New York Herald* reporter, who purportedly paraphrased the young man's experiences for his readers:

> Master William T. Carter, 10 years old, who was rescued with his father, mother and sister, says that when they got on deck the officers were keeping men back from the boats with drawn revolvers. Once the men made a dash and there was a lot of shooting. A man standing by him had his whole lower jaw shot away. He said his mother rowed in the lifeboat until her hands were too blistered to hold the oars.[5]

The next day a reporter from the *Brooklyn Daily Eagle* supposedly recorded a verbatim interview with young Carter describing the events that were merely paraphrased by the *Herald* man the day before:

> Master Carter seemed to remember most vividly the shooting of men who tried to get into the lifeboats with the women.
>
> 'The men were separate from the women,' he said, 'and the little boys and all the girls were with the women. The officers threatened to shoot any man who disobeyed and attempted to board a lifeboat.
>
> 'Once in a while a man would try to break through and there would be some shooting, for officers armed with gleaming revolvers stood guard over the men passengers. Once a lot of men got through and there was a lot of shooting. Several of the men fell to the deck. One stood still for a long time. His whole jaw was shot away. Then he fell to the deck. Just then it came time for mother and I to get aboard a boat and I saw no more of the shooting, but I could hear it at intervals.'[6]

Another newspaper phrased young Carter's account slightly differently even though the gist was the same:

> All the boys and girls were with the women, and while the people were getting into the boats a man would try to break through the line and then there would be some shooting.
>
> Once a lot of men got through and there was some shooting, and some of the men fell on the deck while everyone cried out very loudly. One of the men stood still for some time and all of his jaw was shot away. I was watching him holding on to mother's skirt when it came our turn to get into the boat.[7]

Young William Carter and his parents were congregated at the forward end of the boat deck and were at least in the general area of the ship where the purported shootings took place. However, Carter and his mother were waiting to enter lifeboat #4 on the *Titanic*'s port boat deck, whereas First Officer Murdoch was in charge of loading boats on the starboard side. More importantly, neither of the boy's parents mentioned seeing any shooting during the evacuation of the *Titanic*. (It also pays to remember that 10-year-old boys rarely resort to using terms like 'gleaming revolvers' while speaking to reporters.) In short, William Carter Jr's alleged 'jaw shot story' seems to have been something he heard from other survivors but which was now being put into his own mouth by overeager reporters who wanted to turn him into an actual 'eyewitness' to the event.

John Collins

Assistant Cook John Collins escaped the sinking on Collapsible B and testified at the US inquiry, and in the 1930s he told the following account to Alice Braithwaite, who wrote it down:

> Collins came to Lifeboat #16, and noticed 'that one of the officers on the scene was "the senior mate, the one next to the captain".' Collins wasn't allowed in this boat, and 'he then headed for the starboard side, where he heard there was a collapsible boat being gotten out'. He encountered a woman and her two children, headed toward the last collapsible and saw that 'the situation was chaotic', and that there were three officers trying to control the situation, including the one whom he had seen at Lifeboat #16. At that point, according to the Collins story, an officer shot two men, and then turned the revolver on himself. Collins believed that the officer was the same one who he had earlier seen at Lifeboat #16.[8]

This account agrees with Collins' testimony at the US inquiry, the one exception being that in 1912 he did not offer any voluntary testimony about shots being fired. (Note: when Collins mentioned 'the senior mate, the one next to the Captain', ordinarily we'd assume he was talking about Chief Officer Henry Wilde. As will be seen presently, however, this confusion about the officer's true rank – and therefore his identity – has a very mundane explanation.)

Robert Daniel

Mr Daniel claimed to have jumped from the *Titanic* near the very end, but different reporters recorded different versions of what he heard about incidents of gunfire on the ship. The evidence seems to show that Mr Daniel *might* have heard reports about the 'jaw shot' incident but did not see it occur himself:

> Maj. Butt and Clarence Moore showed themselves to be men all through. We all stood near the captain, and he told us that the way we could help best was to see that no men entered the first boats.
>
> That's what we did. There was a rush for the boats by some of the men in the steerage, but the guards fired a shot at them and drove them back. I do not know how many were killed; not many, I think. One man had his jaw blown off.[9]

> As to the reports that many persons had been shot to prevent them from rushing the lifeboats, Mr Daniel said several shots had been fired in the air to frighten the steerage passengers and keep them in order, but that he did not know or hear of anyone being hit by a bullet.[10]

Vera Dick

Mrs Dick left the *Titanic* in boat #3 at about 12.55 a.m. and was apparently told about the shooting while on board the *Carpathia*:

> A band was playing on the *Titanic* when it went down. The captain had ordered the band to play, and to play continuously, so that the women would not feel that they were in danger. The bandsmen were loyal. They kept on playing jolly, happy tunes. They were playing some American air when the guards shot the jaw off an immigrant who tried to crowd into one of the boats, brushing the women aside.[11]

Ruth Dodge

Mrs Dodge left the *Titanic* in boat #5 at about 12.45 a.m. (long before any alleged shooting incidents took place) and must have heard about them while on board the *Carpathia*:

> There was complete order among the passengers and crew. We really didn't think there was any danger. We were assured that the ship would float and that there were plenty vessels in the reach of wireless to come to our aid if that should become necessary.
>
> Then the sinking of the *Titanic* by the head began and the crew was ordered to man the boats. There was no panic. The officers told the men to stand back and they obeyed. A few men were ordered into the boats. Two men who attempted to rush beyond the restraint line were shot down by an officer who then turned the revolver on himself.[12]

Edward Dorkings

Like John Collins, third-class passenger Edward Dorkings jumped from the *Titanic* at the end and survived on Collapsible B:

> An officer stood beside the life-boats as they were being manned and with a pistol in hand, threatened to kill the first man who got into a boat without orders. The rule of 'women first' was rigidly enforced. Two stewards hustled into a lifeboat that was being launched. They were commanded to get out by the officers and on refusing to obey the command, were shot down.[13]

> Almost at the moment I climbed on the raft I could hear pistol shots sounding from the *Titanic*. The sounds of shots had been distinct during all my swim. I don't know how many were fired, but they kept on during all the time I was within hearing distance. I saw an officer, it may have been the captain or it may not, shoot himself before I got away from the ship.[14]

> Yes, it is true a few were shot because they were attempting to enter the boats before the women and children, but officers did right to do this. I know positively that two stewards and a Chinaman were pushed out of a boat by officers and shot while in the water because they attempted to climb into the boat.[15]

Edward Dorkings' accounts are slightly ambiguous; two of his statements suggest that he saw 'two stewards' shot by an officer who then took his own life, but his third statement claims that these shootings took place in a lifeboat instead of on board the ship. These contradictions suggest that Dorkings might not have been an actual eyewitness to the events in question but heard about them second-hand instead. Nevertheless, Dorkings (like Collins, who saw two men shot) was in the right place at the right time to observe such an event if it did indeed take place, because Dorkings and Collins both found refuge on the overturned Collapsible B.

George Harder

After arriving in New York, Mr Harder spoke with a reporter about things he apparently heard while still on board the *Carpathia*:

> The rumor that Captain Smith committed suicide is not true. I believe the first officer did, but Captain Smith was plainly seen swimming in the water when the boat went down.[16]

Abraham Hyman

Three different accounts attributed to Hyman make mention of a shooting on board the *Titanic*, but only two of them purport to be actual eyewitness accounts of that event:

> Abraham Hyman, of Manchester, England, who was coming to this country to join a brother in Paterson, N.J., is one of the passengers who told about seeing Chief Officer Wilde rushing around with a revolver in his hand. There was not much panic before he left the *Titanic*, he said, except when the chief officer fired into a belligerent group of third class passengers. A man standing next to him had his chin shot off, he said.[17]

> When they got on deck they found a rope drawn closer to their quarters than usual and this made some of them think that there was danger. One or two of the women began to cry, and a panic began to spread. An officer came forward [and] stood close to the rope and waved the people back ... The officer who was standing at the rope had a pistol in his hand and he ordered everybody to keep back. First one woman screamed and then another, and then one man (I think he was an Italian) dashed toward the boat and the officer fired at him and struck him in the chin, and so he came back to where the rest of us were standing. Then the officer said to us to put the women forward and we began picking them out and shoving them beneath the rope.[18]

> 'I got alongside of a boat,' he said, 'and as they lowered it, full of passengers, I just crowded in beside the man at the tiller. They could have taken fifteen more people in our boat. There was no commotion in the first cabin. I heard that a man was shot in a panic in the steerage.'[19]

Instead of alleging that he saw a shooting with his own eyes, Hyman's third account merely states that he 'heard' about a shooting that allegedly took place in third class and which might have involved an Italian passenger. Since Hyman left the ship in boat #13 at around 1.40 a.m. (i.e. long before the 'jaw shot' incident allegedly took place after 2 a.m.), one suspects he merely heard second-hand reports about the shooting after being rescued by the *Carpathia* and that over-zealous reporters later tried to turn him into an actual eyewitness to the event.

Alexander Littlejohn

Although Steward Littlejohn didn't claim to have seen the following incident with his own eyes, it's clear he was talking about the alleged incident in which a fellow member of *Titanic*'s victualling staff was allegedly shot through the jaw:

> The chief officer I think it was, shot one of the Italian waiters belonging to the restaurant because he got into a boat and would not come out of it when he was told to. I think another officer fired his revolver to frighten some foreigners who were looking over the side and intended to jump into a boat as it was being lowered.[20]

George McGough

Seaman George McGough left the *Titanic* in boat #9 at around 1.30 a.m., but he later described an incident that apparently took place after he left the ship and which fellow survivors must have told him about while on board the *Carpathia*:

> Murdoch stood with a drawn pistol and shouted that he would shoot the first man who attempted to force his way into the boats. A crazy steward was warned back, but he jumped into one of the boats at the rail, trampling down a woman and her child. Murdoch shot him through the jaw and he was yanked back on deck.[21]

James McGough

Passenger James McGough left the *Titanic* in boat #7 at around 12.40 a.m. – long before any gunfire took place – and he heard about the alleged shooting incident later on:

> We saw no men shot, but just before the finish we heard several shots. I was told that Captain Smith or one of the officers shot himself on the bridge just before the *Titanic* went under. I heard also that several men had been killed as they made a final rush for the boats, trying to cut off the women and children.[22]

Mr McGough's affidavit at the Senate *Titanic* inquiry modified his above statement very slightly by specifying that he did not actually hear any gunshots with his own ears:

Q. Did you hear any guns or revolvers fired?
A. No.

Arthur Peuchen

Major Peuchen left the *Titanic* in boat #6 at about 1.10 a.m. and didn't hear about the 'jaw shot' incident until later:

> It was stated that the first officer shot himself. As the last boat left, I am told that the people began to jump in on to the women. One of the officers is said to have drawn his revolver and shot a man thru the jaw.[23]

Emily Rugg

Emily Rugg talked to a reporter, who later related how she spoke with a steward, who was one of twenty men saved on a swamped collapsible lifeboat:

> 'One of these twenty men was a ship's steward. He told us that he had seen the captain shoot at two passengers and then shoot himself, and that he had seen the first officer shoot himself.' Miss Rugg does not believe there was any truth in what the man said. 'It was all so confused that no two people could agree on details of what happened. The shots might all have been fired in the air, and excited men imagined the rest,' she said.[24]

Thomas Whiteley

Steward Whiteley was another crewman who was near First Officer Murdoch during the final stages of the evacuation, and when the forward end of the boat deck submerged he found refuge on the overturned Collapsible B. Due to contradictory information contained in his different interviews it's unclear whether or not Whiteley saw any actual shooting with his own eyes, so his interviews are being included here with our second-hand accounts to enable us to err on the side of caution.

> There was a bit of panic when it first happened. The officers had to use their revolvers. The chief officer shot one man – I didn't see this, but three others did – and then he shot himself. But everybody, pretty much, behaved splendidly, especially the firemen.[25]

> I tried not to shirk. I stood by and saw Chief Officer Wilde shoot one of my mates down for trying to get into a boat after being ordered not to. And I went into the water and fought like a rat for a chance.[26]

> 'We lined up the passengers in two lines,' he said. 'The women and children were in the first line and the men in the second. Every now and then a man would try to break through the first line, but all of the officers had revolvers and made them go back. I know of but one case of shooting. One of the boats was filled and several men tried to get in it. The officer in charge stood up in the boat and said that the next man attempting to get in would be shot. Soon afterward a steward rushed over and tried to climb in the descending lifeboat. He was shot in the jaw.'[27]

> The chief officer of the *Titanic* went plumb crazy. He rushed around the decks cracking a pistol from which he had emptied every shot. I saw him plunge overboard after the boats had gone away. He had no life preserver and never came up.[28]

Comment: In interviews elsewhere, Whiteley specifically refers to 'Chief Officer Murdoch' (e.g. *Philadelphia Inquirer*, 22 April 1912), so in our second interview a reporter might have been responsible for adding Henry Wilde's name to Whiteley's mention of the unnamed 'chief officer'. In any case, we'll discuss one reason for the confusion about Murdoch's actual rank later in this essay. It's also worth noting that Whiteley and Fireman John Thompson (to be discussed presently) were berthed together at St Vincent's Hospital in New York, so it's not impossible that Whiteley might have heard about the shooting from Thompson.

The thought might have crossed the reader's mind that these 'shot in the jaw' stories were just an imaginative invention of New York's yellow press, but this was not the case at all. In fact, the story about a steward being shot was being discussed by survivors on board the *Carpathia* before the rescue ship even reached New York.

Carpathia Passenger Accounts

Frank Blackmarr

While the rescue ship was headed back to New York, *Carpathia* passenger Frank Blackmar wrote an account of the rescue that included something he was told by a survivor (Eugene Daly, whose own account will be discussed presently):

> There was no shooting, as I learn, except that a Steerage passenger told me he saw an officer trying to control the maddened rush by shooting two persons. This same officer shot himself a minute later.[29]

Carlos Hurd
Mr Hurd was a *Carpathia* passenger and newspaper reporter who mentioned the shooting in an article he wrote for publication while the rescue ship was still at sea:

> Revolver shots were heard in the ship's last moments. The first report spread among the boats was that Capt. Smith had ended his life with a bullet. Then it was said that a mate had shot a steward who tried to push his way upon a boat against orders. None of these tales has been verified …[30]

Accounts from Unnamed Crew Survivors

Two weeks after the disaster, crewmen returning home to the United Kingdom repeatedly spoke to reporters about First Officer William Murdoch shooting 'Italians' before taking his own life. (Although it's regrettable that these crewmen weren't identified in the interviews, the reason they wished their identities to be kept private was because they hadn't yet given their depositions to the Board of Trade and didn't want to draw unwelcome attention from the White Star Line.) The fact that crewmen were still talking about the shootings so long after the sinking suggests that the men weren't inventing these stories and that sometimes where there's smoke, there might also be fire.

In reading the following accounts, bear in mind that many crewmen referred to First Officer Murdoch as the 'chief officer', because that was his rank up until the last minute when Chief Officer Henry Wilde was added to the *Titanic*'s crew.

Unnamed Crewman #1
After returning home to the United Kingdom, an unnamed crewman spoke with a newspaper reporter:

> I saw Mr Murdoch shoot down an Italian. This officer performed heroic work all through.[31]

Unnamed Crewman #2

In the United Kingdom, a crewman spoke with a reporter, who paraphrased the crewman's words for his readers:

> One man said: During the last scenes on the *Titanic* there was a little panic with the steerage, and one or two Italians tried to rush the boats, but the chief officer kept them back, and finally fired at them, whether he killed them he could not say. Then the officer shot himself. The first shot was fired to frighten them, but the second was directed at them.[32]

Unnamed Crewman #3

On his return to the United Kingdom, a crewman told of things that allegedly happened on the *Titanic* before he left the ship in a (collapsible?) lifeboat:

> All this time the ship was going down in the forward part. When the last but one collapsible boat was ordered away there were some men in it, and the chief officer ordered all the men out. One Italian turned round and said he would not come out, so the officer shot him and pitched him over the side. When the boat was about six feet down, I jumped down into it and heard the captain say 'stand-by to pick up survivors'.
>
> We had 49 [wo]men and children in the boat, and could not take anyone else. There were four men in the boat, and we rowed until we were picked up by the *Carpathia*.[33]

Unnamed Crewmen #4

A group of unnamed crewmen spoke with a reporter for the *London Daily News*:

> Several men spoke of shooting incidents. One of them said: 'There was a panic in the steerage, and one or two Italians tried to rush the boats, but the Chief officer kept them back, and finally fired at them. Then the officer shot himself.'[34]

Unnamed Crewmen #5

After arriving back in the United Kingdom, a group of surviving *Titanic* crewmen gave a coherent story of the sinking to a reporter, who paraphrased their joint account:

> On all hands the bravery of Murdoch, the first officer, was vouched for, though several [crewmen] averred that they saw him shoot himself at the

last. Many spoke of having seen the lights of another ship 'about five miles off our port bow.'[35]

Accounts Worthy of Special Notice

The present writer has found one alleged eyewitness account about the shooting that is worthy of special notice, and two additional accounts (one from an anonymous eyewitness and the other a third-hand account) that provide interesting but inconclusive corroboration. Let's examine the eyewitness account first.

John Thompson

Fireman Thompson remained on the forward end of the *Titanic*'s boat deck until it began to submerge and was in close proximity to where First Officer Murdoch was working beside Collapsible A. Thompson later found refuge on that same boat as it floated off the *Titanic* in a swamped condition, and in New York he told a reporter about his experiences:

> … he was fine, that First Officer Murdoch. I was close to him for half an hour or more. I saw him shoot a steward through the jaw for trying to crowd into a boat full of women. He had the whole crowd under his thumb all the time and he never faltered on the job. I don't believe he shot himself. He was standing at a starboard gangway when I jumped from the ship and that was only a minute or two before she disappeared. I think he was carried under and never came up.[36]

Charles Lightoller

After returning to the United Kingdom, Second Officer Lightoller had occasion to speak with Captain James McGiffin, Marine Superintendent for the White Star and American Lines at Queenstown. McGiffin later spoke with his own son, J.O. McGiffin, about some of the things Lightoller told him, and the son wrote down one of those revelations in a letter to researcher Diana Bristow:

> Murdoch shot one crewman in the jaw as he tried to rush the lifeboats.[37]

Unnamed Crewman (James McGann)

An unnamed crewman described things he saw right before he jumped overboard. Occurrences he described elsewhere in the article make it clear he was Trimmer James McGann:

> While we were loading the boats, I saw the chief officer shoot two Italians who tried to rush one of the boats. He fired in the air first to frighten them, but it was no use.
>
> The Italians tried to scramble over the women and children and get into the boats. Then the chief officer shot one of them. There was very little confusion on board. The officers maintained splendid discipline. After I jumped into the water, so far as I could see, most of those remaining on board tried to get aft, as the ship was sinking rapidly by the head.[38]

Unnamed Steward

After returning to the United Kingdom, an unnamed steward spoke with a newspaper reporter, who described the man's experiences for his readers. He claimed to be an eyewitness to the 'jaw shot':

> One of the stewards last evening described there were many instances among the steerage passengers of attempting to rush the boats … he said that he would have been afraid to have jumped into a lifeboat even if he had felt inclined to do so, as he saw seven men shot for attempting to do so. One had his chin blown off.[39]

It might have been this same unnamed steward whose words were transcribed verbatim by a different reporter:

> Until the very end no one had any idea how serious the affair was. The only panic was among the Dagoes*, one of whom I did see shot through the chin.[40]

We've just presented a newspaper interview with a named eyewitness, a second account recounting something Second Officer Lightoller told a friend about the shooting, and newspaper interviews with an unnamed eyewitness to the shooting. Although these three accounts are rather suggestive regarding the possible reality of the 'jaw shot' incident, they're still a far cry from being the type of solid evidence historians like to hinge their major historical premises upon.

* 'Dago' was a slur aimed at foreigners in general, but Italians in particular.

Did the newspaper reporter quote John Thompson's eyewitness account of the shooting accurately? Although we can never know the answer to that question with certainty, the present writer has always been favourably impressed with Thompson's newspaper interviews and believes the fireman *was* being quoted accurately.

Did J.O. McGiffin accurately quote Second Officer Lightoller's statement about Murdoch shooting a crewman in the jaw on the night of the sinking? It's hard to see how McGiffin could misremember the gist of a single sentence describing such a specific subject, so perhaps a more pertinent question would be this: was Lightoller describing something he saw with his own eyes, or was he describing something he heard *other* survivors discussing while on board the *Carpathia*? The answer to that question is lost to history, but the fact that Lightoller believed the statement to be true is significant.

Did the British newspaper reporters record the unnamed steward's eyewitness account of the shooting accurately? Again, we can never know with certainty, but we *do* know that the steward seems to have witnessed the same shooting that John Thompson claimed to have witnessed. (The fact that the unnamed steward was still talking to reporters about that incident two weeks after the sinking suggests that he was deeply impressed by what he'd seen during *Titanic*'s final moments afloat.)

The accounts written by *Carpathia* passengers Carlos Hurd and Frank Blackmarr prove that stories about a steward being shot on the *Titanic* were circulating on the *Carpathia* before the rescue ship reached New York, and the accounts of John Thompson, Herbert Lightoller and the unknown steward all specify that the man in question was shot in the jaw. Do any additional survivor accounts support the idea of a man or men being shot on the *Titanic* even though the accounts make no specific mention of a 'jaw shot'? The answer is yes.

Primary Sources

Since we know that the 'shot in the jaw' story was being discussed by survivors on board the *Carpathia*, the question we need to ask is: 'How well does this story fit in with first-hand accounts that were written down by survivors themselves? The answer is 'pretty well'.

Eugene Daly

After he was brought on board the *Carpathia* and had a short time to recover from his exposure to the icy water, Eugene Daly told his story to *Carpathia* passenger Frank Blackmarr, who wrote it down for posterity:

> After the accident, we were all held down in steerage. Finally, some of the women and children were let up, but we had quite a number of hot-headed Italians and other peoples who got crazy and made for the stairs. These men tried to rush the stairway, pushing and crowding and pulling the women down. Some of them with weapons in their hands. I saw two dagos [*sic*] shot and some that took punishment from the officers.

Daly's wording here makes it uncertain if the shootings he witnessed took place down in steerage or up on the boat deck, but Dr Blackmarr clarified that point when he wrote another account adding extra details about Daly's experience that he left out of his original written record:

> The only panic at the beginning, as I understand it, was in the steerage, where there were many persons who lacked self-control. There was no shooting, as I learn, except that a steerage passenger [i.e. Daly] told me he saw an officer trying to control the maddened rush by shooting two persons. The same officer shot himself a minute later.[41]

Since the only officer suicide on the *Titanic* was said to have occurred on the boat deck, Dr Blackmarr's account apparently clears up the question of where the two other people were shot as well. Eugene Daly confirmed this boat deck location when he wrote a letter to his sister in Ireland describing his last few minutes on board the *Titanic*:

> At the first cabin [deck] when a boat was being lowered an officer pointed a revolver and said if any man tried to get in, he would shoot him on the spot. I saw the officer shoot two men dead because they tried to get in the boat. Afterwards there was another shot, and I saw the officer himself lying on the deck. They told me he shot himself, but I did not see him. I was up to my knees in the water at the time. Everyone was rushing around, and there were no more boats. I then dived overboard.[42]

On 20 April, Daly went to the home of New York's Mayor Gaynor and related the story of his *Titanic* experiences:

> The officer in charge pointed a revolver and waved his hand and said if any man tried to get in he would shoot him on the spot. Two men tried to break through and he shot them both. I saw him shoot them. I saw them lying on the deck after they were shot. One seemed to be dead. The other was trying to pull himself to the side of the deck, but he could not. I tried to get to the boat also, but was afraid I would be shot and stayed back. The officer shot twice. Afterwards there was another man shot, and I saw the officer himself lying on the deck. They told me he shot himself, but I did not see him. Then I rushed across the deck and there was a sort of canvas craft there. I tried with six or seven other men to get it out but we could not. It was stuck under a wire stay which ran up to the mast. The water was then rushing across the deck. The ship lurched and the water washed the canvas craft off the deck and into the ocean. I was up to my knees in water at the time. Everyone was rushing around, but there were no boats. Then I dived overboard.[43]

In 1915 Daly testified at the Limitation of Liability hearings, and the newspapers summarised the content:

> Eugene Daly of Newark, N.J., was awakened when the *Titanic* struck, but was assured there was no danger. The stewards ordered all hands on deck, and when he reached there he found some of the stewards laughing and smoking cigarettes. He said he returned below and aroused some of his friends. He saw three lifeboats lowered, and when he attempted to get into one an officer threatened him, although the boats were far from full. He said he heard two shots at this time, and later saw two men lying on the deck, and was told that they had been shot. When the ship listed he jumped into the water and clung to an upturned boat until morning.[44]

Perhaps the most surprising thing about Daly's 1915 testimony regarding the shootings is the fact that his statement was simply accepted without comment by his interrogators; it appears that by 1915 the idea of gunplay on board the *Titanic* was disbelieved so completely that nobody paid the slightest attention to Daly's eyewitness testimony or thought his statements were worth bothering with.

George Rheims

Our second primary source about the shooting/suicide on board the *Titanic* comes from George Rheims, who survived the sinking on Collapsible A. On 19 April, after arriving in New York, Rheims wrote a letter to his wife in France describing his experiences:

> While the last boat was leaving, I saw an officer with a revolver fire a shot and kill a man who was trying to climb into it. As there remained nothing more to do, the officer told us, 'Gentlemen, each man for himself, goodbye.' He gave a military salute and then fired a bullet into his head. That's what I call a man!![45]

Mr Rheims was interviewed by the newspapers on that same date and gave the reporter essentially the same story he wrote to his wife:

> 'I was with my brother-in-law, Joseph Loring of No. 811 Fifth Avenue,' said Mr Rheims. 'The majority of men passengers did not attempt to get in the boats. The men assisted the women. But when the boats began to be lowered some men lost their heads. From the lower deck men jumped into crowded boats and others slid down ropes. One officer shot a man who attempted to get into a crowded boat. Immediately afterward the officer said: 'Well, goodbye,' and killed himself.'
>
> Rheims was able to swim to Collapsible A, and was one of the 12 survivors later rescued.[46]

Richard Williams

In later years Mr Williams wrote an account of his final moments on board the *Titanic*:

> We wandered out. The boat was now only about two or three decks above the water. The situation was getting serious. Quite automatically we started up – we happened to be forward; presently we found ourselves on the Captain's bridge – only two other people were there, Captain Smith and a quartermaster – I believe, who presently wandered away. We spoke to the Captain for a few minutes. The ship seemed to give a slight lurch; I turned towards the bow. I saw nothing but water with just a mast sticking out of it. I don't remember the shock of the cold water, I only remember thinking 'suction' and my efforts to swim in the direction of the starboard rail to get away from the ship. Before I had swam more than ten feet I felt the deck come up under me and I found we were high and dry. My father was not more than 12 or 15 feet from me. I heard the crack of a revolver shot from the direction where I had left Captain Smith; I did not look around.[47]

Summary of the Various Accounts

Unattributed Paraphrased Accounts

#1 Murdoch shot two men (one in the jaw).
#2 an officer shot two immigrants (one was killed and one was left moaning with his jaw shot away).
#3 half a dozen men were shot and left dead on deck.

Unnamed Crewman Accounts

Unnamed Crewman #1	saw Murdoch shoot an Italian.
Unnamed Crewman #2	saw the 'chief officer' fire at one or two 'Italians' with unknown results and then shoot himself.
Unnamed Crewman #3	the 'chief officer' shot an 'Italian' and threw his body overboard.
Unnamed Crewmen #4	a group of crewmen said the 'chief officer' fired at one or two 'Italians' and then shot himself.
Unnamed Crewmen #5	several crewmen said they saw Murdoch shoot himself at the end.

Newspaper Survivor Accounts

Beane	heard that two steerage passengers were shot.
Carter	supposedly saw several men shot; one had his jaw shot away.
Collins	saw officer shoot two men and then commit suicide.
Daniel	(a) said steerage men were fired at; one man had his jaw shot off. (b) said he didn't hear of anyone being hit by bullets.
Dick	heard that guards shot the jaw off an immigrant.
Dodge	heard that two men were shot, followed by an officer suicide.
Dorkings	two stewards were shot, after which an officer committed suicide. (One account says the shootings took place in a lifeboat.)

Harder	heard that the 'first officer' took his own life.
Hyman	heard that the 'chief officer' fired at steerage passengers, one of whom (perhaps Italian) had his chin shot off.
Littlejohn	the 'chief officer' shot one of the 'Italian waiters'.
G. McGough	was apparently told that Murdoch shot a steward in the jaw after the man forced his way into a lifeboat.
J. McGough	heard that several men were killed and that Captain Smith or an officer committed suicide.
Peuchen	heard that the first officer shot a man in the jaw and that an officer committed suicide.
Rugg	a steward told her he saw Captain Smith shoot two passengers before he and First Officer Murdoch took their own lives.
Whiteley	(a) said that the chief officer shot a man before committing suicide. (b) said that chief officer 'Wilde' shot one of his mates (i.e. a fellow crewman). (c) said a steward was shot in the jaw.

Carpathia Passenger Accounts

Blackmarr	before the *Carpathia* reached New York, a steerage passenger told him he saw an officer shoot two persons before shooting himself a minute later.
Hurd	while the rescue ship was still at sea, survivors told him about a *Titanic* steward being shot.

Accounts Worthy of Special Notice

Thompson	saw Murdoch shoot a steward through the jaw.
Lightoller	told a friend that Murdoch shot a crewman in the jaw.
McGann	saw the 'chief officer' shoot one (or possibly two) 'Italians'.
Unknown steward	saw seven men shot, one with his chin blown off. In one interview he said the injured man was Italian.

Primary Sources

Daly wrote a letter stating that he saw an officer shoot two men before committing suicide. The facts in his letter were corroborated by his later newspaper interviews and by the things he told Frank Blackmarr while on board the *Carpathia*.

Rheims wrote a letter stating that he saw an officer shoot one man before committing suicide.

Williams heard a shot after the bow rose again after the boat deck's initial submergence.

Discussion

Before we begin our discussion of the evidence, we need to remember the old scientific maxim that 'absence of evidence is not the same thing as evidence of absence'. In other words, if two people are in the same location but only one of them notices an incident taking place, the fact that the second person missed seeing the incident cannot be regarded as ironclad evidence that it never happened. (A good example of this is the fact that several *Titanic* survivors never noticed the ship's band playing music during the evacuation and mistakenly told reporters that the band *did not* play.) In the case of the alleged shooting/suicide incident, we cannot necessarily assume those incidents never took place just because occasional survivors who were 'in the right place at the right time' failed to notice them.

The Second-Hand Accounts

Out of fourteen survivors who heard second-hand reports about the shootings and/or officer suicide while they were on board the *Carpathia*, seven of those survivors mentioned the 'jaw shot'. Although four passengers assumed that *Titanic*'s gunshot victims were third-class passengers, Steward Thomas Whiteley said the 'jaw shot' victim was his 'mate', George McGough said the man was a 'steward', and Alexander Littlejohn said the gunshot victim was an 'Italian waiter' from the restaurant staff. Survivor Edward Dorkings reported that two stewards were shot, and *Carpathia* passenger Carlos Hurd was told by survivors that 'a mate had shot a steward who tried to push his way upon a boat against orders'.

Out of these fifteen second-hand accounts, a steward told Emily Rugg that it was Captain Smith who fired the fatal shots; two crewmen (Whiteley and Littlejohn) heard that it was the 'chief officer' who fired his weapon; another crewman (George McGough) heard it was 'Chief Officer Murdoch', and seven survivors heard that the officer in question committed suicide after firing those shots. (Peuchen and Harder heard that this man was the 'first officer', and in one interview Whiteley supposedly named 'Chief Officer Wilde', even though in other interviews he specifically expressed the commonly held view that William Murdoch was the *Titanic*'s 'chief officer'.)

At any rate, since these fifteen accounts come to us second-hand, all we can conclude from them is that stories were circulating on board the *Carpathia* claiming that *Titanic*'s 'first' or 'chief' officer shot at least one man (perhaps a steward or waiter) in the jaw before taking his own life.

The Purported Eyewitnesses

Out of the four *Titanic* crewmen (Fireman Thompson, Second Officer Lightoller, Trimmer McGann and the unnamed steward) who either saw the shootings/suicide with their own eyes or else were aware of those events, three of those people described the 'jaw shot'. Despite the unnamed steward's eyewitness claim that the man he saw shot in the jaw was a 'Dago', Fireman Thompson and Second Officer Lightoller both agreed that the 'jaw shot' victim was a member of the *Titanic*'s crew (with Thompson specifying he was a steward.) Thompson and Lightoller also specified that First Officer William Murdoch was the officer responsible for the shootings – a significant point, since Thompson and Lightoller were fellow crew members who both knew *Titanic*'s first officer and specifically identified him by name as being the officer in question. When this information is added to the officer suicide information contained in George Rheims' private letter to his family, the idea that a *Titanic* officer really did shoot a couple of people before taking his own life becomes a very real possibility.

The Confusion About Murdoch's Rank

One point of confusion regarding the officer who used his gun in anger that night is the fact that many survivors mistakenly believed that William Murdoch was the *Titanic*'s 'chief officer' instead of its first officer. Whenever a survivor later mentioned the 'chief officer' without actually *naming* that officer, it of course raises the possibility that the officer in question might have been Murdoch instead of Chief Officer Henry Wilde.

The reason for this confusion about Murdoch's rank can be seen in a photograph snapped at Queenstown showing Second Officer Lightoller still wearing his first officer's uniform. The reason Lightoller wore the wrong uniform was because his last-minute demotion from first officer to second officer gave him insufficient time to re-sew the appropriate stripes of rank on his uniform sleeves before the maiden voyage began. It therefore seems likely that First Officer Murdoch (who experienced a similar demotion from chief officer to first officer) was likewise still wearing his chief officer's stripes during the maiden voyage – a fact that explains the occasional stories claiming it was the 'chief officer' who shot two men during the sinking.

Lightoller's Later Story About Murdoch's Deadly Use of a Firearm

Another point of confusion is the fact that even though Second Officer Lightoller claimed in later years that William Murdoch shot a crewman in the jaw, in 1912 Lightoller claimed (in public, at least) that Murdoch's death was not a suicide. In fact, shortly after the sinking, Lightoller wrote a letter to Murdoch's widow saying the following:

> I was practically the last man, and certainly the last officer, to see Mr Murdoch. He was then endeavouring to launch the starboard forward collapsible boat. I had already got mine from off the top of our quarters … Having got my boat down off the top of the house, and there being no time to open it, I left it and ran across to the starboard side, still on top of the quarters. I was then practically looking down on your husband and his men. He was working hard, personally assisting, overhauling the forward boat's fall. At this moment the ship dived, and we were all in the water. Other reports as to the ending are absolutely false. Mr Murdoch died like a man, doing his duty.[48]

This letter to Mrs Murdoch was signed by Lightoller and *Titanic*'s three remaining surviving officers, and many researchers regard the letter and Lightoller's inquiry testimony as absolute proof that Murdoch did not commit suicide. However, in later years Second Officer Lightoller became more voluble on the subject of the officer suicide (just as he became more talkative about Murdoch shooting a crewman in the jaw). Murdoch's biographer, Susanne Störmer, reports the following information:

> It was in 1994, when I talked to somebody who had done lots of research in [the] case of Lightoller and who had been in touch with the Lightoller family. This guy told me that Lightoller had stated that 'somebody he knew committed suicide'. But Lightoller never told who it was. And of course Lightoller did know many people aboard the *Titanic* – nautical officers, engineers, the doctors, the pursers … So Lightoller's statement does not help much in this case. It also does not tell if Lightoller actually observed somebody he knew committing suicide.[49]

Despite Second Officer Lightoller's silence in 1912 about Murdoch shooting two men, and despite his similar silence in 1912 about knowing someone who committed suicide on the *Titanic*, Lightoller's later talkativeness suggests that he knew far more about these incidents than he admitted right after the sinking. It should also be remembered that all four of *Titanic*'s surviving officers affixed their signatures to Lightoller's letter to Mrs Murdoch even though none of the three junior officers had any first-hand knowledge of the veracity of Lightoller's claims. To the present writer, it seems quite possible that the four officers sent that joint letter to Murdoch's widow in a humane attempt to shield her from the knowledge that her husband was the key player in a shooting/suicide incident during the *Titanic*'s final moments.

Where and When Did the Shooting/Suicide Take Place?

One unanswered question about the alleged shootings and subsequent officer suicide concerns the exact time and place these events took place. Fireman John Thompson and Second Officer Lightoller both specified that it was William Murdoch who shot a crewman in the jaw, which suggests that the incident took place on the *Titanic*'s starboard boat deck. Murdoch is known to have fired intimidating shots during the loading of Collapsible C, but the fact that no injuries were reported by anyone in that lifeboat suggests that the shootings took place *after* Collapsible C left the ship at 2 a.m. – i.e. circa 2.10 a.m., while Collapsible A was being wrestled to the davits after being dropped on to the boat deck from the roof of the officers' quarters.

Although Washington Dodge obtained his information second-hand from survivors who were still on board the ship at the end, and even though his unsupported allegation about armed steerage passengers does not pertain to our present discussion, part of Dodge's description of what happened near the last of the collapsible lifeboats might indeed have a bearing on the subject of shootings and an officer suicide:

> Shortly after the launching of the last lifeboat, however, when there was still left four collapsible boats unlaunched, the male steerage passengers swarmed upon the boat deck. Many of these carried drawn daggers and knives in their hands, and others were armed with clubs of wood. They began to fight their way desperately to the collapsible boats, and try to gain possession of the same.
>
> About this time the steamer *suddenly* settled to a very much greater degree forward, so that the waters at the forward end of the boat deck approached to within eight or ten feet of the same. With these conditions prevailing, panic ensued. Those fighting their way to the lifeboats attempted to jump into the same, and several were shot down by officers.[50]

Although Dodge's second-hand account suggests that all four collapsible lifeboats were still on board the *Titanic* when the ship made her sudden dip downward, this downward dip was undoubtedly the one that occurred when the forward boat deck began to submerge and the sea surged toward the passengers and crewmen who were struggling to launch Collapsible A. In support of this premise, Richard Williams wrote that he heard a gunshot from somewhere in the vicinity of the *Titanic*'s bridge a few seconds after the forward boat deck began to submerge, and George Rheims wrote that, 'while the last boat [Collapsible A?] was leaving', he saw an officer shoot a man 'who was trying to climb into it'. For his own part, Fireman John Thompson confirmed that there was a sudden rush of people who attempted to jump on board Collapsible A as the sea surged toward that boat. Thompson said:

> I managed to get into the collapsible boat we had on the planks, in which there were twenty-seven altogether, with one woman from the steerage. We were washed over the side. The boat went right underwater with the weight of us as we rode away from the *Titanic*. She was two or three feet underwater all this time, but, thank God, it was enough to hold us up.[51]

Three additional survivor accounts add general corroboration to our premise that shots were fired just as the forward end of the boat deck began to submerge. Interestingly, our first two accounts show that news of an officer suicide was already circulating among passengers who were still on board the *Titanic* during her final moments – a fact that explains why these stories were being discussed on board the *Carpathia* during the next four days.

Peter Daly

Mr Daly was one of the lucky survivors who managed to swim to Collapsible A:

> There didn't appear to be so much excitement. A certain lot, of course, were panic-stricken and ran from place to place, not knowing which way to run.
>
> While all this was going on a report spread through the ship that an officer had shot himself. I think they said it was the chief officer, or the captain, but we heard that the captain had been flung from his position and landed on his head, fracturing his skull and causing his death.
>
> Standing along the rail I could see the water coming up rapidly. It rose and the passengers became panic-stricken. There were a hundred of them hugging the sides of the captain's and officers' quarters not knowing what to do. The ship went down lower and we realized that it was sinking. Twenty times I thought to myself that I would never see land again.
>
> I saw it was time to do something and jumped into the water. Hundreds did likewise … I have heard that several persons were shot for crowding into the lifeboats ahead of women, but I think those reports which were thought to be pistol shots were the rockets sent up as signals. I saw one officer with a small pistol.[52]

Daly was mistaken about distress rockets being sent up this late in the sinking, since the last rocket was fired by Quartermaster George Rowe shortly before he left the ship in Collapsible C at 2 a.m.

Victor Sunderland

Mr Sunderland managed to swim to Collapsible B as the ship was going down, and a reporter later transcribed his story:

> 'I saw an officer fire his revolver once or twice, killing a man.' Sunderland then claimed he started heading towards the stern of the ship and heard another shot. 'I asked what had happened, and a gentlemen told me that an

officer had shot himself. Seeing that I could not secure a spot in a lifeboat, I leapt from the ship and into the water just a few feet below.'[53]

Unnamed Steward

An interview of unknown reliability was received from an unnamed steward who had just returned to the United Kingdom. Although we cannot use this anonymous account as being evidence of anything specific, the unnamed steward's comment about Murdoch's fate is interesting in the context of our present discussion and in light of the fact that the man claimed to be an eyewitness to the events he was describing:

> A steward who confirmed the statement as to Mr Murdoch, the first officer, having shot himself, averred that in getting back to the bridge after having been washed away once, Captain Smith had to pass the body of his second in command. 'He glanced at it,' said the man, who claimed to be an eyewitness, 'but took no further notice.'[54]*

Why Would First Officer Murdoch Take His Own Life?

It's not the aim of the present author to 'victimise' William Murdoch by suggesting that he was *definitely* the officer who allegedly shot two people before taking his own life. Instead, the author's sole purpose has been to determine if enough evidence exists to support the *possible reality* of the shooting suicide incident and (if so) to try to determine the identity of the officer in question. I'm doing this to counterbalance the large number of people who rely on easily available inquiry testimony (mainly Lightoller's) in order to 'prove' their contention that William Murdoch 'wasn't the kind of man who would take his own life'. After all, what possible reasons (they ask) could Murdoch have had for contemplating such a drastic act?

Regarding the claim that First Officer Murdoch wasn't the kind of man to commit suicide, this argument of course holds no water, because nobody ever knows another person's heart so thoroughly that the possibility of suicide under extraordinary circumstances can be ruled out with absolute certainty.

* This is the only account the present author knows of that alleges Captain Smith crawled back aboard the ship after diving from the bridge. The premise seems unlikely but is being included here just for the sake of completeness.

Also, in past years the idea of suicide was not always regarded as a cowardly act and could sometimes even be regarded as honourable. (We are reminded of the suicide of Captain Wilhelm Langsdorff after he scuttled the German cruiser *Graf Spee* at Buenos Aires in 1939. 'I can now only prove by my death that the fighting services of the Third Reich are ready to die for the honour of the flag,' Langsdorff wrote in a farewell letter shortly before his death. 'I alone bear the responsibility for scuttling the panzerschiff Admiral Graf Spee. I am happy to pay with my life for any possible reflection on the honour of the flag.')

It is interesting to note that Fifth Officer Harold Lowe wasn't averse to the idea of taking his own life in connection with the loss of the *Titanic* and 1,496 of her passengers and crewmen. Survivor Esther Hart was an eyewitness to Lowe's unexpected outburst in lifeboat #14, and she mentioned the incident in a letter she wrote later:

> The officer in charge of our boat was standing on that raised part of it right at the end. We were all women and children aboard (at least I thought so then, but we were not, as I will presently tell you) and we were all crying and sobbing; and the officer said, not roughly, but I think with a kindly desire to keep our minds off the terrible time we had gone through. 'Don't cry, please don't cry. You'll have something else to do than cry; some of you will have to handle the oars. For God's sake stop crying. If I had not the responsibility of looking after you, I would put a bullet through my brain'.[55]

Lowe's contemplation of his own suicide was not a demonstration of cowardice, because the *Titanic*'s fifth officer proved his own courage beyond question that night. Instead, Lowe's outburst to the weeping ladies in his lifeboat was almost certainly a sudden manifestation of the mental anguish he felt at being one of the men who was responsible for the *Titanic*'s navigation and for the tragedy that was now unfolding as a result of that navigation. Just as in the later case of Captain Langsdorff, the taking of one's own life in order to atone for one's perceived shortcomings might sometimes seem to be a man's only honourable option (in the heat of the moment, at least).

Reports of First Officer Murdoch's suicide were not fabricated by New York's yellow press on 19 April, because – as we've already seen – reports of an officer suicide were already circulating on board the sinking *Titanic* as well as on board the *Carpathia* while the rescue ship was bound for New York. (One surviving *Titanic* lookout was even overheard to say, 'No wonder that Murdoch shot himself.')[56] A number of crewmen were still talking about the officer suicide two weeks after the sinking, and one group of crewmen informed a reporter that 'they saw Mr Murdoch fire the fatal shot shortly before the *Titanic* plunged into the darkness of the ocean depths'.[57] Significantly, one crewman also said that, in stopping a rush of panicked passengers, Murdoch patted the barrel of his weapon and grimly advised the unruly passengers that 'There is one left for you and one for myself'.[58]

In light of our many questions about the officer suicide, it has been suggested that First Officer Murdoch had no *reason* to take his own life. In response to this unfounded claim, the present writer has already outlined a few potential reasons that might have occurred to Murdoch while he was working to launch Collapsible A shortly before the *Titanic*'s forward boat deck began to submerge.

Final Conclusions

Given the incomplete and uncertain nature of most of the evidence used to argue both sides of the shooting/suicide debate, we may never know with absolute certainty whether or not a *Titanic* officer fired his revolver in anger before taking his own life. Still, George Rheims and Eugene Daly both wrote first-hand accounts describing how they personally witnessed an officer shoot men on the *Titanic* before taking his own life, and Daly said the same thing to Frank Blackmarr on board the *Carpathia*. If these primary sources are indeed trustworthy, it's the present writer's belief that the officer in question was probably First Officer William Murdoch, that one of the two men Murdoch shot may have been an Italian member of the victualling staff who received a bullet in the jaw, and that the shootings and subsequent officer suicide probably took place just as the forward end of the starboard boat deck began to submerge and panicky passengers and crewmen began jumping into Collapsible A just before that boat was washed into the sea.

If First Officer Murdoch was indeed the officer who took his own life after shooting two men on the boat deck, his death occurred only after he did everything in his power to ensure the survival of as many passengers and crewmen as possible. An unnamed steward put it this way:

> Murdoch was splendid too, but I fear it is true that he did shoot himself. He did not do so, however, till the very end, when he had done everything he could do for others.[59]

11

Diamonds

After the loss of the *Titanic* in April 1912, newspaper stories began claiming that a valuable consignment of diamonds went down with the ship:

> British underwriters will have to bear the greatest part of the loss, though much reinsurance was placed in Germany, and American underwriters probably will have to pay most of the loss on cargo. One Wall Street authority says the *Titanic* carried $3,000,000 in diamonds and $250,000 in rubber, besides securities and specie.[1]

> A dispatch from Antwerp states that a large quantity of diamonds belonging to merchants of that town were on board the *Titanic*. They were insured. Several diamond merchants from Antwerp were among the passengers, but there is no news concerning their safety. In addition to the diamonds there were on board, says a telegram from Leipsic [*sic*], furs valued at £150,000.[2]

> The *Titanic* was insured at Lloyd's for $5,000,000. It is understood that there was no specie aboard the liner, but large insurances had been written on diamonds and other valuables in her cargo.
>
> No definite information is obtainable as to the amount of valuables, but it is understood that the vessel took diamonds of great value consigned to dealers whose estimated value is as high as $5,000,000, but this is admittedly conjecture. She also took a large amount of bonds.[3]

On 9 May 1912, Maurice Farrell (managing editor of Dow, Jones & Co.) testified at the Senate *Titanic* inquiry that at 11.15 a.m. on 15 April his organisation published a report stating, 'London: Information given out here states

Titanic carried about $5,000,000 in bonds and diamonds.' (The report had been received from the Laffin News Service.)[4] The *New York Herald* attributed this report to an unnamed New York broker, and on 17 April the newspaper followed up on this story by interviewing people from the insurance industry and the diamond trade.

A Mr William Prime, from a large insurance agent, discussing the losses to insurers, stated, 'The story that $5,000,000 worth of diamonds were aboard is almost unquestionably wrong.'

In the same issue of that newspaper, an official of the Jewellers Board of Trade stated that his organisation had no knowledge of any shipment of diamonds on board the *Titanic* but admitted that such shipments were not normally publicised.

The *New York Herald* contributed additional details about the alleged *Titanic* diamond consignment as well as describing the usual procedure for shipping such consignments by sea:

> Inquiry among jewelers and importers of precious stones in Maiden Lane yesterday afternoon failed to reveal the names of local firms to which the $5,000,000 worth of diamonds reported to have been carried by the *Titanic*, were consigned. It was known in the district that dealers here expected a heavy shipment of gems and the consignment in question was to be distributed among several firms and individuals.
>
> Such shipments are usually made through the customs division of the Post Office. At the Post Office and Custom House it was said that the authorities had no advance information as to the value of the shipment, or who would receive it. The diamonds are understood to consist for the most part of uncut or unset stones, which were to be made up in settings of special design in this country. English underwriters, it was said, have insured the shipment of jewels for nearly $3,000,000, and the balance of the loss will be distributed about evenly between the American and European owners, The exact value is merely estimated, as no invoice of the entire shipment has arrived in New York as yet.[5]

Within a few weeks of the *Titanic* disaster, debate about the possible existence of a lost consignment of diamonds died down, with the truth of the matter remaining unresolved. Decades passed with no further public mention of the subject, but after the 1985 discovery of the *Titanic*'s wreckage the debate flared up again when salvagers announced they intended to recover a shipment of diamonds that had gone down with the great vessel:

> Divers are scouring the *Titanic* in a desperate attempt to recover up to £200 million of diamonds before the ship finally disintegrates. In a move that recalls the opening to the Oscar-winning film of the disaster, divers are searching for a shipment of diamonds along with passengers' jewellery that experts believe was hurriedly stashed in pursers' bags as the ship was sinking …
>
> The diamonds are at the heart of the search. 'Two brothers were coming out of Switzerland,' said Mr [G. Michael] Harris. 'They had a shipment of diamonds they were bringing back to New York with them that they lost on the *Titanic*, which today would be valued at over $300 million [about £200m].'[6]

Public disagreement about the actual existence of these diamonds arose almost immediately:

> There is no treasure in the dark grave of the *Titanic*, no millionaires' diamonds, as the stories say, no fabled baubles. 'I can assure you there are no valuables down there, nothing that would pay for a salvage expedition,' a leading student of the disaster said yesterday.
>
> Mr John Eaton, historian of the Titanic Historical Society, has examined the *Titanic*'s cargo manifest and insurance claims, and has concluded that nothing of great value went down with the ship which now lies 13,000 feet beneath the surface of the north Atlantic.
>
> Stories of the *Titanic*'s riches are myths, he said … The manifest has only half a page of packages that were kept by the ship's purser and none of these was valued at more than £500 …
>
> Of the $7 million [£5.2 million] worth of diamonds said to be in the *Titanic*'s vault there is no sign on the manifest. 'Yes, there was a diamond merchant aboard,' Mr Eaton said, 'and he had some uncut diamonds with him. But his family made an insurance claim for no more than $5,000 …'
>
> The cargo manifest of the *Titanic* was published in the *New York Times* on April 21, six days after the disaster, and Mr Eaton has compared this list with the original manifest now in an American public records office. The lists matched.[7]*

> The manifest provides no evidence of high value shipments of jewellery or precious metals.[8]

* According to historian Don Lynch, 'Kevin Jones, who is researching the couture on the ship, says the *Times* list is full of inaccuracies.'

Professional Jewellers' Diamond Consignments

Although it is unknown if any individual diamond shipment on the *Titanic* was valued in the millions of dollars, it is known for a fact that multiple smaller consignments were brought aboard the vessel for shipment to the United States. Despite the newspapers' implied suggestion that no shipment of diamonds on the ship exceeded a value of $5,000, we know of one such consignment exceeding that value that was never made public in the newspapers; the existence of this previously unknown diamond shipment came to light at the Limitation of Liability hearings in 1913 when papers were filed by Laura Moore 'as Assignee of the Owners of Certain Cargo':

> In the Matter of the Petition of the Oceanic Steam Navigation Company Ltd., owner of the steamship *Titanic*, for limitation of liability.
> Laura Moore, Claimant, sworn April 11, 1913.
> M.M. Vagner, Nos & Cie, 1 pkg diamonds...... $7,720.00.[9]

At least two smaller shipments of diamonds were listed in other portions of the Limitation of Liability records. On 14 January 1913 Archibald Thacher, a member of the Wallace, Butler and Brown law firm, filed papers asking for restitution on behalf of his clients for the following losses:

Claimant	Owner & Assured	Description of Shipment	Value
H.G. Poland	Ehrmann & Bahlsen	Diamonds	£934.0.8
G.W. Tyser	Richard Roe and others	Diamonds	£775[10]

The possible existence of additional 'undocumented' diamond shipments is supported by a 1912 news report naming the specific intended recipient of a fourth consignment of diamonds:

> As to cargo, it was insured by the shippers. The company has nothing to do with the insurance of the cargo.
>
> The *Titanic* carried a cargo of 1,400 tons, of what is known as case goods, a high class cargo consisting of linen and mercantile goods. It was estimated to-day by an official of the White Star Line that the cargo was worth probably $750,000.

> If there were any diamonds on board, the White Star Line offices here had not been notified to that effect. There was a report in London that the *Titanic* carried about $5,000,000 in bonds and diamonds. This statement could not be verified here. It is known that Ichberg & Company, at No. 65 Maiden Lane, had a consignment of diamonds on the *Titanic*, but nothing like a million dollars' worth. The cargo was insured in London. It was explained that the insurance was carried on what is known as an 'open policy,' that is, the policy was sent to the other side and filled in by agents there.[11]

After learning that Ichberg & Co. supposedly lost a diamond consignment on the *Titanic*, the present author attempted to learn if the firm still exists at 65 Maiden Lane in New York City in order to ask whether or not the company ever collected an insurance claim for its lost diamonds. Unfortunately, by 1917 the Ben Spier Jewelry Company was operating out of 65 Maiden Lane, and all trace of Ichberg & Co. seems to have disappeared by that time. Interestingly, though, the Eichberg & Co. jewellery firm had been conducting business at 65 Nassau since before the turn of the century,[12] and one wonders if the same numerical street address for both firms (65 Maiden Lane and 65 Nassau) was just coincidental or if the Ichberg and Eichberg firms were in reality the same company. (Since several Eichberg & Co. jewellery firms are still operating in California, perhaps some enterprising West Coast researcher can determine if that firm had a lost consignment of diamonds on board the *Titanic* in 1912.)

Another 1912 news report might enable future researchers to track down a fifth diamond consignment that the *Titanic* was allegedly transporting to a Pennsylvania jeweller:

> Pittsburg, Pa., April 16 – W. Wattrell, the oldest and one of the leading jewelers of Pittsburg, dropped dead in a streetcar here today when he heard of the sinking of the *Titanic*, which was bringing him a large consignment of jewels from Paris.[13]

Since we know of at least three documented diamond shipments that definitely existed on board the *Titanic*, sceptics might be wondering why these consignments were not listed on the *Titanic*'s cargo manifest, a copy of which was brought to New York on board the *Mauretania* on 21 April 1912. It has been speculated that diamond shipments might have been placed in the purser's safe instead of being listed on the cargo manifest and consigned to the ship's cargo hold, but in reality, neither the *Titanic*'s cargo handlers nor the *Titanic*'s purser had anything to do with transporting valuable diamond consignments – a fact that the following newspaper article makes clear:

> As no advance invoices had been mailed to New York jewel importers prior to the steaming of the *Titanic*, it is impossible yet to learn to whom $5,000,000 worth of gems reported to have gone down with the steamship were consigned.
>
> Jewelers said today that all they know of the loss of the gems is that they received a report some days ago from London telling of a great shipment of diamonds and other gems in that country which underwriters had insured for $3,000,000. The names of neither the exporters nor the importers were contained in the report.
>
> The jewels were being sent to this country by way of the Customs Department of the Post Office. The loss will be borne evenly by the English and American dealers. Most of the lost jewels were uncut.[14]

In other words, any consignments of diamonds on board the *Titanic* would have been handled by the vessel's postal clerks and were probably being transported inside one of the *Titanic*'s 200 bags of registered post.[15]

Another newspaper article added several extra details describing the exact character of the *Titanic*'s diamond shipments:

> The consignment in question was to be distributed among several firms and individuals … The diamonds are understood to consist for the most part of uncut or unset stones which were to be made up in settings of special design in this country.
>
> English underwriters, it was said, have insured the shipment of jewels for nearly $3,000,000, and the balance of the loss will be distributed about evenly between the American and European owners. The exact value is merely estimated as no invoice of the entire shipment has arrived in New York as yet.[16]

Information about the exact procedure for insuring diamond shipments for ocean crossings was presented in another newspaper article:

> … There were 1,400 tons of small bits of cargo on board. It was also said that the *Titanic* carried diamonds valued at $5,000,000. This bit of news

came from London, with the additional information that the jewels were consigned to dealers on this side. From the same source came information that a large amount of bonds were also on board. But if any jewels of anywhere near the value given were on board they were in the mail bags and not among the freight, and any bonds of great value were also in the custody of the mail authorities. The vessel carried 3,428 bags of mail.

It is the custom of the steamship company to learn by cable the precious nature and value of any freight of more than usual value such as bullion, precious stones or negotiable securities, so that special attention may be paid to them on their arrival. But no word came from over the sea about any freight of more than ordinary value in the hold of the *Titanic*. So it was decisively said yesterday by the White Star Company's manager of incoming freight that whatever of extraordinary value was between the decks of the ship was in the mail bags …

'We never know anything about the freight a ship is carrying until it arrives here,' said one of the freight managers. 'The purser makes up his manifest during the voyage and turns it in when he gets here. Then the various cases and barrels and packages and so forth are checked off and care is taken to see that they get into the proper hands. Then our responsibility ends.

'But whenever any art treasures, bullion, jewels or any other thing of more than ordinary value is shipped our agents on the other side cable the list, the approximate value, the consignors, the name of the consignees, and all other necessary information to us. In the matter of the *Titanic*, we have received no such word and so we do not think that the vessel bore much of value among the freight. Of course, we do not know what is in the mail bags.'[17]

Additional information about the insuring of *Titanic*'s diamond consignments was presented in a second newspaper article on the subject:

In this disaster, too, the underwriters sustain what will rank as one of the most curious and costly single losses ever taken. On the *Titanic* was a $2,000,000 consignment of diamonds. These were insured in London at a total premium for the voyage of $1,100, says the *New York Evening Post*. In point of premium received for the risk taken, therefore, this loss will probably rank as the most disastrous on record for the underwriters. It is possible that the diamonds have been saved and that the precious package

> was immediately transferred with the women passengers. At any rate, the underwriters are figuring on paying over the money to the insured as soon as the loss is definitely established …
>
> Diamonds are covered by special forms of insurance, written chiefly in London. The underwriters assume all the risks encountered from the moment that the diamonds are surrendered by their owners until delivery is made to consignee. Losses have been so few and far between that heavy risks have been taken at very low rates, generally 5 cents per $100 of insurance carried.
>
> Except for the possibility of saving the package of diamonds, insurance men do not expect to get anything out of the *Titanic* wreck …
>
> None of the underwriters knows just what amount they have at stake on the *Titanic*. This was due to the fact that much of the insurance was written on yearly policies which cover cargo sent by various shippers to all parts of the world. Invoices showing the goods sent and the conditions of shipment might have been aboard the lost ship. Cable advices will later clear up these details and make plain just what risks each company carried and what losses it must quickly pay.[18]

We have just established the definite existence of the Laura Moore, Ehrmann & Bahlsen and Richard Roe diamond consignments on board the *Titanic*, and we have listed the possible existence of two additional shipments – the Wattrell and Ichberg consignments. We have also shown that these shipments were not listed on *Titanic*'s cargo manifest because they were given into the custody of the ship's postal clerks and were probably inside bags of registered mail in the ship's post office. (Since the jewel-encrusted *Rubaiyat of Omar Khayyam* was likewise unmentioned in the *Titanic*'s cargo manifest, this valuable edition of the book was probably posted as an insured registered parcel as well and was inside a bag of registered post just like the diamond shipments.)

But what about other caches of diamonds that were on board the *Titanic* during her maiden voyage? One of our earlier newspaper articles suggested that several Amsterdam diamond merchants were transporting their own consignments of diamonds during the *Titanic*'s maiden voyage. Although there were no (literal) Amsterdam diamond merchants on board the *Titanic*, does any evidence prove that such private diamond consignments really did exist?

Before we examine the evidence pertaining to this topic, the presence of two alleged private consignments of diamonds on the *Titanic* can be disproved without difficulty.

Non-Existent Private Caches of Diamonds

Madeleine Astor

After the *Titanic* went down it was rumoured that survivor Mrs John Jacob Astor had a fortune in diamonds with her on board the great vessel:

> Paris, April 30 – It is reported here that Mrs John Jacob Astor had with her on the *Titanic* diamonds of the value of 15,000,000 francs, or $3,000,000, which she bought from Cartier, the Paris jeweller. The latter refuses to confirm or deny this statement that he sold that amount of diamonds to her.[19]

This report about the rumoured Astor diamonds is included here just for the sake of completeness, because (1) these diamonds were probably set in pieces of jewellery and were not uncut stones, and (2) they were personal items not intended for resale via commercial diamond merchants. This latter fact is confirmed by another newspaper article that appeared shortly after the disaster:

> Mrs John Jacob Astor has gained enough strength to tell the detailed story of how she was saved from the *Titanic* just before the great White Star steamship went to the bottom a week ago today. The young woman's grief and illness resulting from the terrible experience made it imperative for her physicians to order that she do but little talking, but bit by bit she has told all details of what she knew of the wreck. The fractional parts of her story were told to her mother, Mrs W.H. Force, her sister, Miss Katherine Force, and her Physician, Dr Ruel B. Kimball …
>
> Colonel Astor returned in about five minutes and told his wife that the damage was far more serious than he had at first thought. He had talked with Captain Smith and thought it best that she should go at once to the boat deck. Before they left the suite Colonel Astor opened his wife's jewel case and took from it her most valuable gems, including a string of pearls, her engagement ring and several other pieces of great value and told her to take them with her.[20]

A few days later, Colonel Astor's son Vincent made it clear to reporters that his stepmother did not lose a fortune in jewellery on board the *Titanic*:

> There is another matter concerning the reported loss of Mrs Astor's jewels, which is – whatever jewels are bought by any member of the family are not

carried by them. The jewels of the family are always carried and cared for by agents of the family. Mrs Astor had very few jewels with her.[21]

Evalyn McLean

A tiny article in the *New York Herald* claimed that the infamous Hope diamond (owned by socialite Evalyn McLean) was reportedly lost on the *Titanic*. However, a longer follow-up article in the same issue of the newspaper made it clear that the jewel was still safe with its owner in Washington, D.C.[22]

Authentic Private Consignments of Diamonds

Now that we've examined and dismissed these two mistaken accounts of lost diamonds, let's consider a number of diamond consignments that definitely existed and remained in the possession of their owners during the *Titanic*'s maiden voyage.

Jakob Birnbaum

Jakob Birnbaum was a diamond merchant who headed the jewellery firm of J. Birnbaum & Co. In January 1912 Birnbaum sailed for the United Kingdom on a European buying trip for his jewellery firm, and on 11 April 1912 he wrote to a young friend from the *Titanic* fulfilling his promise to send the boy some foreign coins with holes in their centres. Birnbaum's letter provides indirect evidence that he also purchased a fair number of diamonds while he was in Europe:

> Going back to America. I remind myself of the promise I gave you to send you some Belgian money with holes. As I spent a whole lot of money in Europe I cannot send you more than the amount you will find enclosed.[23]

Despite having spent 'a whole lot of money' during his buying trip, no diamonds were reported to have been found on Birnbaum's body when it was recovered after the disaster. In light of information that will be discussed momentarily, it seems that Birnbaum must have concealed his diamonds somewhere in his first-class stateroom.

It also appears that Birnbaum was transporting a second consignment of diamonds in addition to the stones he acquired for his own business:

> David Zaslave, the well-known local jeweler, had his diamond agent on the steamship *Titanic* … The agent was Jacob Birnbaum of New York,

whose body … was picked up by the Mackey-Bennett … Mr Birnbaum was coming to this country with a consignment of diamonds, some of them for Mr Zaslave, and he was scheduled to come to Waterbury three days after the docking of the ship in New York …

Said Mr Zaslave Saturday, 'I couldn't sleep at all last night after I read in the papers that Mr Birnbaum was drowned. I thought he would be on the *Titanic*, but I didn't read his name until last night. I am glad that his body was recovered, however.'

Mr Zaslave intends to go to New York when the body arrives there … The diamonds intended for Mr Zaslave were lost, it is supposed, with the rest. Just what amount is represented by Mr Zaslave's loss he does not care to say. 'I lost some diamonds, but I don't want to name the amount of money involved,' he said.

Some of Mr Zaslave's own diamonds were lost, too. He gave them to Mr Birnbaum to match in Europe … for similar size and quality.

'I wanted those stones matched for a special reason,' said Mr Zaslave, 'but now they are lost. I do not feel a half, or a quarter, so sorry to lose them, though, as I do to lose my good friend, Jake Birnbaum.'[24]

After the *Titanic* went down it was reported that Birnbaum was bringing a consignment of diamonds with him to America:

San Francisco. Cal., April 26 – Jacob Birnbaum, whose body was recovered by the *Mackay-Bennett*, was a San Francisco jeweler and was bringing a quantity of jewelry from Antwerp. Letters of administration in his estate were filed here Monday.[25]

In May 1912 steps were taken to recover financial remuneration for the death of Mr Birnbaum and the loss of his property:

SAN FRANCISCO, May 7 – The public administrator is laying plans to bring suit against the White Star Line, owners of the steamship Titanic, as a result of the death of Jacob Birnbaum, a diamond importer of this city. Birnbaum lost his life while he was a passenger on the ship and is numbered among the heroes who went down. He is believed to have had a large quantity of diamonds with him.

The action will be brought by the administrator in the event that he discovers relatives for whom he is now searching. It is probable that suit will

> be brought for damages for loss of life on the part of the decedent as well as for the jewels which went down with the vessel.[26]

The National Archives at Bayonne, New Jersey, once possessed the records of the 1913 *Titanic* Limitation of Liability hearings, and a notation in those records recorded that Birnbaum was transporting $2,000 worth of diamonds during the *Titanic*'s maiden voyage.[27]

Henry Blank

Henry Blank was a partner in the manufacturing jewellery firm of Whiteside & Blank in Newark, New Jersey. In spring 1912 he travelled to Europe to conduct business with watch movement manufacturers in Switzerland and with stone dealers in Paris, Belgium and Amsterdam:

> By the time of the *Titanic* disaster in 1912, Blank had become a distinguished jeweler, [Sam] Joseph said. He was on his way to Europe to buy diamonds.
>
> 'He made watch casings for Tiffany and Cartier when money was flowing like bootleg liquor,' Joseph said.[28]*

Charlotte Cardeza

After the disaster Mrs Cardeza filed a claim for the loss of the following item that she had deposited with the *Titanic*'s purser:

> Pink diamond, 6-7/16 carats. Tiffany, New York. $20,000.[29]

Walter Hawksford

Hawksford's specific profession is a bit uncertain. The 1911 census lists him as living in Kingston, Surrey, and making his living as an export representative, but *Hampshire Magazine* of July 1991 says he was working for Schweppes and was on a business trip for them. Moreover, the *Surrey Advertiser* of 20 April 1912 said Hawksford was a diamond merchant who was travelling to New York on business. (His wife was to have accompanied him, but the sister in Canada with whom she was to stay became ill.) There is not yet any direct evidence that Hawksford had diamonds with him on board the *Titanic*, but if the *Surrey Advertiser* was correct about his being a diamond merchant the possibility cannot be ruled out.

---

* Sam Joseph was a Montclair, New Jersey realtor who used to live in Henry Blank's home.

Erwin Lewy

Ervin Lewy and his two brothers owned and operated Lewy Brothers Jewelers in Chicago. On 15 January 1912 Ervin departed for Amsterdam on a diamond purchasing trip, and for his return to Chicago he boarded the *Titanic* as a first-class passenger in Cherbourg:

> Erwin J. Lewy of 5628 South Park Avenue and W. Irwin G. Lewy, members of the jewelry firm of Lewy Brothers, State and Adams Streets, are thought to have been drowned. W. Irwin G. Lewy left Chicago five weeks ago to purchase jewelry in Europe for the firm of Lewy Brothers. Mr Lewy's brother and partner, M. D. Lewy, today said:
>
> 'My brother sailed about five weeks ago for the annual purchase of diamonds and other jewelry. He visited Paris, Naples, and Amsterdam while in Europe. We have had no word from the White Star, nor any messages from my brother.'[30]

A hint about the possible value of Mr Lewy's lost diamonds is contained in a newspaper article that appeared a year after the *Titanic* went down:

> A claim of $100,000 has been made by Mark Levy and J. D. Levy for the death of Irving G. Levy of Chicago, and $5,460 for property.[31]

The centenary of the *Titanic* disaster saw renewed interest in Lewy's lost consignment of diamonds:

> As the world commemorates the 100th anniversary of the sinking of the *Titanic*, the descendants of a jeweler who made the fateful trip still hope that his lost inventory will be found …
>
> In 1912, Ervin Lewy, the youngest brother, went to Europe on a diamond buying trip. After poor luck purchasing diamonds in Amsterdam, Ervin decided to stay in Europe a few extra days and take the *Titanic* back to the United States. 'I'll be here about a week yet to see if I can't do better …' Ervin wrote in a letter he sent home.
>
> Ervin died when the ship sunk and never made it back to America, but a gift he sent his mother arrived in the post shortly after the voyage. 'He was in Paris and saw a sapphire with a cameo carved into it at Cartier and sent it to my grandmother through mail,' Stanley Lewy, Ervin's great-nephew, says. 'When the sapphire arrived my grandfather set the stone in a ring surrounded by baguette diamonds.'

The family heirloom has been passed down from generation to generation. Originally worn by Stanley's grandmother, it has since been worn by his mother and now belongs to his daughter. However, the diamonds that Ervin purchased in Europe remain a mystery. 'It was possible that he purchased quite a bit of diamonds when he was on his trip,' Stanley says.

Although the diamonds have yet to be found, Stanley was contacted in 2000 with favorable news. 'Historians contacted me and told me that they had located two probable areas where the diamonds may have been,' he says. 'It is thought that the diamonds may reside in the captain's safe or the bursar's bag at the bottom of the ocean.'[32]

David Livshin

For some unknown reason, Mr Livshin was travelling on the *Titanic* under the pseudonym 'Abraham Harmer'. Although we have no concrete evidence he was transporting a shipment of diamonds, researcher Geoff Whitfield has written, 'David Livshin from Manchester, [was] going ahead of his pregnant wife, Chyna, to set up a jewelry business in the USA.'[33] When asked by fellow researcher Randy Bigham if Livshin might have used an assumed name because he didn't want to be robbed of a large amount of jewellery, Whitfield replied:

> I don't think that Livshin would have had diamonds – although – you've got me thinking here Randy! – he may have been carrying them for someone else? If that was the case, wouldn't his first reaction be to put them in his pocket – he didn't know he was going to drown, after all!
>
> The Livshin family are under the impression that he was not so much a jeweler as a watch and clock repairer – though he may have been hoping to branch out once in America.[34]

Milton Long

On 22 February 1999, Milton J. Long (a modern-day relative of the *Titanic* passenger) of Gahanna, Ohio, wrote a letter to the Titanic Historical Society regarding something his grandfather, jeweller Henry B. Long, told him. The gist of the story was this:

> Early in 1912 Judge Charles L. Long spoke with his relative Henry Long and told him that his son Milton was planning to hide some jewels and gold in his steamer trunk in order to avoid paying customs duties on those items when he returned from overseas. Although the judge disapproved of his son's plan, he nevertheless asked Henry the jeweler if Milton could dispose

of the smuggled jewels and gold in his hometown without any unforeseen legal problems arising. After the *Titanic* went down the Judge never mentioned the matter to Henry Long again.[35]

Samuel and Emma Risien

Samuel and Emma Risien were residents of Corsicana, Texas. Researcher Craig Stringer writes:

> In South Africa they [the Risiens] had collected diamonds, some of which were presumably for Johnathon [Samuel's brother, a diamond dealer], although it seems Samuel had some of his own … Samuel and Emma boarded the *Titanic* at Southampton on April 10th. They had booked to travel third class, believing they no one would think a third class passenger would be carrying valuable diamonds.[36]

Researcher Phil Gowan, a resident of Corsicana, writes:

> 'When I was 4, my grandma had a lady friend [Rosa Risien] over to visit one morning, and I was sitting on the floor playing with a plastic boat,' said Phillip Gowan, now 59 and a retired telecommunications engineer living in suburban Nashville.
>
> 'This lady told me, "My husband's mother and daddy got drowned on a boat one time and they were bringing diamonds with them,"' he recalled Tuesday. '"When you grow up, you have to find those diamonds."'[37]
>
> ---
>
> As a long-time *Titanic* buff I have always been interested in this couple as my parents were friends for a time with Charlie and Rosa (Bostick) Risien of Corsicana, Texas (where I was born and raised). My mother's best friend was Mrs Daisy Bostick whose husband would have been a stepson of Charlie Risien. I was born in 1952 – 4 years after Charlie's death but Rosa lived until about 1984 and I remember her well … Daisy Bostick and her husband Earl once told me that Samuel and Emma had been on a trip to Durban, South Africa to buy diamonds and all went down on the *Titanic* …[38]
>
> ---
>
> After the death of Mary Louise Risien, Samuel remarried to Emma (maiden name unknown), who was a native of Durban, South Africa where her family apparently had an interest in diamond mines. Late in 1910, Samuel and Emma went back to Durban and stayed for about 14 months. Family lore has them bringing back diamonds and travelling third class so no one

> would guess what they were carrying in their huge suitcases – this may be true as they were a fairly well-to-do family in northeastern Texas and it is curious that they were travelling steerage.[39]

Frances Reynolds, the Risiens' great-granddaughter, writes:

> Samuel Beard Risien was my great-grandfather ... There is no definite confirmation whether Samuel and Emma were bringing diamonds back. This is part of the story my mother, Sadie Louise Risien Reynolds Shumway, told me. It might be logical that they were since Jonathan Risien was a diamond merchant in London. It is conjecture that they sailed third class because that is all they could get. We (my sister and cousins) think they might have had passage on another ship, but because of the coal strike they could not sail on that ship, so took what they could get on the *Titanic*.[40]

Laura Myhre, another of the Risiens' great-granddaughters, writes:

> According to my grandmother [Sadie Louise Risien who is Charles J.'s* only daughter], Emma and Samuel were bringing back diamonds from a family diamond mine in Johannesburg, South Africa and sailed third class so as not to draw suspicion to their heavy luggage.[41]

Civil War researcher Terry Foenander writes:

> Emma's family is noted as having an interest in some diamond mines in Durban, South Africa, where they were resident at the time. Sam and Emma had apparently gone to Durban in 1910 to visit the family, and were on their way home, via London, when they decided to travel aboard the *Titanic* on its maiden voyage to America. They embarked aboard the *Titanic* on April 10, 1912, at Southampton. Family lore speculates that they were carrying some diamonds from the Lellyet family mines, when they boarded the vessel, and were using the third class facilities so as not to arouse suspicion.[42]

In observing the centennial of the *Titanic* disaster, a reporter for the *Corsicana Daily Sun* wrote:

---

* Charles J. Risien was a son of Samuel and Emma Risien.

With the difficulty in obtaining coal and therefore a limited number of opportunities to sail, Risien and Emma Jane made the return to the United States as third-class passengers aboard the *Titanic*'s maiden voyage. Their station in life certainly afforded them higher accommodations, [their great-granddaughter Fran] Reynolds said, and it's believed a third-class passage was all they could obtain, although that 'fact' is one that also involves a story or two – one that has the couple transporting diamonds from South Africa and not wishing to be 'discovered,' although Reynolds doesn't believe that to be the case.

'I think they would have taken first or second class, because they had the means to do that,' Reynolds said.

Reynolds does, however, have a diamond that was handed down to her – an engagement diamond from her grandmother, she said.[43]

Mrs Edward Robert

After arriving back in St Louis, Mrs Robert told newspaper reporters about a collection of 'jewels' or 'gems' she had been bringing back to the States. It's uncertain if these 'jewels' were actually pieces of jewellery instead, but we include the newspaper report here for the sake of completeness:

> Mrs Robert is mourning the loss of a valuable collection of jewels which went down with the *Titanic*. It was not until the party returned to St. Louis that their friends learned details of the loss. Although Mrs Robert declines to state the exact value of the gems, it is known to be considerable.
>
> After the liner had crashed into the iceberg and the women had been ordered into the lifeboats, Mrs Robert's maid, Emilie Kreuchen, 3453 Iowa Avenue, remembered the jewels. She hastened back to their cabin and seized a black handbag in which they were usually carried on their travels.
>
> Throughout the exciting incidents that followed, the maid clung to the bag. When she was being taken up a ladder by the side of the rescue ship, the *Carpathia*, with a rope from above under her arms, a lurch of the vessel caused her to drop the bag. It was caught by a seaman in the lifeboat beneath. When the maid proudly put the bag into the hands of Mrs Robert, she was dismayed to learn that the jewels and about $1,000 in cash had been locked up in the purser's safe aboard the *Titanic* and had gone down with the ship. The bag contained only a few trifling toilet articles.[44]

Austin van Billiard

Speculation about Mr van Billiard's lost diamonds began almost immediately after the *Titanic* disaster. James W. van Billiard, Chief Burgess of North Wales, Pennsylvania, was interviewed in the newspapers about the loss of his son, Austin:

> Two grandchildren and a son of James W. van Billiard of North Wales, Pa., who were passengers on the *Titanic*, were vainly sought in New York yesterday by the children's uncle, James van Billiard Jr. Austin van Billiard, the father, with his son James and Walter, aged eleven and nine, sailed from Liverpool [*sic*] on the *Titanic* according to a cablegram received from Mrs Maude van Billiard in London. They were on the *Titanic*'s steerage list, but missing in the list of survivors.
>
> James van Billiard Jr. told a reporter for *The World* yesterday that his brother had been for many years in the diamond fields of the Congo Free State, Central Africa, and had amassed there a fortune in uncut stones. In the hope of realizing good prices on the diamonds in New York he and his two eldest boys left Mrs van Billiard in London with her little daughter and baby boy. They wanted to surprise the family Austin van Billiard had not seen for many years and whom his children did not know.
>
> The plan was upset by Mrs van Billiard's illness, and Austin van Billiard then wrote his father that he might soon be expected. He had several of his diamonds cut in Amsterdam, then wrote that he would sail for the United States the latter part of April. It is believed he brought his diamonds with him and that they went down with the *Titanic*.[45]

James van Billiard was interviewed by a second newspaper about the loss of his son:

> He said that his son probably had a great many valuable uncut diamonds with him, as he had spent the past five years in the African diamond fields.[46]

General stories were also written about the loss of Austin van Billiard.

> Although travelling in the steerage, it is believed by the family that Austin van Billiard was returning home with many thousand dollars' worth of diamonds, mostly uncut stones. He was extremely fortunate in his mining ventures in Africa. It is believed that the man sailed earlier with the expectation of surprising his relatives.[47]

> While the exact amount is not known, it is believed that Austin van Billiard was returning home with many thousand dollars' worth of diamonds, mostly uncut stones. For the last six years he has been in the diamond fields in Congo Free State, Central Africa, and, judging from numerous letters received, his father believed that he had been extremely fortunate in his mining ventures.[48]

Researcher Craig Stringer has written a brief biography of van Billiard in which he says:

> In 1906 the van Billiard family decided to move to Africa. Austin purchased a part share in a diamond mine in the Congo Free State, and took his young family with him … Austin's venture proved successful, but by 1912 the family … decided to return to the van Billiard family in America. However, on arriving back in England the family discovered that their travel plans would have to be delayed … Austin used the delay to travel to Amsterdam, where he could have the diamonds he had with him valued, or even sold … They boarded the *Titanic* as third class passengers … Austin had with him a quantity of diamonds.[49]

According to a recent article about van Billiard:

> Austin had with him at least a dozen large uncut diamonds with which he likely planned to start a new business in this country. He reportedly stored others in the ship's safe.[50]

In October 1958, Maud Helen van Billiard (Austin's widow) wrote a one-page typed memoir that contained the following statement:

> Our prospecting was successful, and we continued north to Rhodesia. From there we entrained for Elizabeth Villa. There we found our children were the only white ones in the village. At that time our family consisted of four boys and one girl. After a short stay here we decided to return to London, this being a three weeks trip. My husband, having successfully contacted diamond brokers in New York City, booked passage for himself and the two older boys on the *Titanic*.[51]

After van Billiard's body was recovered, the list of personal effects found on his body was as follows:

> EFFECTS – Pipe; £3. 5s. in purse; gold watch, 'J.B.' on back; 12 loose diamonds; 1 pair cuff links.[52]

At one time the National Archives at Bayonne, New Jersey, possessed the records of the 1913 *Titanic* Limitation of Liability hearings, and one notation in those papers stated that van Billiard was transporting twelve diamonds that were valued at $800.[53]

Van Billiard died intestate, and the papers administrating his estate were filed on 10 June 1912. The final papers of administration contained the following notation:

> 1913, May: Received from sale of rough and uncut diamonds, $637.90.[54]

August Wennerström

In later years August Wennerström gave lectures about his experiences on the *Titanic* that included the following information:

> Wennerström and 'a couple girls' with him did not have lifebelts yet, and began searching for some, 'knowing now that they surely would be needed.' Eventually, their search led them into one of the First Class suites. There were 'magnificent suits, clothing thrown all over, on the table were jewels and diamonds, and on other tables champagne …' In the second room of this suite, August found his life preserver, right next to a pitcher of water.[55]

Three Additional Personal Diamond Caches?

When the bodies of *Titanic* victims were recovered by the *Mackay-Bennett* and the *Minia*, it became apparent that possibly three different passengers lost their lives while carrying hidden caches of diamonds on their persons.

Francis Dyke

Francis Dyke was serving as the *Minia*'s temporary wireless operator when he wrote a letter to his mother describing his vessel's recovery of the bodies of *Titanic* victims:

> They say there was tons of money on some of the bodies when they were picked up. Astor had $10,000 & another man had a bag of diamonds hung

> around his neck worth $250,000. Some of the jewels that went down in her were worth enough to buy ½ doz *Minias*, one woman's pearls alone were worth $450,000.[56]

No mention of this bag of diamonds appears on the official list of recovered bodies and personal effects.

Arminias Wiseman

A second diamond-carrying *Titanic* victim was written about by Arminias Wiseman, a fireman on the recovery ship *Mackay-Bennett*:

> During the search of the bodies various things were found, trinkets of all kinds, and souvenirs. I very clearly recall a mass of wet tissue paper taken from the pocket of one victim and when it was opened a small handful of sparkling jewels of some kind fell to the deck and rolled down in the scuppers. They were quickly gathered up of course and packaged with the rest of the belongings.[57]

A description of (apparently) the same passenger appeared in a book compilation of 1912 newspaper accounts of the disaster:

> The little repair shop on the *Mackay-Bennett* was a treasure house when she came to port. Fifteen thousand dollars in money was found on the recovered bodies and jewelry that will be worth a king's ransom. One of the crew related his experience with one dead man whose pockets he turned inside out only to have seventeen diamonds roll out in every direction upon the littered deck.[58]

The body described by Wiseman and the unknown *Mackay-Bennett* crewman might possibly have been that of Austin van Billiard, even though the present body was supposedly carrying seventeen diamonds whereas van Billiard's body was carrying only twelve. If the present body was not van Billiard's, it should be noted that no mention of this victim's seventeen recovered diamonds appears on the official list of recovered bodies and personal effects.

Gerald Ross

A third diamond-carrying *Titanic* victim was recovered by the *Mackay-Bennett* and was described by the vessel's electrician in 1912:

> 'We came across a diamond smuggler,' said Electrician Ross, 'a Swede travelling in the steerage. He was among the 116 consigned to ocean graves.
>
> 'I felt a peculiar hard lump in the back of his coat. I told my workmate and we ripped the lining and found a half dozen fine diamonds sewn there. This man was not identified. The diamonds were turned over to the purser with the other valuables taken from the unidentified bodies and all placed in the custody of the White Star Line.'[59]

No mention of this sewn cache of diamonds appears on the official list of recovered bodies and personal effects.

Summary and Conclusions

Unconfirmed reports of diamond shipments worth anywhere from $2 million to $5 million dollars surfaced after the loss of the *Titanic*, but these reports remained unconfirmed and a number of jewellery experts felt they were probably mistaken. Although it was reportedly well known in New York's diamond district that a number of local jewellers were expecting consignments of diamonds on the *Titanic*, subsequent queries failed to turn up the specific names of those local firms. This lack of information about the intended recipients was apparently due to the fact that much of the insurance was written on yearly policies covering cargo that was sent by various shippers to all parts of the world, and it was also believed that invoices showing the consignments and the conditions of shipment might have been lost in the sinking.

Even so, newspaper reports claimed that the firm of Ichberg & Company lost a consignment of diamonds that was worth considerably less than a million dollars, and Pittsburgh jeweller W. Wattrell died of a heart attack after learning about the loss of a second consignment of diamonds that was reportedly being transported to him from Paris.

Despite the uncertainty surrounding the two diamond shipments being sent to specific consignees in the United States, at least three additional shipments of diamonds *definitely* existed on board the *Titanic* – the Laura Moore, Ehrmann & Bahlsen and Richard Roe shipments worth $7,720, £934.0.8 and £775 respectively. No record of these shipments appeared on the *Titanic*'s cargo manifest because such shipments were customarily consigned to the ship's postal clerks and were probably being transported as insured pieces of registered post instead of in the cargo hold. Since these three consignments of diamonds are known to have existed despite the lack of pre-sinking records to that effect, additional diamond consignments could easily have existed right alongside them inside the bags of registered post in the *Titanic*'s mail room. In other words, the 1912 newspaper reports about expensive diamond consignments on board the *Titanic* might have had a solid basis in fact.

Regarding personal diamond consignments that passengers retained in their own possession, we have shown that the alleged Madeleine Astor and Hope diamond cases had no basis in fact, and it's presently unknown if Henry Blank, David Livshin, Walter Hawksford and Milton Long were transporting diamonds at all. In later years third-class passenger August Wennerström claimed to have seen 'jewels and diamonds' scattered on a table in a first-class suite, but – although he might have been telling the truth – it's also possible he was embellishing his account for dramatic effect.

On the other hand, seemingly reliable family stories claim that Samuel and Emma Risien were transporting diamonds they'd gleaned from their mining interests in South Africa, but the truth of these accounts cannot yet be verified.

We know that Jacob Birnbaum was transporting $2,000 worth of diamonds for his own firm, but this sum doesn't include the additional consignment of diamonds he was transporting for his friend David Zaslave. Charlotte Cardeza filed a claim for $20,000 for the loss of a single pink 6½-carat diamond, and Ervin Lewy was transporting diamonds that his brothers apparently valued at $5,460. Austin van Billiard was reportedly transporting 'many thousands of dollars' worth of diamonds that he obtained in the Congo Free State, but the twelve stones recovered on his body were valued at only $800 and were sold for only $637.90 (although it was later said that van Billiard had entrusted additional diamonds to the *Titanic*'s safe).

The *Minia* supposedly recovered the body of a male victim with a bag of diamonds worth $250,000 hung around his neck. The *Mackay-Bennett* recovered the body of another man who was carrying seventeen diamonds in the pocket of his trousers, and the same vessel picked up the body of a 'Swede' who had half a dozen diamonds sewn into the lining of his coat and whose body was later consigned to the deep.

One wonders how many additional *Titanic* passengers might have had diamonds in their possession when the great ship went down, and how many additional European jewellery firms might have entrusted 'unknown' diamond consignments to the ship's post office without knowing that their stones were destined to remain hidden in *Titanic*'s registered mail bags for all time.

12

Dinner

We present a selection of survivor accounts describing dinner in *Titanic*'s Ritz restaurant and in the first-class dining room on the evening of 14 April 1912. We also present a selection of accounts describing how various passengers occupied their time after finishing their dinner.

The Restaurant

Mahala Douglas wrote:

> On Sunday we had a delightful day; everyone in the best of spirits; the time the boat was making was considered very good, and all were interested in getting into New York early. We dined in the restaurant, going in about 8 o'clock. We found the people dining, as follows: (See sketch of dining room.) As far as I have been able to learn, not a man in that room [was saved]; all those who served, from the head steward down, including Mr Gatti, in charge; the musicians who played in the corridor outside, and all the guests were lost except Sir Cosmo Duff Gordon, Mr Carter, and Mr Ismay. All stories of excessive gaiety are, to my mind, absolutely unfounded.[1]

In later years Mrs Douglas wrote:

> On the *Titanic*. We dined the last night in the Ritz restaurant. It was the last word in luxury. The tables were gay with pink roses and white daisies, the women in their beautiful shimmering gowns of satin and silk, the men immaculate and well-groomed, the stringed orchestra playing music from

Puccini and Tchaikovsky. The food was superb: caviar, lobster, quail from Egypt, plover's eggs, and hothouse grapes and fresh peaches. The night was cold and clear, the sea like glass.[2]

Lady Duff Gordon wrote:

I remember that last meal on the Titanic very well. We had a big vase of beautiful daffodils on the table, which were as fresh as if they had just been picked. Everybody was very gay, and at neighboring tables people were making bets on the probable time of this record-breaking run. Bruce Ismay, Chairman of the White Star Line, was dining with the ship's doctor [William O'Loughlin] next to our table, and I remember that several men appealed to him as to how much longer we should be at sea. Various opinions were put forward, but none dreamed that the Titanic would make her harbor that night. Mr Ismay was most confident, and said that undoubtedly the ship would establish a record.

Further along the room the [George] Wideners and the Thayers (American multi-millionaires both of them) were dining with the Captain and others, and there was a great deal of laughter and chatter from their table. It was the last time I saw them. At another table sat Colonel Jacob Astor and his young bride. They were coming back to New York after a honeymoon in Europe, and I thought how much in love they were – poor things, it was the last few hours they were to have together. They were joined by Isidor Straus, the multi-millionaire and his wife. These two so openly adored one another that we used to call them 'Darby and Joan' on the ship. They told us laughingly that in their long years of married life they had never been separated for one day or night …[3]

May Futrelle wrote:

There was not the slightest thought of danger in the minds of those who sat around the tables on the luxurious saloon after-deck. It was a brilliant crowd. Jewels flashed from the gowns of the women. And oh, the dear women, how fondly they wore their latest Parisian gowns. It was the first time that most of them had an opportunity to display their newly acquired finery. The soft sweet odors of rare flowers pervaded the atmosphere. I remember at our table was a great bunch of American Beauty roses. The orchestra played popular music. It was a buoyant, oh, such a jolly crowd.[4]

Rene Harris remembered:

> When I entered the Ritz Room I had a reception from all the diners, most of whom I had not met. It made me feel that a broken arm was an asset. The table to which we were shown was next to that of Bruce Ismay, the managing director of the White Star Line. His party numbered ten or twelve. I had just sat down at our table when Captain Smith came into the room. I had not before met the captain. In passing our table, he stopped, complimented me on my spirit, and went to an unoccupied place at the Ismay table. He was not there five minutes, for on his passing me again I asked him if he wasn't going to stay to enjoy the festivities. He answered that he was going back to the bridge because of the presence of icebergs in the region where we were. Captain Smith had not indulged in any drinking bout, as has been the general impression. On the contrary, he was one hundred percent on his job.[5]

Daisy Minahan wrote:

> My brother, his wife, and myself went to the cafe for dinner at about 7:15 p.m. (ship's time). When we entered there was a dinner party already dining, consisting of perhaps a dozen men and three women. Capt. Smith was a guest, as also were Mr and Mrs Widener, Mr and Mrs Blair [Thayer], and Maj. Butt. Capt. Smith was continuously with his party from the time we entered until between 9:25 and 9:45, when he bid the women good night and left. I know this time positively, for at 9:25 my brother suggested my going to bed. We waited for one more piece of the orchestra, and it was between 9:25 and 9:45 (the time we departed), that Capt. Smith left. Sitting within a few feet of this party were also Sir Cosmo and Lady Duff Gordon, a Mrs Meyer of New York, and Mrs Smith of Virginia. Mr and Mrs Harris were also dining in the café at the same time.[6]

Mary Eloise Smith wrote:

> At 7.30 p.m., as usual, my husband and I went to dinner in the cafe … At a quarter of 9 o'clock … we left the dining room. There was a coffee room directly outside of the cafe, in which people sat and listened to the music and drank coffee and cordials after dinner.[7]

Marian Thayer wrote:

My husband and I were guests at a dinner in the restaurant on Sunday evening, the 14th of April, given by Mr and Mrs Widener. Captain Smith was there, also Major Butt and others. We entered the restaurant at 7:35 p.m. I am sure that our party, including Captain Smith, left the restaurant, to have coffee, before 8:30 p.m., as the dinner was served very quickly. We went out into the hall by the companionway for that purpose. Captain Smith had left our party and gone towards his own quarters by a quarter of nine o'clock, at the latest.

My husband, my son and I were the only persons at the Captain's table in the Saloon. The Captain usually took his meals in the Saloon, but did not do so for about the first day and a half after sailing. I noticed that the Captain never took any alcoholic liquor of any kind at any meal.

I do not remember hearing, during the dinner on Sunday night, any mention made by any person of ice being in the neighborhood, or that we might expect to see ice, as Mr Widener, Major Butt and I were deeply engrossed in conversation on other subjects during the entire time of the dinner.[8]

The First-Class Dining Room

Helen Candee recorded:

And after dinner there was coffee served to all at little tables around the great general lounging place, for here the orchestra played. Some said it was poor on its Wagner work, others said the violin was weak. But that was for conversation's sake, for nothing on board was more popular than the orchestra. You could see that by the way everyone refused to leave it. And everyone asked of it some favourite hit. The prettiest girl asked for dance music, and clicked her satin heels and swayed her adolescent arms to the rhythm.

He of the Two [Edward Kent] who had walked the deck asked for Dvorak, while she asked for Puccini, and both got their liking, for the orchestra was adroit and willing. At eleven, folk drifted off to their big cabins, with happy 'see-you-in-the-mornings,' until a group formed itself alone, and the only sounds the musicians made were those of instruments being shut in their velvet beds.[9]

Archibald Gracie wrote:

> That night after dinner, with my table companions, Messrs. James Clinch Smith and Edward A. Kent, according to the usual custom, we adjourned to the palm room, with many others, for the usual coffee at individual tables where we listened to the always delightful music of the *Titanic*'s band.[10]

Elsewhere Gracie was recorded as saying, 'The band or orchestra had been playing ragtime just before the collision.'[11]

Violet Jessop wrote:

> On that Sunday evening, the music was at its gayest, led by young Jock [Hume] the first violin; when I ran into him during the interval, he laughingly called out to me in his rich Scotch accent, that he was about to give them a 'real tune, a Scotch tune, to finish up with.' Always so eager and full of life was Jock.[12]

Helen Ostby recalled:

> There was the usual Sunday evening concert by the ship's orchestra in the main lounge, and after that nearly everybody retired early to their cabins.[13]

Arthur Peuchen testified:

> Sunday evening I dined with my friends, Markleham [Markland] Molson, Mr Allison, and Mrs Allison; and their daughter was there for a short time. The dinner was an exceptionally good dinner. It seemed to be a better bill of fare than usual, although they are all good. After dinner my friends and I went to the sitting-out room and had some coffee. I left the friends I had dined with about 9 o'clock, I think, or a little later.[14]

Edith Rosenbaum wrote:

> Sunday night, the night of the wreck, there was a gala dinner. The lounge presented a very beautiful spectacle; everyone in evening clothes and the orchestra playing sacred as well as other music. The sight of this gaily dressed crowd contrasted vividly with the pathos of the following night aboard the *Carpathia*. At 9:30 I went to the drawing-room and started to write letters.[15]

The Countess of Rothes and her cousin, **Gladys Cherry**, listened to the concert in the first-class reception room. The countess recalled that the bandsmen played a selection from Jacques Offenbach's 'The Tales of Hoffman' as their 'last piece of after-dinner music' that night.[16]

Elizabeth Shutes wrote:

> We passed by the palm room, where two short hours before we had listened to a beautiful concert, just as one might sit in one's own home.[17]

Margaretta Spedden wrote in her diary:

> Read and puttered most of the P.M. Listened to the music till 10 after dinner.[18]

Martha Stephenson wrote:

> We spent our evening in the reception room listening to a fine musical program, many whom we knew sitting about us. About nine-thirty we went up to the lounge, a most beautiful room with open fire.[19]

John Thayer Jr wrote:

> I was sitting in the room outside the main dining saloon, waiting for the music to begin. I had dined alone and was sitting alone, my father and mother having been invited out to dine in the restaurant.[20]

Anna Warren said:

> After dinner in the evening and until about 10 p.m. we were seated in the lounge on the dining saloon deck listening to the music.[21]

Thomas Whiteley was a first-class dining room steward. Although certain details in his newspaper interviews are inconsistent with the facts as established from primary sources (e.g. Captain Smith dining in the dining room on the night of 14 April),* it's possible Whiteley's memories are applicable to dinners

---

* Captain Smith dined in the restaurant on 14 April, so Thomas Whiteley's account of dinner in the first-class dining room is a bit of a puzzle.

on previous evenings. In any case, his two accounts are included here for the sake of completeness.

People lingered over their dinners Sunday night. Just before the doors closed at 9:30 Chief Surgeon O'Loughlin got up in his chair at the head of his table, which was next to the one I served. In his hand was a glass of champagne.

'Here's to the mighty *Titanic*!' he said. 'Long may she defy the seas.'

Captain Smith dined as usual at the head of his own table. Mr. Andrews was on his right, on his left a very beautiful woman who always wore white furs of great richness but whose name I did not know. Mr. Ismay during the whole trip sat at one of the small tables for two persons. Throughout the voyage he was always served by the head waiter; always he ate alone.[22]

It was the gayest night of the trip among the diners. We had made great time, and the probability the trip would be a record-breaker. Orders had been issued Sunday to make the dinner the finest ever served on a ship regardless of expense, and the orders were carried out.

I believe it was soon after half-past six when the passengers strolled in. Mr Ismay sat alone at a table a few feet away from the table of Mr and Mrs Astor, and he was in a corner. The Astor table was to the right, and the captain's table was in the centre just abutting the Astor table.

At the Astor table sat Dr O'Loughlin, the ship's surgeon, and his assistant. There were some other people there, but I don't know who they were.

Soon after the dinner was served the fun commenced. Wine was served at the Astor table and the conversation was very animated. The captain talked and joked with Mr Astor and Mr Ismay spoke. The one topic of conversation was the new boat and the speed she was making.

I did not see the captain drink anything and I don't think he ever indulged. As dinner progressed the gaiety increased, and I believe some bets were made as to the speed of the boat. At one time Dr O'Loughlin stood up and raising a glass of champagne cried, 'Let us drink to the mighty *Titanic*.' With cries of approval everyone stood and drank the toast.

I believe it was generally believed by all of those at the tables that the *Titanic* would reach New York late Tuesday or early Wednesday morning, and the captain and other officers were planning a big banquet after the landing in anticipation of the trip being a record-breaker.

The dinner broke up shortly before nine o'clock and the men retired to the smoking room, while some of the women went to their staterooms, and others strolled along the promenade. We cleared the dining room about ten o'clock, and soon after I went to bed, to be awakened by the shock when we struck the iceberg.[23]

13

Death by Funnel

A number of passenger and crew accounts suggest that swimmers struggling in the water near the forward end of the boat deck lost their lives when the first and second funnels collapsed and fell into the sea. In connection with this belief, we'll mention Archibald Gracie's 1912 suggestion that fellow passenger John Jacob Astor was killed during the violent break-up of the *Titanic*:

> From the fact that I never saw Colonel Astor on the Boat Deck later, and also because his body, when found, was crushed (according to the statement of one who saw it at Halifax, Mr Harry K. White, of Boston, Mr Edward A. Kent's brother-in-law, my schoolmate and friend from boyhood), I am of the opinion that he met his fate on the ship when the boilers tore through it, as described later.[1]

A modern-day variation of Gracie's story claims that Colonel Astor's crushed body was also blackened by soot from the collapsed funnel,[2] but – as we've already seen – this imaginative elaboration has no basis in fact. Since John Jacob Astor was not killed by a falling funnel, do we know if any other passengers were killed by the collapse of these giant structures? At the present time we know of only one, Charles Williams, whose death was described by his son, Richard.

Richard Williams

After arriving in New York, Richard Williams told a reporter how his father, Charles Williams, was killed by the collapse of the forward funnel while the two men stood together on the forward boat deck:

'We stood on deck watching the life-boats of the *Titanic* being filled and lowered into the water,' said Mr Williams. 'The water was nearly up to our waists and the ship was about at her last. Suddenly one of the great funnels fell. I sprang aside, endeavoring to pull father with me. A moment later the funnel was swept overboard and the body of father went with it.

'I sprang overboard and swam through the ice to a life-raft, and was pulled aboard. There were five men and one woman on the raft.'[3]

In later years Richard Williams wrote a lengthy personal account containing a description of how his father was killed:

> Still remembering 'suction' I yelled to my father 'quick – jump.' He started towards me just as I saw one of the four great funnels come crashing down on top of him. Just for one instant I stood there transfixed – not because it had only missed me by a few feet – this did not even occur to me; curiously enough not because it had killed my father for whom I had a far more than normal feeling of love and attachment; but there I was transfixed wondering at the enormous size of this funnel, still belching smoke. It seemed to me that two cars could have been driven through it side by side. It was probably but a fraction of a second, then I jumped to the rail; the water was about two and a half to three decks down. I climbed over the rail and jumped clear.[4]

In at least one 1912 interview, Mr Williams said nothing about the collapsing funnel causing his father's death:

> 'The boat listed badly,' said Mr Williams, 'and we saw that the situation was dangerous. I believe that this was the first thought we had given to it. The big ship listed still farther, and confusion spread upon the decks. The officers tried to keep order but it was hard. The lifeboats were lowered and the women began to pass in line towards the little craft. We thought that there would be enough boats for all, but they filled up quickly. Then we gave up hope. I had on my fur coat, for it was bitterly cold. Father and I were talking together. We were at the forward end. This began to sink rapidly. We agreed to jump and to keep together as long as we could. A wave ripped over the deck, and when it passed my father had disappeared. The water swept him off before we could jump.'[5]

Since it appears that all four of *Titanic*'s funnels collapsed during the sinking, let us subdivide our eyewitness accounts and look at each funnel separately.

First, however, we'll look at one preliminary account that mentions the ship's funnels but does not describe their actual collapse.

Eugene Daly
While on board the *Carpathia*, survivor Eugene Daly wrote an account of his survival for Dr Frank Blackmarr:

> As I looked over my shoulder, as I was still hanging to this oar, I could see the enormous funnels of the *Titanic* being submerged in the water. These poor people that covered the water were sucked down among those funnels, each of which was 25 feet in diameter, like flies. I managed to get away and succeeded in reaching the same boat that I had tried to set free from the deck of the *Titanic*.[6]

Funnel #1

Archibald Gracie
In 1912 Colonel Gracie described what he saw after he was swept overboard from the *Titanic*:

> When I reached the surface finally, there was nothing to be seen about me but a great field of wreckage of every sort and description. I learned later that one of the funnels had fallen from the ship before I reached the surface, and splashed its waves over young Mr Thayer and the second officer, who thought that the funnel would fall upon him.[7]

Elin Hakkarainen
In later years Miss Hakkarainen's son wrote an account of her *Titanic* experiences based on what she told him over the years and what he had read for himself:

> As the stern of the ship rose higher and higher, everything within the ship broke loose and went crashing downward to the bow. There was a mad rush of passengers and crew to the rear of the well and poop decks. There seemed to be a mad rush of people from below. The locked doors that I had encountered must have been opened at the last moment. Many hundreds more must have been trapped below decks and crushed by the breaking up of the ship. One of the giant funnels toppled to the deck crushing many passengers as it

> slid into the water. The screaming and moaning of the trapped passengers was beyond description.[8]

Albert Horswill

Seaman Horswill left the ship in lifeboat #1, and in speaking with a reporter later on, he just inferred what had happened when the forward funnel collapsed:

> Just before the end the *Titanic* separated between the third and fourth funnels. The foremost funnel had previously fallen into the water on the starboard side with a terrific splash, unquestionably doing a great deal of injury to people struggling in the water.[9]

Walter Hurst

In 1956 Mr Hurst gave the following interview to the BBC:

> Well, I saw the forward part of the boat deck dip underwater so I jumped overboard ... [I] swim away from the ship, turned round to look at her and down come the funnel smashed into the water right in front of my face. I got a gush of wind and dirt that nearly blinded me and I felt the cap go off my head and one slipper off my foot.[10]

Mr Hurst also wrote a letter to historian Walter Lord:

> The ship's bows were now under water. There was a group of officers in corner of the bridge and I never saw one move from there. A man just in front of me jumped overboard and I, without a thought, did the same. The Ship's Lights were still on from the Emergency Dynamo. There came a terrible crashing of machinery falling forward and one Propellor [*sic*] fell off the After [i.e. forward] funnel fell in the sea near me and I was half blinded by soot and water. Then came the raft we had cut adrift. It fell within a dozen feet of me and some men were clinging to it. There were terrible screams all round and I plainly heard screaming 'save one Life'. I've never forgotten that.[11]

Violet Jessop

In later years Miss Jessop wrote an autobiography in which she described *Titanic*'s last moments:

A tiny breeze, the first we had felt on this calm night, blew an icy blast across my face; it felt like a knife in its penetrating coldness. I sat paralyzed with cold and misery as I watched *Titanic* give a lurch forward. One of the huge funnels toppled off like a cardboard model, falling into the sea with a fearful roar. A few cries came to us across the water, then silence, as the ship seemed to right herself like a hurt animal with a broken back.[12]

Charles Lightoller

Second Officer Lightoller swam away from the *Titanic* and later testified at the British inquiry into the disaster:

14068. [*The Solicitor-General*] When you came up where did you find yourself? – I found myself alongside of the collapsible boat, which I had previously launched on the port side, the one I had thrown on to the boat deck.

14069. The one still shut up? – Yes, still shut up, bottom up.

14070. Were you able to make use of it to clamber on to it? – Not at that time. I just held on to something, a piece of rope or something, and was there for a little while, and then the forward funnel fell down. It fell within 3 or 4 inches of the boat. It lifted the boat bodily and threw her about 20 feet clear of the ship as near as I could judge.

14074. [*The Solicitor-General*] I do not know whether you can help us at all in describing what happened to the ship. You were engaged and had other things to think about; but what did happen to the ship? Can you tell us at all? – Are you referring to the reports of the ship breaking in two?

14075. Yes? – It is utterly untrue. The ship did not and could not have broken in two.

14076. [*The Commissioner*] If you saw it – if you saw what happened, tell us what it was? – After the funnel fell there was some little time elapsed. I do not know exactly what came or went, but the next thing I remember I was alongside this collapsible boat again, and there were about half a dozen standing on it. I climbed on it, and then turned my attention to the ship. The third if not the second funnel was still visible, certainly the third funnel was still visible. The stern was then clear of the water.

14077. Which do you call the second and third? – Numbering them from forward, my Lord.

14078. The second was visible? – The third was visible – I am not sure if the second was visible, but I am certain the third was visible, and she was

> gradually raising her stern out of the water. Even at that time I think the propellers were clear of the water. That I will not be certain of.
> **14079**. Had the funnel broken away? – Only the forward one.
> **14080**. But you are not sure about the second one? – I am not sure whether that was below water or not, that I cannot say.
> **14081**. That is what I mean. I want to know from you. Was it below water in the sense that the ship had sunk so as to immerse it in the water, or had it broken adrift? – No, the second funnel was immersed.
> **14082**. It appears to me, looking at that model, that if that was so the stern must have been very well up in the air? – Well, I daresay it was, my Lord; it would be.
> **14083**. And the propellers all visible? – Yes, clear of the water. That is my impression.
> **14084**. [*The Solicitor-General.*] When you say the third funnel was visible I understand you to mean part of it? – Yes, some part of the funnel. As a matter of fact, I am rather under the impression that the whole of the third funnel was visible.[13]

Later in the year Lightoller wrote a letter for publication by the *Christian Science Monitor*:

> I want it to be understood that during this time in the water the fact came calmly and clearly that there was a divine power which could be utilized in a practical manner, and also it seemed perfectly natural to rely on this power with the spiritual understanding which is so often spoken of in the Bible, and which is explained in Science and Health with Key to the Scriptures by Mrs Eddy. Now, with the sinking of a great ship like the *Titanic*, there was also the fear of suction to overcome, and at this time the forward funnel fell, throwing the boat, myself, and other survivors about twenty feet clear of the ship, so that of suction we felt nothing.[14]

In later years Lightoller twice wrote about passenger and crew deaths that he presumably saw with his own eyes:

> The terrific strain of bringing the after end of that huge hull clear out of the water, caused the expansion joint abaft No. 1 funnel to open up … The fact that the two wire stays to this funnel, on the after part led over and abaft the expansion joint, threw on them an extraordinary strain, eventually carrying away the port wire guy, to be followed almost immediately by

> the starboard one. Instantly the port one parted, the funnel started to fall, but the fact that the starboard one held a moment or two longer, gave this huge structure a pull over to that side of the ship, causing it to fall, with its scores of tons, right amongst the struggling mass of humanity already in the water. It struck the water between the Engelhardt and the ship, actually missing me by inches.[15]

> A bit later the for-ard funnel guys carried away, and the funnel (weighing perhaps fifty or sixty tons) fell down with a crash on the water. It missed the raft and some of us hanging on to it by inches – there was a good many it didn't miss.[16]

Harry Oliver

Fireman Harry Oliver was in lifeboat #9 when *Titanic* began to break up:

> Suddenly there was a terrible crash, and the great ship appeared to split in twain, if not in three distinct sections, the rending of her timbers and steel plates making a noise that carried terror into the hearts of all. The end came swiftly. One of the huge funnels toppled over the side, and then the bow parted just in a line with the bridge. Tilting forward, the *Titanic* appeared to be going down slowly by the head, when there was a rush and a roar which led the horrified onlookers to come to the conclusion that the machinery had burst through the bulkhead and had fallen out of the ship.[17]

John Poingdestre

After his rescue, Mr Poingdestre testified at the British *Titanic* inquiry:

> **3107**. How far away were you when she sank? – About 150 yards.
> **3108**. Now will you describe to us what you saw happen when she sank? – Well, I thought when I looked that the ship broke at the foremost funnel.
> **3109**. What led you to that conclusion? – Because I had seen that part disappear.
> **3110**. If she sank by the head you would see that part disappear, would you not? – Yes.

Harry Senior

After arriving back in the United Kingdom, Mr Senior described the collapse of the first funnel:

> The ship was pretty near sinking then, and the captain shouted 'Each man for himself'... When that order came I dived over the side, leaving a boat which I had been helping to lower. The boat floated off, overturned, and after a time I got on her ... Before I dived off the ship one of the forward boilers burst and blew up the forward funnel.[18]

Mr Senior granted an anonymous interview in which he suggests that the forward funnel may have collapsed *after* he dived into the sea and that it produced a wave that swept over him while he was swimming away from the ship:

> After the last boat had gone I was standing by the bridge, and the ship was just on the point of sinking. The captain shouted, 'Everyone for himself!' An Italian woman was standing by me. She had two children. I took one from her. We jumped into the water at the same time. By this time all the boats were gone. Before I jumped I saw the men left on the ship running aft because the poop was rising out of the water. The cold of the water soon killed the baby. I had to leave it. As I swam about there was a wave which carried me clear of the wreck. She lunged straight down to the bottom.[19]

Eustace Snow
After returning to England, Trimmer Snow made a deposition for the British *Titanic* inquiry:

> I jumped into the water and clung to the upturned boat with 9 or 10 others. One of the funnels fell near the boat and some of the men let go and sank.[20]

Victor Sunderland
After the sinking Mr Sunderland described how he was saved on Collapsible B:

> The ship had dropped down in the water until the boat deck was awash, and the officer, fireman and myself tried to lower away a boat that stood in the blocks on the starboard side. The water was then gushing up through the gangway through which the firemen enter and leave the fire room. Just as we had the boat ready to lower, the ship trembled and dropped suddenly. The fireman jumped over the starboard side.
>
> 'Here she goes,' shouted Lightoller and jumped over the port side. I followed. A lifeboat, bottom-up and evidently one of those which had overturned under its load, floated up to the rail and we grabbed for it. We climbed upon it and it drifted over the submerged part of the *Titanic*. We passed under

the forward funnel, and just as we were clear it fell. At that minute the *Titanic* broke in two just aft of amidships, and the stern stood straight in the air.

'Make for the stern. It looks like she will float,' Lightoller shouted, but just as he spoke the stern plunged down.[21]

John Thompson

Fireman Thompson witnessed the falling funnel at close hand:

> One man discovered a collapsible lifeboat, which he took from its place and adjusted. He forgot to see that the plug was in place. I was the last to get into the lifeboat, and while I was stepping into it one of the funnels broke loose and fell to the water with a roar, causing so great a wash that our boat was sent spinning and I was knocked violently against one of the davits.[22]

Unnamed Crewman

After returning to the United Kingdom, George Cavell and a couple of other crewmen spoke with a reporter, and one of them (whether or not it was Cavell is unclear) spoke about the death of an unnamed fellow crewman:

> A funnel fell over onto lots of people in the water. It must have killed a tidy few. I was picked up.[23]

Unnamed Crewmen

> Several members of the crew declared that just before the ship made her fatal dive, the foremost funnel broke off and fell into the sea, killing and injuring a number of men who were already in the water struggling and swimming towards the boats.[24]

Unnamed Fireman

After arriving back in the United Kingdom an unnamed fireman described the collapse of the first funnel:

> Another fireman came up from below quite at the last. An officer shouted to him to help to launch a collapsible boat which was fastened above the officers' quarters. They managed to launch it, but it turned turtle. One of the ship's funnels fell close, and the wash caused by this swept the boat clear. This was the boat of which so much has been heard, to which 30 men clung and were saved.[25]

Unnamed Passenger
After arriving in Boston, a passenger who preferred to remain anonymous spoke with a local reporter, who paraphrased his words:

> He states that before the *Titanic* sank the forward stack crashed down on a stack of passengers on the forward deck, killing and maiming many; that the shrieks of those drowning in the water were so terrible that women in the lifeboats were driven into hysteria.[26]

'Robert Williams'
After arriving back in the United Kingdom, an unnamed crewman used the pseudonym 'Robert Williams' to speak with a reporter without incurring the wrath of the White Star Line:

> It was awful to see the ship go down. We heard a muffled roar of an explosion, and one of the funnels fell, and then came another explosion, and the boat slid down out of sight.[27]

Funnel #2

Percival Keen
In 1912 Steward Keen spoke with a British newspaper reporter about what he observed during the sinking:

> The second funnel broke off and killed a number of people in its fall.[28]

Eino Lindqvist
In 1930 Mr Lindqvist recounted his *Titanic* experience for his local newspaper and described the absence of the ship's first two funnels:

> The *Titanic* was equipped with four funnels. It was when she had sank so that the two forward stacks were under water that the monster ship exploded, breaking in two. Quickly after the concussion, the stern righted itself, held steady for a moment, then keeled over and sank![29]

Edward Ryan
Prior to 1970 Mr Ryan wrote an undated memoir of his *Titanic* experience describing his impression of the ship's forward funnels:

> The forward part of the ship was now all submerged, the water was up to the bottom of the first two funnels and people were climbing up the slippery deck to get clear of the water.[30]

Emily Ryerson

On 9 May 1912 Mrs Ryerson submitted the following deposition to the Senate *Titanic* inquiry:

> Then suddenly, when we still seemed very near, we saw the ship was sinking rapidly. I was in the bow of the boat with my daughter and turned to see the great ship take a plunge toward the bow, the two forward funnels seemed to lean and then she seemed to break in half as if cut with a knife, and as the bow went under the lights went out; the stern stood up for several minutes, black against the stars, and then that, too, plunged down, and there was no sound for what seemed like hours, and then began the cries for help of people drowning all around us, which seemed to go on forever.[31]

John Thayer Jr

In later years Mr Thayer described what he saw after he jumped overboard and attempted to swim away from the *Titanic*:

> The water was over the base of the first funnel. The mass of people on board were surging back, always back toward the floating stern. The rumble and roar continued, with even louder distinct wrenching and tearings of boilers and engines from their beds. Suddenly the whole superstructure of the ship appeared to split, well forward to midship, and blow or buckle upwards. The second funnel, large enough for two automobiles to pass through abreast, seemed to be lifted off, emitting a cloud of sparks. It looked as if it would fall on top of me. It missed me by only twenty or thirty feet. The suction of it drew me down and down, struggling and swimming, practically spent.[32]

In 1932 Mr Thayer wrote a brief account of the *Titanic* disaster that contained the following description:

> I was trying to get away from the ship. I looked back and the second funnel fell and missed me by about ten yards. This funnel, large enough for two automobiles to go through abreast, made a tremendous additional wash and suction. I was drawn down again …[33]

Unnamed Third-Class Steward

This young man went into the water and found refuge on the upturned Collapsible B:

> I saw the *Titanic* go down. Two of her funnels fell off and after an explosion, which I distinctly heard, being only a short distance away at the time, she smashed in the middle. Her bows went down, and then her stern, which was almost upright when it sank.[34]

Funnel #3

It seems likely that the sparks observed by some of the following survivors were emitted from *Titanic*'s third funnel while it was collapsing during the break-up of the ship.

Charlotte Collyer

Mrs Collyer wrote an account of the *Titanic* disaster:

> Something in the very bowels of the *Titanic* exploded, and millions of sparks shot up to the sky, like rockets in a park on the night of a summer holiday. This red spurt was fan-shaped as it went up, but the sparks descended in every direction in the shape of a fountain of fire. Two other explosions followed, dull and heavy, as if below the surface. The *Titanic* broke in two before my eyes. The fore part was already partly under the water. It wallowed over and disappeared instantly. The stern reared straight on end and stood poised on the ocean for many seconds – they seemed minutes to me.[35]

It's uncertain if Mrs Collyer was initially describing the collapse of a funnel or if this entire scenario denoted the actual break-up of the ship.

Joseph Scarrott

In May 1912 Mr Scarrott wrote an account of his experiences which indicates that the third funnel's base was partially submerged when it collapsed during the subsequent break-up of the ship:

> The ship sank shortly afterwards, I should say about 2:20 a. m. on the 15th, which would be two hours and forty minutes after she struck. The sight of

> that grand ship going down will never be forgotten. She slowly went down bow first with a slight list to starboard until the water reached the bridge, then she went quicker. When the third funnel had nearly disappeared I heard four explosions, which I took to be the bursting of the boilers. The ship was right up on end then.
>
> Suddenly she broke in two between the third and fourth funnel. The after part of the ship came down on the water in its normal position and seemed as if it was going to remain afloat, but it only remained a minute or two and then sank. The lights were burning right up till she broke in two.[36]

Spencer Silverthorne
Mr Silverthorne appears to have observed the collapse of the third funnel when the ship broke in two:

> Mr Silverthorne said the ship slowly sank and as it went down showers of rockets flew far into the sky from its deck in the faint hope that their blaze would attract succour from a passing ship. The front part of the *Titanic* had entirely disappeared when two explosions came which seemed to break the liner in part amidships. Showers of sparks came from the funnels, indicating that the boilers had blown up.[37]

Funnel #4

Thomas Dillon
In his testimony at the British inquiry Mr Dillon described how the fourth funnel fell aft toward him when the ship broke up:

> **3859**. She gave a plunge and righted herself again? – Yes.
> **3860**. Did you notice anything about the funnel? – Not then.
> **3861**. Did you afterwards notice something about the funnel? – Yes.
> **3862**. What? – When she went down.
> **3863**. Was that after you had left the ship? – Before I left the ship.
> **3864**. What did you notice? – Well, the funnel seemed to cant up towards me.
> **3865**. It seemed to fall aft? – Yes; it seemed to fall up this way.
> **3866**. Was that the aftermost funnel? – Yes.
> **3867**. Did you get the idea that the ship was breaking in two? – No.
> **3868**. Did the funnel seem to fall towards you? – Yes.
> **3869**. [*The Commissioner*] That is the after funnel? – Yes, my Lord.[38]

Albert Major

Mr Major observed the collapse of the fourth funnel from the safety of his lifeboat:

> The ship broke off at the nose and began to settle at the head so the passengers were driven off. The stern lifted so that the people were actually dumped into the water. There was a series of explosions, one of which blew off the aft funnel. The masthead light was the last to go out.[39]

John Thayer Jr

Twenty-eight years after the disaster Mr Thayer described what he recalled seeing while swimming near the *Titanic*:

> It seemed as though hours had passed since I left the ship; yet it was probably not more than four minutes, if that long. There was the gigantic mass, about fifty or sixty yards away. The forward motion had stopped. She was pivoting on a point just abaft of midship. Her stern was gradually rising into the air, seemingly in no hurry, just slowly and deliberately. The last funnel was on the surface of the water. It was the dummy funnel, and I do not believe it fell.[40]

Conclusions

As we've just seen, many passengers and crewmen claimed that falling funnels took the lives of a large number of swimmers as the *Titanic* was going down. Although these claims might well be true, Charles Williams is the only person we can presently identify by name whose life was snuffed out when a falling funnel crushed him and swept his body overboard.

14

The Hämäläinen Family

Anna Wartiainen was born in Finland around 1889 and came to the United States around 1904. She spent time in Brooklyn in New York City, but eventually she met a fellow Finn named John Hämäläinen, to whom she was married around 1909. In 1910 the couple was living in Essex, Massachusetts, but they seem to have moved to Hartford, Connecticut, later that same year. On 4 February 1911 the young couple was blessed with a little son, whom they named Wiljo, and in August of that same year Anna travelled back to Finland with Wiljo so that her parents in the old country could meet their little grandson.

Anna, Wiljo and John Hämäläinen. (Author's collection)

In September 1911 John Hämäläinen moved from Connecticut to Detroit, Michigan, where he began working as an auto factory copper worker and began preparing a new home for his little family. In spring 1912 John received a letter from Anna saying that she and 13-month-old Wiljo would be returning to America in April and that they and their friend Martta Hiltunen would be travelling on the new White Star liner *Titanic*.

That was the last word John Hämäläinen received from his wife and little son until after the *Titanic* carried 1,496 of her passengers and crewmen to their deaths on 15 April 1912.

Miraculously, Anna and her infant son survived the disaster and, after travelling by train to her new hometown of Detroit, Anna described the things she had seen, heard and experienced during the *Titanic*'s first and last voyage:

> Captain Smith of the steamer *Titanic* did everything in his power for the safety of the passengers who could leave the sinking ship and then deliberately jumped into the sea. The coolness and bravery of Captain Smith was wonderful. I was placed in the last boat which left the *Titanic* and had a good opportunity to watch the man's actions in the time of greatest danger. He was as solicitous of the welfare of the helpless people in his care as though he were showing visitors over his ship when she was tied to a dock.
>
> There was no excitement and certainly no fear in his face as he went about doing what he could to assure the safety of the few who could be crowded into the lifeboats. He had seen ten boats filled to overflowing with humanity lowered from the upper decks of the ship and started away over the ice-strewn sea, to what fate God alone knew. There had been heart-rending scenes at the parting of husband and wife, father and children. Captain Smith had seen men go mad with fear and throw themselves overboard to what was almost certain death. Perhaps he had seen panic-stricken men shot down when they tried to crowd into the boats reserved for the women; there are stories that this happened though I saw no such occurrence. I heard two shots but am unable to say whether the bullets found human marks.
>
> Through all this grief and terror and panic the master of the giant steamship had not lost his head or his nerve for one minute. His only thought was to do what he could toward starting the frail boatloads of humanity on their only chance for life. He walked about in the crowds lining the rails, speaking quietly here and there, suggesting a change in the preparations here, ordering one there.
>
> As the last boat, the one in which I and my baby were placed, was about to be lowered, Captain Smith walked over and asked another officer who

the men of the crew who were to man the oars were. The names were called off to him, one by one.

'It is well,' he said quietly. 'They are good men and will do all they can.' And then to the oarsmen who sat, with white drawn faces looking up at him, he said, 'Men, these women and children are in your hands. Do your very best by them. Take good care of them.'

When the boat was lowered and even as we struck the water, I heard the captain's low, calm voice above the other noises.

'It's every man for himself now, friends,' he said, as calmly as though he were bidding an acquaintance good morning. 'Each man look out for himself. The last boat's gone.'

And then while I was locking up, that man of men, whose courage seemed to be exceeded only by his kindness of heart and sense of duty, walked to the rail and threw himself into the sea. It is not true, as some of the survivors have said, that Captain Smith had a child in his arms when he leaped. He plunged to his death alone. It seemed as though the end were just a matter of that duty to which he had adhered so religiously all during that terrible ordeal when he saw hundreds, whose lives had been in his hands a few minutes before, facing certain death.

No one can blame Captain Smith for the end he chose. He had done everything a human being in his position could do, and when there was no more chance to save his passengers and crew he went to his death calmly and deliberately.

I had attended church services in the second class dining salon during the evening, joining in the singing and praying. It must have been after 10 o'clock when poor Martta Hiltunen and I retired to our stateroom all unawares of what was impending.

Martta occupied one of the berths, but because my baby had been restless I lay down on the couch with him. I had just dropped asleep when the jar of the ship as she struck the iceberg awakened me. It was not a hard collision, just a little bump and then a grinding that lasted for a minute or two. So slight was the shock that I didn't consider it of enough importance to investigate, even when I felt the engines stop. I dropped asleep again, as did Martta.

Within a few minutes, however, we were awakened by a pounding on the stateroom door and a man's voice telling us to get up and dress, that the ship had collided with an iceberg. Even then we could not realize that anything serious had occurred but took our leisure dressing. Martta and I put on warm clothing and I dressed the baby warmly. Though we were later in getting on deck, arriving there just as the last lifeboat was ready to be lowered, I was glad later that we had taken the time. The warm clothing prevented suffering when we were floating on the ice-strewn sea.

Telling Martta to stay close to me, as the girl knew no English and was nervous, I made my way to the deck. There was not much confusion or evidence of panic, as I consider now what danger those people were in. Men and women stood about in a big group conversing quietly, though here and there a poor steerage passenger was wailing and praying.

'Here's a woman with a baby!' shouted one of the ship's officers as I came into view. 'Hurry and get into the boat,' he said to me. I turned and handed Martta my handbag, expecting that the girl would follow me into the boat. The last I ever saw of her was when she stood near a group of men and women when our boat was lowered over the side.

I found myself in a boat loaded with forty or fifty women of all classes, first, second and third class passengers. Some of them were dressed only in their night gowns; one or two had furs and heavy wraps. The sailors who were at the oars were loath to leave the side of the ship when we struck the water, declaring that they should stay near at hand and pick up whoever might be in the water.

But the women knew the awful danger of the suction should the ship sink and begged and prayed the men to row out of danger.

'There are other lives just as precious as yours,' the sailors said in answer to the prayers and entreating, but finally they heeded and rowed away from the *Titanic*. The big steamer was listing badly, we saw, so we rowed away from her, and her bows were deep in the water. When we had reached a point about three hundred feet away, I should say, the boilers exploded and then the work of destruction was swift.

The *Titanic* seemed to heave into the air and split open. The bows settled rapidly, and then the whole ship sank. The wave which was thrown up just rocked our boat gently; we were not in danger of capsizing at all.

The wailing and crying and praying which had been increasing in volume from the time I came on deck until the ship sank, became the most terrible sound I have ever heard. The whole sea seemed to be filled with the death cries of hundreds of people. It was an indescribable sound, but one to strike terror and pity in the stoutest heart.

There must have been scores of people in the water near our boat, floating about among the small icebergs, clinging to whatever they could seize when the crisis came. Our boat picked up eight poor fellows, all steerage passengers, within a few minutes. Two of them died after being hauled in.

For eight hours we drifted and rowed about among the ice and in an atmosphere that was freezing. The half-clad women in the boat kept up a continuous moaning and crying, the French women especially wailing continually. After the first excitement we looked about to see what there might be done toward relieving suffering and protecting the refugees from the bitter cold. Seeing several women with nothing but their night dresses I asked a Mrs Brown, a first class passenger to whom I had been talking, how many skirts she had on.

'I have on two skirts,' was the answer.

'Then give one of them to one of those freezing women; they need it worse than you do,' I told her. Mrs Brown didn't hesitate a second but gave up one of her skirts and other parts of her clothing. We soon had the available clothing in the boat divided and then settled down to wait for dawn and the *Carpathia*. It seemed ages before the relief ship came and we were taken aboard to warmth and safety.

A man and his wife, passengers on the *Carpathia*, offered to give up their berth to me, but I knew there were many sick aboard and contented myself with a mattress which had been placed on the floor of the dining room. We were very comfortable until New York was reached.

I am sure there were many women who went down with the *Titanic*. I saw several in the crowds on deck, many of them refusing to leave their husbands for the lifeboats. One case in particular was very pathetic.

This was the case of Mrs William Lahtinen, whose husband was pastor of a Lutheran church in Minneapolis and with whom I had become acquainted on the voyage. Rev. and Mrs Lahtinen had been visiting in his old home Finland for several months, and last January their daughter died there. When the time came for her to get into a boat she refused, choosing to die in her husband's arms to living without him. There were many such cases, and I have been told that many women did not leave their staterooms at all, but were drawn down ignorant of their danger until death was upon them.

When we arrived in New York I intended to go to the home of friends in Brooklyn, with which city I am familiar. But I found another friend waiting for me on the dock and she took me home with her. I stayed there from Thursday night until Friday evening and then took the train for Detroit.

This friend was very indignant with the officers of the White Star Line, declaring that she had tried for two days to get a wireless message to me on the *Carpathia*. She says the officials told her they had no time for private messages and refused to accept it.

> Of course I am happy that my baby and myself were saved, but the loss of poor little Martta, who started for the strange country with such high hopes is hard to think of. And the loss of other lives on that ship is absolutely appalling.
>
> I have been trying to rest since my arrival in Detroit and feel much better than I have at any time since the accident. The baby has a slight cold, but I do not think it is serious. [1]

After living through her heart-shaking experience on board the *Titanic*, one would like to think that Anna Hämäläinen, her husband John and their little son Wiljo lived happily together for the remainder of their time on earth. Sadly, Swedish researcher Peter Engberg has discovered that this was not destined to be the case at all, because on 18 March 1914, 3-year-old Wiljo died of endocarditis and was buried in Gethsemane Cemetery in Detroit.

It was apparently sometime during this same time period that Anna and John divorced. Both remarried in 1917, with Anna being wed to auto worker Frank Sarlin in Detroit on 22 September. At the time of the wedding, Frank had a 5-year-old son from a previous marriage, and in 1930 Frank, Anna and Anna's stepson were making their home together in Elkhart, Indiana. In 1940 the Sarlins were living in Baltimore, Maryland.

On 28 December 1945 Anna Hämäläinen Sarlin passed away in Baltimore at the age of 55 and was buried in that city's Loudon Park Cemetery. Her mortal remains rest far from those of her little son Wiljo, in whose company she survived one of the greatest maritime disasters in history.

15

'I Had No Knowledge At All'

After the *Carpathia* brought *Titanic*'s survivors into New York, newspaper stories suggested that White Star Chairman Bruce Ismay knew that several additional boilers were to be connected to *Titanic*'s engines on the evening of 14 April with a consequent increase in the vessel's speed. Since these stories originated with *Titanic* survivors who conversed with fellow survivor Emily Ryerson on board the *Carpathia*, let us look at how these claims first came to public notice.

Arthur Peuchen

> Sunday it was very cold, and we knew we were in the ice zone. But there was no checking of speed. When we struck the berg we were running at 25 miles an hour.
>
> I know that the wireless warned of danger from the ice. Why. Ismay told Miss Ryerson that we would pass bergs. She asked him if he would slow down and he is reported to have told her that he 'guessed not.'[1]
>
> ---
>
> 'J. Bruce Ismay knew of the presence of icebergs, but arrogantly disregarded the danger of them. And when the *Titanic* was every instant facing the possibility of running into an ice mountain, Mr Ismay was dining with Captain Smith.'
>
> Asked the source of his information, he said he was told by Mrs Ryerson of Philadelphia. He quoted Mrs Ryerson as saying to him: 'Late Sunday afternoon, while the *Titanic* was going along at a fast rate, I went to Mr Ismay

and said: "Oh, Mr Ismay, I have heard that the wireless has reported a large number of icebergs in the path of our ship. Are you not going to order her to slow down?"

'He replied: "On the contrary, Mrs Ryerson, we are going to go along faster than we have been going." And we did go faster.'[2]

A reporter for a different New York newspaper summarised Major Peuchen's statements as follows:

> The proximity of icebergs was well known to Mr Ismay on Sunday, the day of the accident, Major Peuchen said, but he refused to sacrifice speed for safety. Major Peuchen said that he had received this information from Mrs Ryerson, whose husband and son perished with the *Titanic*.
>
> It was on the *Carpathia* that Mrs Ryerson told him of her talk with Mr Ismay, Major Peuchen said. He quoted her as having asked Mr Ismay whether the *Titanic* would reduce her speed on approaching the icebergs that had been reported ahead.
>
> 'On the contrary,' Mr Ismay was said to have answered, 'we will speed up.'[3]

Mahala Douglas

'Mrs Ryerson, of Philadelphia, who was in the boat with me, told me in the presence of Major Peuchen and others whom I can name that in daytime on Sunday before the night of the wreck she was walking on the upper deck and met Mr Ismay, who handed her a Marconigram, which she did not read.

'"What does it say?" she said she asked, and he replied; "I have just had word that we are in the icebergs."'

'"Of course you are going to slow down," she said.

'"Oh, no,"' said Mr Ismay. "'We are going to put on two more boilers and get out of it."'[4]

Mrs Douglas was in the same lifeboat with Mrs Arthur Ryerson of Philadelphia, formerly of Chicago, who also lost her husband. Mrs Douglas expects to be called to testify before the senate investigating committee as to her knowledge of conditions on board the *Titanic*.

She thought J. Bruce Ismay was, in part, responsible for the disaster to the *Titanic*. She told her brother-in-law that Mr Ismay had ordered the speed of the vessel increased when he learned it was in the neighborhood of ice bergs. Mrs Douglas' brother-in-law related her story …

'On Sunday before the night of the wreck Mrs Ryerson and I were walking on the upper deck. She told me she had met Mr Ismay and that he had handed her a Marconigram which she had not read.

'"What does it show?" Mrs Ryerson asked him.

'"I have just had word that we are in the icebergs," he answered.

'"Of course you are going to slow down?" Mrs Ryerson said.

'"Oh, no," Mr Ismay said, "we are going to put on two more boilers and get out of it."'[5]

J. Bruce Ismay is said to be partly responsible for the *Titanic* disaster by Mrs Walter D. Douglas of Minneapolis, whose husband was drowned in the wreck. Mrs Douglas was rescued in a lifeboat with Mrs Arthur Ryerson of Philadelphia. 'Everybody knew we were near icebergs because it grew so cold,' said Mrs Douglas.

'On Sunday before the wreck, Mrs Ryerson told me Mr Ismay said to her, "I have just had word that we are in the icebergs."

'Mrs Ryerson said: "Of course, you are going to slow down?"

'"Oh, no," Mr Ismay replied, "we are going to put on two more boilers and get out of it."'[6]

Mrs Douglas went so far as to submit an affidavit to the Senate *Titanic* inquiry describing this incident for the investigators:

We heard many stories of the rescue from many sources. These I tried to keep in my mind clearly, as they seemed important. Among them I will quote Mrs Ryerson, of Philadelphia. This story was told in the presence of Mrs Meyers [*sic*], of New York, and others.

[Mrs Ryerson speaking.] 'Sunday afternoon Mr Ismay, whom I know very slightly, passed me on the deck. He showed me, in his brusque manner, a Marconigram, saying, "We have just had news that we are in the icebergs."

'"Of course, you will slow down," I said.

'"Oh, no," he replied, "we will put on more boilers and get out of it."'[7]

Bruce Ismay

Perhaps unsurprisingly, Bruce Ismay availed himself of his first opportunity to deny the specifics of the Peuchen and Douglas interviews. Mr Ismay was questioned piecemeal about the alleged incident at the Senate *Titanic* inquiry, but an accurate summary of his pertinent testimony appeared in at least one New York newspaper:

Senator Burton. Did you have any conversation with a passenger on the *Titanic* about slackening or increasing speed when you heard of the ice?
Mr Ismay. No, sir; not that I have any recollection of. I presume you refer to what Mrs Ryerson said. I testified in New York, the day after we arrived, that it was our intention on Monday or Tuesday, assuming the weather conditions to suit, and everything was working satisfactorily down below, to probably run the ship for about four or six hours full speed to see what she could do.
Senator Perkins. You did not have any conversation on that Sunday about increasing the speed, did you?
Mr Ismay. Not in regard to increasing the speed going through the ice, sir.
Senator Burton. That is all.

Shortly afterwards, Mr Ismay submitted a formal statement to the press addressing what he felt were unjust accusations that were being made against him in the newspapers:

> It is absolutely and unqualifiedly false that I ever said that I wished that the *Titanic* should make a speed record or should increase her daily runs. I deny absolutely having said to any person that we would increase our speed in order to get out of the ice zone, or any words to that effect.[8]

Emily Ryerson
Mrs Ryerson herself never spoke with the press in 1912 to clarify the details of Bruce Ismay's alleged conversation with her, but on 18 April 1913 she wrote a letter regarding her requested testimony at the Limitation of Liability hearings:

> As far as I can now recall all I could say would be that I was on deck in the afternoon of April 14 between 5–6 o'clock & Mr Ismay came up & inquired if our staterooms were comfortable & the service satisfactory etc. & then thrust a Marconigram at me, saying, we were in among the icebergs. Something was said about speed & he said that the ship had not been going fast now that they were going to start up extra boilers that afternoon or evening (I forget when.) The telegram also spoke of the *Deutschland* a ship out of coal & asking for a tow, & when I asked him what they were going to do about that he said they had no time for such matters, our ship wanted to do her best & something was said about getting in Tuesday night. I was not much interested & cannot remember the exact words & details but repeated the conversation immediately to my husband & to Miss Bowen when I went

down to my cabin & she remembers it & the strong impression which was left on my mind & on hers was that they were speeding the ship up – to get away from the ice – & that we would probably get in late Tuesday night or early Wednesday morning – Mr Ismay's manner was that of one in authority & the owner of the ship & that what he said was law.[9]

Not long afterwards, Mrs Ryerson was asked to testify about this incident at the Limitation of Liability hearings:

A. He [Ismay] produced from his pocket a telegram blank on which some words were written in type-writing, and he said that we were in among the icebergs – he said as he handed the telegram to me, 'We are in among the icebergs.'
Q. Did you look at the telegram and see what it said?
A. I don't remember what it said. It had the word 'Deutschland' and something was said about speed, whether I said it I don't know; but he said 'We are not going very fast, 20 or 21 knots, but we are going to start up some extra boilers this evening' how many there were I don't know, it was two or three, but I wouldn't swear to that – I know the fact of the extra boilers because I didn't know what it meant except going faster.
Q. Anything said about getting in, or not being able to stop?
A. Yes, I said 'What is the rest of the telegram?' He said 'It is the *Deutschland* wanting a tow, not under control' or something of that sort, and they wanted a tow, and I remember saying, 'What are you going to do about that?' and he said they weren't going to do anything about it. Can't remember his exact words; I am only giving the impression left on my mind, that 'we are going to get in [early] and surprise everybody'. I don't know whether he used the word 'record' but that was left on my mind, that we had no time to delay aiding other steamers.
Q. Did he say anything about expecting to get in any particular time in New York?
A. There was some discussion about it, and my impression was it would be very late Tuesday night, or early Wednesday morning, because I discussed it with my husband after I went down stairs and the question was what we would do if we got in so very late. But as I say, at the time the conversation had no importance to me; I was very much over-burdened with other things that were on my mind – I carried on the conversation merely to keep the ball going, and the words have faded from my mind; but the strong impression left on my mind I can remember perfectly, but not the words …

Q. Do you remember Mr Ismay stating you were among the icebergs at that time when he handed you this message?
A. Yes.
Q. How long did he stay talking to you at that time?
A. Oh, it wasn't very long, he sat down beside us, and he talked about one or two other things I don't remember, he was not a friend of mine, and I didn't want to talk to him, and he was talking to Mrs Thayer and me, and presently Mr Ryerson and Mr Thayer came up, and he stood up and went down stairs, and as we went down he was at the foot of that first flight, near the restaurant – he wasn't talking to us over ten minutes, I couldn't positively tell …
Q. Do you recollect hearing anything – his saying whether you were going ahead at full speed that night?
A. No, he merely said as I said before.
Q. Repeat your answer?
A. He said 'We are going to start some extra boilers to-night,' or 'this evening,' I don't remember which time …
Q. In telling of your conversation with Mr Ismay have you given the substance of what he said and what you said?
A. Yes, so far as I can now recall it. About my attitude in the matter, I was under great mental distress, and the conversation didn't make any impression on me, and I didn't care anything about it, and it wasn't until afterwards that certain things came back to me, and it wasn't important at any time; only if it is any value in bringing out the facts I am glad to give it.
Q. Did you speak of this conversation to any of the other passengers on the Carpathia?
A. Yes …
Q. Do you recollect whether Mr Ismay said anything about the effect of the additional boilers on the speed of the boat?
A. No …
Q. You had been induced by your friend Mrs Thayer to go out on deck for a little walk, and he came up and spoke to you both?
A. Yes.
Q. And it was – I suppose his conversation was partly with Mrs Thayer?
A. Yes, the conversation about the telegram was partly with her, but mostly with me …
Q. Was Miss [Grace] Bowen there too?
A. She passed, and saw him sitting there …
Q. He [Ismay] said something in addition to showing you the telegram?
A. First he showed the telegram – then he said 'We are in among the

icebergs.' The impression he gave to me was we were in the region of the icebergs and that was the reason it was so cold; but he didn't say so.
Q. Did he say 'We expect to get into ice?' Do you remember that expression? You can't say positively he said 'We are among the icebergs'?
A. He said 'We are in among the icebergs' or 'We are in the ice.'
Q. Wasn't it 'We are going in the ice?'
A. No, 'We are in among ice,' or 'in among the icebergs.' He wasn't talking officially at all, he was talking to two women.
Q. And this matter of the knots you were making, was that with regards to the time you would get in?
A. No, with regards to how fast we were going. Something was said about speed and he said we hadn't been making much speed, twenty or twenty-one knots, and he said 'We are going to start up some new boilers this evening' – that was the impression left on my mind – that was the substance of what he said. I didn't know what starting up new boilers meant unless going faster. He didn't make any explanation of it …
Q. Now you have given the whole of the conversation with Mr Ismay as you remember it, but it is more an impression rather than a distinct recollection – is that right?
A. Yes, it is more than an impression, it is a record of the impression it left on my mind, a very distinct recollection on every single point.
Q. You didn't say anything to him about slowing the boat down?
A. No.
Q. He didn't say anything to you about speeding the ship up to get out of the ice?
A. No, that was merely the impression that was left on my mind.
Q. My question is not whether he spoke about their putting on more boilers and going faster; but I am confining my question to whether he said, or suggested to you, anything that indicated that they were going to increase their speed in order to get out of the ice?
A. As I say, that was merely the impression left on my mind.
Q. Nothing was said?
A. No, not in so many words – that was the impression left on my mind.
Q. You don't wish to be understood the Titanic was trying to make a speed record across the Atlantic?
A. I should say my impression was they were going to show – surprise us all by what she could do, on that voyage.
Q. As a matter of fact, was it discussed whether she should get in on Tuesday night, or Wednesday morning?

A. Yes.
Q. Among passengers?
A. Yes, and in this conversation with Mr Ismay also, there was some question about it, because I discussed it with my husband after I got down to the cabin.
Q. You wouldn't say Mr Ismay said they were going to make a record?
A. No, I wouldn't say he said those words – his attitude, or his language, was assumed that that was – that we were trying to make a record. I wouldn't say he used those words.
Q. When you say your impression, you mean your recollection of incidents now, Mrs Ryerson?
A. Yes, the impression it left on my mind, as I went down with it on my mind directly afterwards; the impression I gave the other people. As I say now, the other coming in since, and all, I couldn't say exactly the words that Mr Ismay said to me.
Q. You have correctly stated the substance of what he said, have you not?
A. Yes.[10]

Grace Bowen

Grace Bowen, Mrs Ryerson's maid, gave her own testimony about this incident at the Limitation of Liability hearings.

A. I saw a man come up and speak to Mrs Thayer and Mrs Ryèrson and sit down on the end of a steamer-chair and talk to them for some minutes; he had a white slip of paper in his hand, which he appeared to show to them …
Q. Did you afterwards have any conversation with Mrs Ryerson when you went down below, that afternoon?
A. Yes, directly after we went down …
Q. When was that?
A. Only a short time.
Q. Did Mrs Ryerson speak to you about her conversation with Mr Ismay?
A. Yes. She said …
Q. Now will you tell us what was said?
A. She said that Mr Ismay had come and spoken to her, she didn't know him very well, and objected to talking to people.
Q. Did she say anything about boilers?
A. I don't wish to be understood as quoting exactly what she said, because a long time has passed; I paid more attention to the fact she was bored by him than the rest.

Q. Just give us the substance of what was said?
A. As I remember, she said he said we were among the icebergs; and some of us said that was why it was so cold; but I don't mean, necessarily, he said so; and that the Deutschland had sent a message she was out of coal, and that we weren't going to bother about that, because – well, I can't remember whether she said because they wanted to make this a record trip, or because they wanted to see how soon we could get in. I should say she said a record trip and didn't want to be delayed. And she also said we hadn't been going at our best speed, and they were expecting to start up three more boilers; she didn't say Mr Ismay said they were going to start up the boilers in order to go faster, that was the impression I …[11]

Bruce Ismay Again

Mr Ismay's own testimony at the Limitation of Liability hearings took exception to the claims being made by his fellow *Titanic* survivors:

Q. Do you remember speaking on the afternoon of Sunday on deck to Mrs Ryerson, and showing her the message you had?
A. I remember speaking to Mrs Thayer.
Q. Was another lady with her?
A. Mrs Ryerson, I believe, was sitting on the other side of her.
Q. Was this the message you showed to them?
A. I believe I held it up to them …
A. I think I referred to the *Deutschland* being broken down.
Q. What did you understand from this telegram about the presence of the ice?
A. I do not think the telegram made very much impression on me with regard to the ice; what I was more impressed about was the steamer being broken down.
Q. Did not the message convey to you the fact that you were approaching the region of ice?
A. I naturally would assume that if the *Baltic* sent that message there must have been ice about somewhere …
Q. I think you have said that you produced the message in the presence of two ladies?
A. Yes.
Q. And talked to them about it?
A. Yes.
Q. Mrs Thayer and Mrs Ryerson?

A. Yes.
Q. Do you remember at all what you said to those ladies, either of them, with regard to the message?
A. No, I have very little recollection of what I said.
Q. Were you sufficiently acquainted with the locality of the ice referred to in the message, relatively to the position of the *Titanic*, to express any opinion as to how near it was?
A. I was not.
Q. Had you any belief as to how near or how far it was?
A. I had not.
Q. I think it would be convenient to put in the text of that message. I will read it from page 377 of Lord Mersey's report: 'From s.s. Baltic, April 14th to Capt. Smith, Titanic. Sent 11.52 a.m. Capt. Smith, Titanic. Have had moderate variable winds and clear fine weather since leaving. Greek steamer Athenai reports passing icebergs and large quantities of field ice to-day in latitude 41 degrees 51 minutes north, longitude 49 degrees 52 minutes west. Last night we spoke German oil tank steamer Deutschland, Stettin to Philadelphia, not under control short of coal, latitude 40 degrees 42 minutes north, longitude 55 degrees 11 minutes west. Wishes to be reported to New York and other steamers. Wish you and Titanic all success. Commander'. You were asked some questions as to dining with the captain. Had the captain a table which was called the captain's table?
A. In the saloon, yes.
Q. Yes, I know. Did you know that most of the boilers would have to be put on in order to test her out on this Monday and Tuesday?
A. I naturally assume if they were going to have a test of speed that they would put all the boilers on.
Q. Did you know that they were firing up some of the boilers on the Sunday?
A. I had no knowledge at all as to what was being done below.
Q. Was there any slowing down of the speed of the vessel on Sunday after the ice report that Captain Smith handed you?
A. I have no knowledge at all with regard to the speed of the ship.
Q. There was no slowing down that you knew of, was there?
A. No, not that I knew of. I say I had no knowledge with regard to the speed the ship was making.[12]

John Thayer Jr
On 25 June 1915 Mr Thayer testified at the Limitation of Liability hearings and described a conversation he and his father had had with Bruce Ismay on 14 April 1912. While discussing *Titanic*'s speed and arrival time in New York, Mr Ismay told the Thayers that the vessel's speed was scheduled to be increased very soon when 'Two more boilers are to be opened up today'.[13]

Discussion and Conclusions

The original newspaper reports describing Bruce Ismay's conversation with Emily Ryerson were second-hand accounts relayed to the press by Arthur Peuchen and Mahala Douglas. Whereas Peuchen merely said it was Ismay's intention to 'speed up' the ship, Mrs Douglas specified that *Titanic*'s speed was being increased in order to 'get out' of the icefield that everyone knew lay ahead of the ship. Although Mrs Ryerson might have mentioned this interpretation when she spoke with Mrs Douglas, it appears she did so based solely on her own *impression* of what Ismay told her instead of on his actual words:

> **Q.** He didn't say anything to you about speeding the ship up to get out of the ice?
> **Mrs Ryerson:** No, that was merely the impression that was left on my mind.

Bruce Ismay's own testimony at the Limitation of Liability hearings confirmed the accuracy of Mrs Ryerson's testimony on this particular point.

> **Senator Perkins**. You did not have any conversation on that Sunday about increasing the speed, did you?
> **Mr Ismay**. Not in regard to increasing the speed going through the ice, sir.

That this interpretation of events is correct is confirmed by John Thayer Jr, who said that Mr Ismay told him and his father that 'Two more boilers are to be opened up today' with no mention of 'getting out' of the approaching icefield. Indeed, for better or worse, the addition of these new boilers was a regularly scheduled event, since they had been lit and warmed up for a full twelve hours before being connected to the engines.

Even so, it is reasonably clear that Bruce Ismay was guilty of telling half-truths at the inquiries regarding the connection of new boilers on the evening of 14 April. Ismay carefully (and truthfully) denied having told Mrs Ryerson that the extra boilers were for the purpose of 'getting out' of the ice zone quicker, but he was apparently hoping to convince the court that he never mentioned the impending addition of new boilers *at all*.

'I had no knowledge at all as to what was being done below [in the boiler rooms],' Ismay insisted at the inquiries. 'I have no knowledge at all with regard to the speed of the ship.' The falsity of Ismay's two claims is made clear by the fact that he told Mrs Ryerson that the ship was making '20 or 21 knots' and also told Mrs Ryerson and the two Thayers that additional boilers were to be connected to *Titanic*'s engines that same evening. Too many people (including Arthur Peuchen, Mahala Douglas, Grace Bowen and Leila Meyer) were aware of Ismay's statement about the additional boilers for him to get away with his denials in the long run.

In truth, it seems unlikely that Ismay was involved in the actual decision-making process regarding extra boilers and impending speed increases and that he merely *relayed* that information to fellow passengers after receiving it from Captain Smith. This probability is illustrated by the way Ismay obtained the ice warning that he later showed to Mrs Ryerson.

Shortly after 1.40 on the afternoon of 14 April, George and Eleanor Widener were talking with Ismay on A deck when Captain Smith walked past the group and casually handed Ismay an ice warning received from the White Star liner *Baltic*. Smith continued on his way aft without saying a word, and Ismay simply put the ice message in his pocket as he bade farewell to the Wideners and headed below.[14]

Needless to say, the handing of this ice warning to Ismay was not something Captain Smith would have done for an ordinary passenger, so it seems likely he kept Ismay apprised of all significant occurrences that were scheduled to take place during the maiden voyage – such as adding new boilers and increasing the ship's speed. In turn, Ismay sometimes shared this type of information with fellow passengers like Mrs Ryerson and the Thayers as a simple matter of courtesy and good public relations.

Ismay's sense of courtesy also extended to soothing any fears and anxieties that might be exhibited by his fellow passengers. A later report alleged that on the afternoon of 14 April, George Widener and Mr Ismay were conversing together in one of *Titanic*'s public rooms when Widener remembered hearing about several Marconi messages warning of a large icefield directly ahead of the *Titanic*. Widener asked Ismay if the increasing chill outside wasn't a sign that the vessel was getting close to the icefield and he offered his opinion that it might be a safe precaution for the ship's speed to be decreased until she was clear of the danger zone.

'Oh, there is no danger,' Mr Ismay insisted as he casually dismissed George Widener's topic of conversation.

'Well,' Widener replied, 'if there is an ice pack in the course of this vessel we should slow down. I for one don't wish to be a passenger on a vessel to hit an iceberg.'[15]

Widener reportedly told his wife about this conversation later that same afternoon. Although Ismay's final response to Widener's misgivings is not on record, it *is* known that at seven o'clock that same evening three additional boilers were connected to *Titanic*'s engines and the vessel's speed increased to the fastest yet achieved during her maiden voyage.[16]

To repeat an earlier point, we doubt if Ismay was involved in the actual decision-making process about adding extra boilers or impending speed increases even though he definitely knew about these planned events in advance. Instead, we feel Ismay probably just *relayed* such information to fellow passengers after he received it from Captain Smith. (In the author's book *There's Talk of an Iceberg*, we investigate the possibility that increasing speed in order to 'get out' of ice regions was actually Captain Smith's *own* preferred method of operation instead of Ismay's.)

Nevertheless, Ismay definitely tried to give the Court of Inquiry the impression he was unaware of the impending addition of new boilers on 14 April and that *Titanic*'s speed would be increasing even though the ship was known to be approaching an icefield. Not everyone was taken in by Ismay's half-truths, because on 1 September 1913 *Titanic* survivors submitted a claim to the Limitation of Liability hearings that included the following codicil (with the author's emphasis in bold type):

> **17.** J. Bruce Ismay was the chairman and managing director of petitioner, and was on board the *Titanic* not as a passenger, but as the representative of the petitioner; that said Ismay participated in the navigation of the vessel and instructed, advised and influenced the master and the chief engineer with regard to the navigation of the vessel and the speed thereof, and was consulted by the master with respect to the navigation of the vessel. That said Ismay had full knowledge of the speed of said vessel on each day of her voyage, and immediately prior to the collision, and was also aware of the fact that on the evening of the disaster the vessel would reach the area in which ice was known by him to be, and that the vessel's course was not

> to be changed so as to avoid such area. Notwithstanding such knowledge, said **Ismay permitted the speed of the vessel to be maintained and increased in spite of the known danger of such a course, in view of the presence of ice, and the said Ismay, representing the petitioner, had knowledge of and acquiesced in the maintenance of speed and course of the *Titanic* by the master of the *Titanic* at the time of and prior to the disaster, knowing the risk that was incurred thereby, and assumed responsibility therefore on the part of the petitioner.**[17]

Whether or not *Titanic*'s increase in speed was a direct result of Ismay's own acquiescence, in the 1913 legal case of *Ryan vs the Oceanic Steam Navigation Company*, a court of law found *Titanic*'s officers guilty of negligence in running their ship at high speed under the conditions that prevailed on 14 April 1912. According to the *London Times* of 26 June 1913:

> In the action for damages for negligence brought against the Oceanic Steam Navigation Company by a man whose son was lost in the *Titanic* disaster, the jury returned a verdict to the effect that the navigation of the vessel had not been negligent as regards keeping a good look-out, but that there had been negligence as regards speed.

Naturally, the Oceanic Steam Navigation Company Ltd appealed this verdict to the Court of Appeals in November 1913 on points of law, but the appeal was unsuccessful. The company's next appeal was to the House of Lords, where its grounds of appeal were held to be without merit and were dismissed in February 1914. The verdict of negligence regarding the *Titanic*'s navigation with unjustified speed in a known icefield was therefore acknowledged and upheld for all time.[18]

16

Alice Johnson's *Titanic* Experience[1]

Elisabeth Backberg (known as 'Alice') was born in Finland on 24 January 1885 and by 1908 was married to Oscar Johnson (who was born in Sweden). In 1911 the couple lived in St Charles, Illinois, with their 3-year-old son Harold and 9-month-old daughter Eleanor. Oscar worked as an editor while Alice stayed at home and cared for their two children.

One day in 1911 Alice received a letter from her father in Finland saying that he was very ill and wanted to see her again before he died. Even though he knew he would miss his family terribly, Oscar agreed to his wife's request to visit her father, so in March of that year Alice packed up Harold and Eleanor, bade her husband goodbye and took a train to New York, where they boarded a ship for Europe.

By the time the three travellers reached Finland Alice's father had already passed away, so they spent the next nine months visiting relatives in Finland and Sweden. In Sweden they met 18-year-old Elin Braf and 26-year-old Helmina Nilsson, both of whom wanted to emigrate to America.

Alice's visit to Finland and Sweden passed all too quickly, and in the spring 1912 Oscar sent her money to purchase second-class tickets on a ship returning to the United States. Alice and her two children travelled to Southampton in company with Miss Braf and Miss Nilsson, but when they arrived there she learned that her ship's sailing had been cancelled due to the coal strike but that she could still book her passage on the *Titanic*. Being a practical woman, Alice decided that travelling in second class was a needless waste of money, so she decided to return to America in third class – a plan that would permit her to travel in company with Miss Braf and Miss Nilsson. Alice traded her family's three second-class tickets for five third-class tickets, and the five travellers shared third-class quarters on the ship, which set sail from Southampton on 10 April. In the meantime, Oscar Johnson was purchasing new rugs, furniture and other household fixtures with which to furnish his new home as a surprise for his wife and children when they returned to St Charles.

It was at 11.40 p.m. on 14 April 1912 when *Titanic* struck an iceberg, and young Harold was reportedly thrown off his upper bunk and awoke everyone in the cabin. Soon Alice could hear the sounds of voices and people rushing around in the passageway outside her steerage compartment. Realising that something unusual must have occurred, the young woman arose from her warm bed, stepped outside her cabin and asked passersby what was going on. A young immigrant girl from the cabin across the hall replied that the *Titanic* had reached New York and that everyone must hurry and get ready to go ashore; the girl even returned to her room to pack a big lunch, explaining to Alice that she had a three-day rail journey ahead of her after she finally stepped ashore in the New World.

Alice realised that the girl's unlikely explanation didn't make sense, but Elin Braf and Helmina Nilsson went up on deck to investigate and playfully kicked around some chunks of ice that had fallen from the iceberg. When officers told them to return to their cabins because the ship would soon be under way again, the two girls obeyed and headed back down toward their cabin.

Time passed, and eventually the gravity of the situation made itself known when a steward knocked at the cabin door with instructions for Alice and her companions. The steward told everyone the ship was sinking and that they must put on lifebelts and hurry to the upper decks, where passengers were being taken off in lifeboats. He added that there wasn't time for anyone to gather their belongings.

The frightened women quickly grabbed some blankets while Alice grabbed Harold and little Eleanor, and the group hurried to the *Titanic*'s upper decks as quickly as they could manage with two small children in tow. After reaching the boat deck the five travellers stepped outside the warm companionway into the chilly night air, and Alice looked out past the ship's railing into the darkness beyond and realised how vast the ocean seemed at that particular moment. The people standing around her were all talking in whispers, and Alice was impressed by how pale everyone looked. Clearly the situation was very serious, and Alice knew the time had come for her to try to save herself and her two little children.

Spying what seemed to be the very last lifeboat on board the ship, Alice Johnson started walking toward it even as the officer in charge decided the boat was filled to capacity and ordered it to be lowered away. As the boat began creaking downwards toward the sea Alice hurried to the officer's side and clung to his arm as she begged him to permit her and her children to enter the boat. The officer noticed that a man in the boat was just in the process of seating himself there, so he ordered the lowering to be halted and instructed the man to relinquish his seat to Mrs Johnson. The gentleman climbed back on to the *Titanic*'s deck without complaint, and Alice gratefully carried little Eleanor with her into the boat while hoping the man whose place she'd just taken would find a place of safety in another boat.

A young woman clad in a kimono now approached the deck officer and asked his permission to enter the lifeboat, but he replied that the boat was filled to capacity and couldn't carry even one more passenger safely. Once again the officer ordered the lifeboat to be lowered away, and once again it began creaking downward along the ship's side toward the black water below.

The boat had descended about 30ft below the boat deck when Alice happened to glance upward, and her eyes widened in sudden terror as she saw Elin Braf still standing beside the ship's railing holding 4-year-old Harold in her arms.

'Save my boy!' Alice screamed. Little Harold, who was crying his eyes out, reached for his mother who he could see sitting in the lifeboat below, but Elin was frozen into immobility, her fright having completely overwhelmed her. A man standing nearby realised what was happening in front of his eyes and knew that immediate action was required if the little boy was to be saved. Grabbing Harold by an arm and a leg, the gentleman lifted him over the railing and dropped him into the arms of several men who were waiting to catch him 30ft below. Alice was grateful beyond words to be reunited with her little boy, but the last she saw of Elin her friend was still standing on deck with her hands clasped over her eyes as if unable to cope with the reality of what was going on around her.

The lifeboat finally reached the water, and after the falls were released it began moving slowly away from the *Titanic*'s side. As the boat crept away into the darkness, Alice looked up at the *Titanic* again and saw the young kimono-clad woman standing at the railing watching the boat depart. The young woman put her head down on the railing and began to cry, and Alice continued to watch her as the lifeboat clunked and splashed its way further and further away from the ship.

The cold night air soon began to affect Alice and her two children, all of whom were barefoot and clad only in their nightclothes, and the fact that their bare feet were immersed in icy water that was slowly accumulating in the bottom of the boat only made matters worse. A woman seated near Alice was carrying a baby wrapped in a shawl, and the woman allowed her to wrap part of the shawl around little Eleanor to help protect her from the cold.

The men in Alice's lifeboat were rowing as fast as they could in order to avoid the suction they felt would occur when the *Titanic* went down. Even so, the boat had only moved 500 yards away from the *Titanic*'s side when the ship's lights suddenly went out, and then the great vessel herself vanished into the black depths of the North Atlantic.

'The sight was awful,' Alice recalled later. 'The sounds were worse.' She was referring, of course, to the heart-shaking, hopeless cries of the 1,496 human beings who had been left on board the *Titanic* and who were now freezing to death in the icy water over the spot where the largest ship in the world had just gone down.

One voice from somewhere out there in the darkness slowly became more distinct than the others. 'Save me! Save me!' a man cried as loudly as he could while he swam in the general direction of Alice's lifeboat. The man finally came within sight of the boat and desperately floundered toward it.

'Save me!' he panted. 'I've got a quart of whiskey!' The men in the lifeboat reportedly pulled the Italian gentleman out of the water, and the boat's oarsmen used the liquor as a stimulant for the next five hours until they were all taken on board the rescue ship *Carpathia*.

Back in St Charles, Illinois, Alice's husband Oscar continued to make preparations for his family's return home. He was undoubtedly appalled by the news that the *Titanic* had gone down, but his interest in the tragedy was only academic at that point because his wife and children were coming home from Sweden on another ship after being gone for an entire year. On the evening of 15 April, though, Oscar received a letter his wife had written before she and the children sailed for America, and the young husband was horror-stricken when he read: 'We have secured third-class passage on the White Star liner *Titanic* ...'

Staggered by this revelation, Oscar began the long wait for reliable news of his family's fate. Numb with anxiety, he spoke with a local reporter on the evening of 16 April.

'I have not yet given up hope,' Oscar said, 'but things look pretty tough for my wife and babies just now.'

On 17 April Oscar Johnson tried to take comfort in early newspaper reports claiming that practically all of the *Titanic*'s first- and second-class women and children had been saved, but finally the terrible strain of not knowing his family's fate took its toll: Oscar fainted into a semi-conscious condition for more than an hour, and his employer, John Daly, took him into his own home and confined him to bed there.

On 18 April early editions of the newspapers contained partial lists of the *Titanic*'s third-class passengers who were still unaccounted for. One list contained the entry, 'Elias Johnson and family', while the name 'Oscar Johnson' appeared in another list. Oscar realised that either of these names could be referring to his wife and their two children, and the knowledge that they might have gone down with the *Titanic* continued to gnaw away at his very soul. Oscar remained under the care of two physicians and was watched closely by Mr Daly, who began to fear that the terrible anxiety would undermine Oscar's reason.

On the night of 18 April the *Carpathia* finally arrived in New York Harbor and docked at the Cunard pier, and the *Titanic*'s survivors walked down the gangplank on to dry land.

'When we reached New York they thought we were immigrants and did not want to let us in,' Eleanor said in later years. 'Mother, with her broken English, had a hard time convincing the immigration officials that we were United States citizens. After they finally let us in they took us to a hospital. Mother was suffering from pneumonia.'

At 1.30 a.m. on the morning of 19 April Oscar Johnson's terrible anxiety about his family's fate disappeared when a cable addressed to him arrived at John Daly's home in St Charles, Illinois. The cable was from the White Star Line and read: 'Wife and children safe. Are at St Luke's . Oscar broke down and wept when he read the message confirming that his family was safe, but he received an even more welcome cable shortly thereafter: 'We are safe and sound. Don't worry. Will be home soon. Alice.'

When daylight came Oscar was feeling well enough to be up and around again, and he scanned all the newspaper accounts describing the landing of *Titanic*'s survivors the night before. Oscar left for New York that same day and was finally reunited with his family on the evening of Saturday, 20 April.

Alice, Harold and Eleanor were able to leave St John's Hospital on 22 April, and Oscar escorted his wife and children to the train for the journey back to Illinois. The family arrived safely in St Charles at 7.30 p.m. on 24 April. Alice, who had celebrated her 27th birthday three days before, was very tired; neither she nor little Eleanor were feeling well, but Harold was in high spirits and had already forgotten the events that he, his sister and mother had gone through just a few nights before.

Oscar guided his wife and children through the crowded Chicago Great Western train station to a waiting car and proceeded to take them to

John Daly's home for a celebratory meal. Soon the home was filled with visitors, and Alice began to tell her story of how she and her children had survived the sinking of the *Titanic*. Later that evening Oscar took his wife and children to the new home he'd furnished and decorated as a surprise for them when they returned from Europe.

Little Eleanor Johnson was only 6 years old when her father, Oscar, passed away in 1917; in later years Alice remarried several times but, as a family member recalled, she 'kept outliving husbands'. Alice eventually had a total of five sons and two daughters.

The years passed, and Eleanor grew up, married Delbert Shuman and had a son they named Earl. In later years Alice, Harold and Eleanor occasionally participated in *Titanic*-related events, and in 1959 they attended a special Chicago showing of the film *A Night to Remember*.

Harold passed away on 10 April 1968, exactly fifty-six years after the *Titanic* sailed from Southampton, and Alice died just eight months later on 19 December. After their deaths Eleanor continued to attend occasional survivor reunions and conventions, and in August 1996 she visited the disaster site on board the cruise ship *Royal Majesty* and scattered flowers on the water in memory of Elin Braf. In 1997 Eleanor was a guest of filmmaker James Cameron at the Chicago premiere of his blockbuster film *Titanic*.

Even though Eleanor was just a small child in 1912, in later years she was able to recall a couple of things from her time in the lifeboat after the *Titanic* went down. 'I have a memory of looking down and seeing all of these heads in the water and hearing all of this noise,' she told one reporter in 1996. To another reporter in 1962 she said, 'My cold feet and the screams, I can remember.'

Eleanor Johnson Shuman lived her entire life in the part of Illinois where her family lived in 1912, and she worked in Elgin as a switchboard operator and at Auto Meter products. On 7 March 1998 Eleanor passed away at Sherman Hospital in Elgin.

17

Michael 'Ty' Joseph, Titanic Survivor

The present author wrote the following obituary of Mr Joseph for the summer 1991 issue of the Commutator, *Vol. 15, No. 2.*

Michael J. Joseph, 84 years old, passed away of heart failure at Bi-County Hospital on Saturday, 18 May 1991 in Warren, Michigan.

Mr Joseph was only 4 years old when, along with his 24-year-old mother Catherine and 1-year-old sister Mary, he ended his visit to Syria and boarded the *Titanic* at Cherbourg in order to rejoin his father in the United States.

Mother and children were asleep when *Titanic* collided with the iceberg. Catherine Joseph was awakened by the impact, and shortly thereafter stewards circulated among the third class passengers ordering them to get out of bed while at the same time insisting that nothing was seriously wrong with the ship. Mrs Joseph got her children dressed, picked up little Mary and told Michael to hang onto her skirt tails as she started for the upper decks. The little boy did his best, but in the confusion he somehow lost his grip and became separated from his mother. At that point a man who Mr Joseph later described as his 'Guardian Angel' grabbed the little boy's hand and hurried him through the crowd towards the upper decks. Catherine Joseph apparently saw her son vanish in the throng ahead of her, and she rushed along as best as she could with her infant daughter; by the time she reached the lifeboats, however, Michael was nowhere to be seen.

Mrs Joseph and Mary got into a lifeboat carrying about twenty women and children and four men at the oars. The boat reached the water safely and was rowed away from the ship's side before she went down, and Catherine and the little Mary spent the rest of the night crying – Mary for herself and Catherine for her son Michael, who she thought had gone down with the ship. However, when Mrs Joseph and her daughter were taken on board the *Carpathia* Michael was already there waiting for them; he had left the *Titanic* in another lifeboat and made the trip to the rescue ship all by himself.

Mary and Michael both contracted measles while on the *Carpathia*, but this brief bout with illness had no lasting effect on either child. When Michael later attended St Peter and Paul School in Detroit, the nuns who learned of his experience on the *Titanic* bestowed the nickname 'Ty' on him and considered him a 'miracle child'. The nickname stuck all his life.

Michael Joseph was survived by his wife, Catherine, a daughter, Liela Dunlap and three sons, Peter, Tony, and Louis. He was a beer and soft drink delivery driver in Detroit and retired from Vernor's in 1967, but he never tired of telling friends and relatives how he escaped from the sea. He left nine grandchildren and two great-grandchildren, and today he is remembered with a beautiful pictorial headstone in Resurrection Cemetery in Clinton Township, Michigan. The stone shows a beautiful engraving of the *Titanic* steaming along in all her glory just as she did right up until the evening of 14 April 1912.

18

The Man Who Dressed as a Woman

The Coward

Somewhere in the shadow of the appalling *Titanic* disaster slinks – still living by the inexplicable grace of God – a cur in human shape, to-day the most despicable human being in all the world.

In that grim midnight hour, already great in history, he found himself hemmed in by the band of heroes whose watchword and countersign rang out across the deep – 'Women and children first!'

What did he do? He scuttled to the stateroom deck, put on a woman's skirt, a woman's hat and a woman's veil, and picking his crafty way back among the brave and chivalric men who guarded the rail of the doomed ship, he filched a seat in one of the life-boats and saved his skin.

His name is on that list of branded rescued men who were neither picked up from the sea when the ship went down nor were in the boats under orders to help get them safe away. His identity is not yet known, though it will be in good time. So foul an act as that will out like murder.[1]

Sentiments like the one expressed above by Logan Marshall were based on graphic stories told by the *Titanic*'s surviving passengers and crewmen after their rescue by the *Carpathia*. In later years, survivor Annie McGowan related one such story to the newspapers, even though she did not claim to be an actual eyewitness to the events she was speaking about:

> 'Women wouldn't leave their husbands,' McGowan said. 'They were screaming, and I could hear gunshots in the background. Apparently, some of the men had tried to dress like women in order to be rescued, and they were shot.'[2]

It has generally been regarded as lurid fiction that – in order to save his own life – an unidentified man disguised himself as a woman in order to secure a place in one of the *Titanic*'s lifeboats. But is the old story really just a legend?

No, it isn't.

As is the case with several other so-called 'legends' surrounding the *Titanic* tragedy, the 'man dressed as a woman' story is based on a true incident. In fact, it is based on separate incidents involving at least two different men who used the art of deception in order to survive the sinking of the *Titanic*. Although neither of the men in question went to the extreme length of donning a woman's dress in order to find a place in a lifeboat, the measures they *did* resort to resulted in their being mistaken for women – a ploy that permitted each man to enter a lifeboat unchallenged or remain in the boat unnoticed. Let's examine the known facts connected with each of these two men.

Men Known to Have Utilised Female Disguises

Edward Ryan

Edward Ryan (born 28 January 1888) was a young Irishman who boarded the *Titanic* at Queenstown in the hope of starting a new life in America. Ryan was one of the male steerage passengers lucky enough to survive the sinking of the *Titanic*, and on 6 May 1912 he wrote a letter to his parents telling them how his life had been spared:

> I stood on the *Titanic* and kept cool, although she was sinking fast. She had gone down about forty feet by now. The last boat was about being rowed away when I thought in a second if I could only pass out [i.e. get into the lifeboat] I'd be all right. I had a towel round my neck. I just threw this over my head and left it hang in the back. I wore my waterproof overcoat. I then walked very stiff past the officers, who had declared they'd shoot the first man that dare pass out. They didn't notice me. They thought I was a woman. I grasped a girl who was standing by in despair, and jumped with her thirty feet into the boat.[3]

Daniel Buckley

Daniel Buckley (born 28 September 1890) was a young Irishman who was travelling to America in the *Titanic*'s steerage section. After the collision Buckley went up to the boat deck and stood near several of the ship's lifeboats while they were being loaded with passengers and lowered away.

During the latter stages of the sinking a big crowd of men was standing on the boat deck while the 'sixth lifeboat' was being prepared for lowering. When a number of these men attempted to save themselves by jumping into the boat, Buckley decided to take his chances and jumped into the boat with them.

Suddenly two officers approached the lifeboat escorting a large number of steerage passengers of both sexes, and the officers ordered the men in the boat to get out of it again in order to make room for the ladies. Most of the men complied with the officers' order, but half a dozen firemen and sailors remained where they were and Buckley decided to remain in the boat with them. As he told his parents in a letter written on board the *Carpathia* on 18 April, '... I hid in the lower part of the boat'.[4]

Buckley's later testimony at the Senate inquiry revealed what happened next:

> I was crying. There was a woman in the boat, and she had thrown her shawl over me, and she told me to stay in there. I believe she was Mrs Astor. Then they did not see me, and the boat was lowered down into the water, and we rowed away out from the steamer.
>
> The men that were in the boat at first fought and would not get out, but the officers drew their revolvers and fired shots over our heads, and then the men got out. When the boat was ready, we were lowered down into the water and rowed away out from the steamer. We were only about 15 minutes out when she sank.[5]

Before we move on, it might prove instructive to compare Buckley's official Senate testimony with an unofficial newspaper version of what he supposedly said in that same testimony; the huge differences between these two versions of his story will highlight the uncertainty of our having to rely on newspaper stories containing supposedly verbatim survivor interviews that were actually filtered through the pen of a newspaper reporter:

> 'I was crying when I jumped into the boat and fell on the floor. Then I heard two officers who were in command order the men out. They

> refused to go till the officers drew their revolvers and began to fire over our heads.
>
> '"Here, stop your crying," said Mrs Astor, "and let me cover you." She put something over me like a shawl as I lay near her in the bottom of the boat. I could not stop crying, but peered from under the shawl and saw the officers firing over the men's heads and saw the men leaving the boat.'[6]

The first-hand admissions of Edward Ryan and Daniel Buckley provide the best proof imaginable that the so-called 'legend' of the man who dressed as a woman is based on fact instead of fiction. Both men freely admitted that a shawl (or a suitable substitute) was instrumental in permitting them to find (or keep) a seat in a lifeboat. Clearly the *Titanic*'s boat deck was illuminated so poorly during the evacuation that a shawl-like head covering altered a man's appearance just enough to disarm the suspicion of crewmen who were preoccupied with filling the lifeboats with women and children.

Which Lifeboat was Edward Ryan in?

Since Edward Ryan and Daniel Buckley freely admitted to wearing deceptive headgear in order to disguise themselves as women, can we determine which lifeboat each of these two men occupied? Let's look at evidence pertaining to several possible lifeboats.

Boat #13
Several eyewitnesses in boat #13 made observations pertaining to a man in their boat who they said was dressed in women's clothing.

Mary Glynn
In a 1912 newspaper interview, Miss Glynn was quoted as saying the following:

> Most persons think the report that one of the men disguised himself as a woman in order to escape is a manufactured tale. It is not. That man occupied a seat in the boat I was in, and I never looked with greater disdain upon any creature than he. He was an object of scorn to every man, woman, and child in our boat. Just imagine, a strapping man, twenty-two years old, who admitted that he donned feminine attire and wrapped a towel around his head in order to fool the officers who were placing the passengers in the boats.[7]

Julia Smyth
On 16 April 1962 a group of *Titanic* survivors attended a memorial service at the New York Seamen's Church Institute. A reporter said that Julia Smyth White, a survivor rescued in lifeboat #13, 'kept alive the legend of a man in woman's clothing who escaped by lifeboat'.

'I remember him,' she said. 'He was a lad from Dublin, and he got into our life boat, number 13, the last to leave the ship.'[8]

Agnes Sandström
Sometime between 1963 and 1973 Mrs Sandström wrote the following:

> I never heard any music from the *Titanic*, but two women in the boat, English speaking, with shawls around their heads appeared to be men and they were put to the oars. We were only a few hundred yards from the *Titanic* when she went down.[9]

Anna Nysten
In 1972 Miss Nysten granted a newspaper interview in which she said:

> They kept telling us not to worry, that everything would be all right. Lots of things I can't remember now. I can't remember getting in the lifeboat, but I remember being in it from 2 a.m. to 7 a.m. I saw a man in woman's clothing in the bottom of another lifeboat. I wasn't hurt, but I was nervous.[10]

It's difficult for us to know how much reliance can be placed on the reminiscences of Agnes Sandström and Anna Nysten, since both ladies were interviewed more than half a century after the *Titanic* went down – plus Miss Nysten claimed to have seen her 'man dressed as a woman' hiding in the bottom of *another* lifeboat instead of in boat #13. Perhaps the key facts in the Sandström and Nysten interviews are simply these: both ladies were saved in boat #13, and both ladies remembered seeing a man who disguised himself as a woman in order to obtain a seat in a lifeboat.

The most helpful information pertaining to boat #13 seems to be contained in the accounts of Mary Glynn and Julia Smyth – i.e. that the man disguised as a woman in boat #13 was a 22-year-old Irishman. Although this description fits Daniel Buckley almost perfectly (he was aged 21 years and 7 months), Buckley testified that he was wearing a shawl in his own lifeboat instead of the towel described by Mary Glynn. On the other hand, 24-year-old Edward Ryan freely admitted to wearing a towel around his own head just like the towel-wearing man in boat #13. Furthermore, Edward Ryan made no mention of shots being fired at his own lifeboat, and we know that no shots were fired during the loading of boat #13. (Daniel Buckley said shots were fired during the loading of his own lifeboat – a circumstance that eliminates boat #13 from our consideration in regard to Buckley's survival.)

Although the specific lifeboat that saved Edward Ryan can never be determined with 100 per cent certainty, the present author is inclined to believe that the towel-wearing Ryan was the same towel-wearing man who was seen in lifeboat #13.

Which Boat was Daniel Buckley in?

Boat #14

At the Senate inquiry, Senator William Alden Smith interrogated Fifth Officer Harold Lowe regarding Lowe's participation in the evacuation of the *Titanic*. When Lowe, who was in charge of lifeboat #14, told Senator Smith that his boat contained fifty-eight people, the senator asked him if all of those people had been women:

> **Mr Lowe**: They were all women and children, bar one passenger, who was an Italian, and he sneaked in, and he was dressed like a woman.
> **Senator Smith**: Had woman's clothing on?
> **Mr Lowe**: He had a shawl over his head, and everything else, and I only found out at the last moment.

Fifth Officer Lowe testified how he began transferring people from his own lifeboat into several other boats so that he could row back to the scene of the sinking and attempt to pick up survivors. Lowe then described how he came to discover the disguised man in question:

> **Mr Lowe**: I then asked for volunteers to go with me to the wreck, and it was at this time that I found this Italian. He came aft, and he had a shawl over his head, and I suppose he had skirts. Anyhow, I pulled this shawl off his face and saw he was a man. He was in a great hurry to get into the other boat, and I caught hold of him and pitched him in.
> **Senator Smith**: Pitched him in?
> **Mr Lowe**: Yes, because he was not worthy of being handled better.
> **Senator Smith**: You pitched him in among the women?

Mr Lowe: No, sir, in the fore part of the lifeboat in which I transferred my passengers.
Senator Smith: Did you use some pretty emphatic language when you did that?
Mr Lowe: No, sir; I did not say a word to him.
Senator Smith: Just picked him up and pitched him into this other lifeboat?
Mr Lowe: Yes.[11]

Lowe's observation that the man wore a 'shawl' instead of a towel strongly suggests he was talking about Daniel Buckley, who freely admitted that a woman threw her shawl over him in order to keep him from being ejected from his lifeboat during the loading process. It seems likely that Buckley would have kept that shawl over his head while transferring to another lifeboat, too, since his fear of Lowe's Browning automatic would certainly not have vanished after boat #14 left the *Titanic*'s side.

Buckley's statement that 'officers drew their revolvers and fired shots over our heads' while his lifeboat was being filled with passengers is strongly reminiscent of boat #14. According to Able-Bodied Seaman Joseph Scarrott's testimony at the British inquiry:

381: Who was taking charge of that boat when you got there – was there anybody?
Scarrott: When I got there I put myself in charge as the only sailorman there. I was afterwards relieved by the Fifth Officer, Mr Lowe.
383: … Now having got to boat 14, which was your boat, what was done about that?
Scarrott: Directly I got to my boat I jumped in, saw the plug in, and saw my dropping ladder was ready to be worked at a moment's notice; and then Mr Wilde, the Chief Officer, came along and said, 'All right; take the women and children,' and we started taking the women and children. There would be 20 women got into the boat, I should say, when some men tried to rush the boats, foreigners they were, because they could not understand the order which I gave them, and I had to use a bit of persuasion. The only thing I could use was the boat's tiller.
384: [*The Commissioner*] When you say that foreigners tried to rush the boat, were they passengers?
Scarrott: By their dress I should say yes, my Lord.
385: [*Mr Butler Aspinall*] Did the Fifth Officer assist you in this persuasion?
Scarrott: He was not there then.

386: Did you get these men out of your boat, or prevent them getting in?
Scarrott: Yes, I prevented five getting in. One man jumped in twice and I had to throw him out the third time …
393: Was Mr Lowe, the Fifth Officer, also in the boat?
Scarrott: We were practically full up. I was taking the women in when Mr Lowe came. There was another officer with him on the boat deck, but I do not know which one that was, and he said to this other officer: 'All right, you go in that boat and I will go in this.' That would mean No. 16 boat; she was abaft us, the next boat. Mr Lowe came in our boat. I told him that I had had a bit of trouble through the rushing business, and he said, 'All right.' He pulled out his revolver and he fired two shots between the ship and the boat's side, and issued a warning to the remainder of the men that were about there. He told them that if there was any more rushing he would use it. When he fired the two shots he fired them into the water. He asked me, 'How many got into the boat?' I told him as near as I could count that that was the number, and he said to me, 'Do you think the boat will stand it?' I said, 'Yes, she is hanging all right.' 'All right,' he said, 'Lower away 14.'

We know for a fact that a young man wearing a shawl somehow managed to remain unnoticed in boat #14 until his discovery by Fifth Officer Lowe. (Lowe felt the man was 'Italian', a term he used freely when referring to immigrants 'of the types of the Latin races'.[12] In other words, Lowe did not know the passenger's nationality but simply felt he *looked* foreign.) We also know that Joseph Scarrott scuffled with male passengers who rushed boat #14 and that Fifth Officer Lowe fired a number of shots to discourage more men from leaping into that same boat. If the shawl-wearing young man in boat #14 was indeed Daniel Buckley, the fact that he was hidden by the woman's shawl with (probably) his face averted from the officers might have prevented him from seeing the specific details of Scarrott's scuffle with unruly passengers and Lowe's gunfire to discourage further disorder. This might explain why certain details of Buckley's story differ a bit from the testimony of Harold Lowe and Joseph Scarrott.

In his book *The Irish Aboard Titanic*, author Senan Molony alleges that 'a consensus of scholars' believes Edward Ryan was the shawl-wearing man in boat #14, but the present writer is unaware of any such consensus comprised of reputable researchers. It's likely that the shawl-wearing Daniel Buckley and the shawl-wearing young man in boat #14 were one and the same.

Did Men Disguise Themselves as Women in Other Lifeboats?

It should be noted that Daniel Buckley's presence in boat #14 is not an absolute certainty because, according to Buckley, the *Titanic* went down just fifteen minutes after his lifeboat left the ship. That fact, plus Buckley's memory of men being physically ejected from the boat after shots were fired, raises the possibility that the young Irishman might have been saved in Collapsible C, since First Officer Murdoch did indeed fire shots in order to quell disorder at Collapsible C before that boat was launched just twenty minutes before the *Titanic* foundered.[13]

The main (and perhaps fatal) weakness in the belief that Buckley was in Collapsible C is that – unlike boats #13 and #14 – not a single survivor in 1912 ever mentioned seeing a man wearing articles of women's clothing in that boat. Even so, it must be acknowledged that – aside from Fifth Officer Lowe's chance observation – we have no other eyewitnesses to the presence of a shawl-wearing man in boat #14. This means a remote possibility exists that Buckley might have been saved in Collapsible C while somehow remaining completely unnoticed (or unmentioned) by that boat's occupants in 1912.

Let's take a look at a small body of uncertain evidence that might possibly pertain to a man who resorted to disguising himself as a woman in Collapsible C.

Collapsible C

Shawneene Abi-Saab

In a 1937 interview with the *Sharon Herald*, survivor Shawneene Abi-Saab mentioned a young man who entered her lifeboat (the lifeboat number being uncertain):

> 'I saw Gerios Youssef, one of my cousins. He pushed me toward one of the lifeboats. Sailors armed with revolvers drove the men away from the boats shouting, "Women and children first!" They shot into the air to frighten the men. Many passengers were overcome with fright. Banoura [Ayoub] and I were placed into the next to the last lifeboat to be lowered from the ship. A scared young man leaped over the side of the liner and landed in the bottom of the lifeboat. Women shielded him with their night clothing so the sailors wouldn't see him. They would have shot him.'[14]

Shawneene's comment about being in 'the next to last lifeboat' would of course apply to Collapsible C, as would her comments about shots being fired (by First Officer Murdoch) in order to control unruly passengers. However, her comment applies equally well to boat #14, which was the 'next to last' lifeboat positioned on the ship's aft port side and where Fifth Officer Lowe fired shots to control passengers in that location. In any case, Shawneene's statement about women shielding the frightened young man with their clothing is strikingly similar to Daniel Buckley's statement that a woman threw her shawl over him in order to keep him from being seen and thrown out of her lifeboat.

Helga Hirvonen

One account that might possibly be connected with Collapsible C is that of Helga Hirvonen, who claimed to have left the ship in that boat, even though the Encyclopedia Titanica website claims she was in lifeboat #15:

> Finally when I got to the deck I could see people being put in life boats. Two or three men when they found out they couldn't get off the doomed steamer until after the women robed themselves in women's clothing. I saw a man disappear from my side. A few seconds later he reappeared with a boy whom he had dressed in girl's clothing. The boy was saved. I was the last woman to be given a place in the last life boat. I was very carefully picked up because I had my baby with me. Mrs Hakkarainen was seized by the neck and foot, I believe, and tossed in a life boat. She fainted. Her husband bade her a fond goodbye. He intended to get into a lifeboat but heroically gave way to others.
>
> I suppose we had been away from the *Titanic* 20 minutes when it went down. I saw it plainly ... I was in the boat with the managing director of the steamship company, J. Bruce Ismay, although at the time I didn't know it.[15]*

It's important to note that Miss Hirvonen never claimed to have seen the two or three disguised men with her own eyes, so it's possible she heard rumours about these things later on after being picked up by the *Carpathia*. The claim about the boy dressed in girl's clothing is harder to explain away, but to the best of this writer's knowledge no such person was ever noticed by any eyewitness known without doubt to have been saved in either Collapsible C or

---

* There is no way to know if her informant was accurate in telling her she was in the same boat as Ismay.

lifeboat #15. The boy could not have been Daniel Buckley, who did not don a woman's shawl until after he was already crouched and hiding in his own lifeboat. The only similar incident of a boy disguised as a girl we are presently aware of was that of 11-year-old William Carter, who was denied entry into lifeboat #4 before his mother put a woman's hat on his head so that he would be counted as a female.

Fatimah Muslamani

One account possibly connected with Collapsible C alleges that a man dressed in woman's garb *attempted* to enter that boat during the evacuation, but the reliability of this account is open to question. In 1980 Janette Goutimy wrote a letter to a newspaper regarding her aunt, Fatimah Muslamani, who the Encyclopedia Titanica website claims was 'most likely' saved in Collapsible C:

> She risked her own life by returning to the room she was sharing with a woman who had a 4-year-old child. She didn't see them anywhere around, so she sensed something must have happened to the mother and the child was still in bed. Sure enough, she was right. She grabbed the child out of bed and ran to the lifeboat. She also had two cousins who died on the ship. One was shot because he tried to disguise himself as a woman. The other was thrown overboard because he was trying to get on the lifeboat. She shed so many tears over the way they died.[16]

Aside from the fact that Fatimah Muslamani's presence in Collapsible C is conjectural, and despite the fact that Mrs Goutemy's 1980 statement seems pretty straightforward, one can't help but wonder if the facts might have become slightly garbled after decades of retelling. We know that First Officer Murdoch did indeed fire shots in the air at Collapsible C and that Hugh Woolner and other men forcibly ejected male passengers who refused to leave the boat, so perhaps the cousin wearing women's apparel was merely *deterred* from entering the lifeboat by Murdoch's gunfire and perhaps the other cousin was forcibly thrown out of the boat without being thrown overboard. The present writer is proposing this tentative 'toned-down' scenario because of a 1912 newspaper story about Fatimah Muslamani that was considerably less dramatic than her niece's 1980 statement describing how her two cousins lost their lives:

> She [Fatimah Muslamani] was being accompanied to this country by two cousins, but they were left aboard the *Titanic* when she was placed in a lifeboat and they perished in the ocean.[17]

If Fatimah Muslamani's cousins really died by gunfire and by being thrown overboard as Mrs Goutemy believed in 1980, it would have been perfectly understandable if Muslamani wished to hide those facts from the press when she was interviewed in 1912. However, the present author suspects that Muslamani's 1912 interview was probably pretty close to the truth and that her niece simply misremembered a few details of her aunt's story by the time she wrote them down in 1980.

Thamine Tannous

According to the Encyclopedia Titanica website, some researchers believe that Mrs Tannous (Thelma Thomas) was saved in Collapsible C, but others believe she was rescued in boat #14. In any case, in 1962 Thelma Thomas granted an interview describing how she boarded her lifeboat and seated herself next to a person who turned out to be a man dressed in woman's clothing. Far from despising the man for his deceit, however, the ensuing years imbued Mrs Thomas with a certain feeling of gratitude:

> 'If that impersonator had not been with us to help pull the boat away from the ship, I probably would not be here,' she said. 'We would have capsized like so many others ... I had spoken to him on the ship. He was coming from Lebanon but not from my province ...'
>
> After the [life]boat was lowered to the water Mrs Thomas said three crewmen at the oars had difficulty in trying to move it away from the sinking ship.
>
> 'We should have another man to help us out of here,' one of the crewmen shouted.
>
> Mrs Thomas wanted to know what the shouting was about. She nudged the person next to her in the lifeboat.
>
> 'Then I recognized this fellow,' she said. 'He was wearing a babushka and a lady's coat. I remembered him from the ship where I had spoken to him in Lebanese.
>
> 'I asked him: "What did they say?"
>
> 'They need another man but I am afraid to help because they may throw me over the side,' she said the man replied.
>
> 'I reached over and pulled the babushka from his head,' Mrs Thomas said. 'I prodded him and told him to go ahead and help the men. He finally did. The crewmen did not throw him overboard. All they said was: "Come on, row. Let's get out of here."'[18]

Mrs Thomas had already told a different reporter the same thing four years previously:

> Mrs Thomas said a man disguised as a woman jumped on their life boat, and it wasn't until they were underway that she personally discovered the impersonator.
>
> 'He turned out to be our savior after all,' she added. 'It took a great deal of effort to row away from the sinking ship, and if he hadn't been aboard we probably would have capsized also.'[19]

Hanne Touma

One second-hand account recorded in 2012 comes from an interview with Phyllis Thomas (wife of Hanne Touma's grandson) and Kimberly Gazso (Hanne Touma's great-granddaughter):

> They [Hanne Touma and her two children] found themselves on the second-to-last life boat, watching the *Titanic* break in half and sink below the surface, sitting with a man who'd dressed himself in a woman's coat and wig to escape with the women and children. It was his boots, Anna would later tell her family, that gave him away.[20]

Kimberly Gazso and Phyllis Thomas both believe their relative was saved in 'the second-to-last lifeboat' based on the belief of Hanne Touma's son Michael that his mother was saved in Collapsible C.[21] Although this could be a reference to Collapsible C, it could just as easily be referring to the 'second to last lifeboat' in any of the four quads of lifeboats that existed on the ship. To complicate matters, researcher Michael Poirier has provided the author with an article claiming that Hanne Touma heard pistol shots 'just as we were being rowed away'.[22] Since the last undisputed use of firearms on the *Titanic* took place right beside Collapsible C while that boat was still in the process of being loaded with passengers, Touma's information about hearing shots as her boat rowed away from the ship might indicate one of two things: (1) an officer fired shots after Collapsible C left the ship (a possible reference to reports that an officer shot passengers before taking his own life?), or (2) Hanne Touma was not in Collapsible C but was in another lifeboat that was rowing away from the ship when Fifth Officer Lowe fired his pistol at lifeboat #14.

In addition to the above-listed uncertainties, Archibald Gracie's book claims that Hanne Touma and her two children were the 'foreign family' saved in lifeboat #2, and Joseph Thomas (Touma's grandson) subscribes to that opinion.[23] However, researcher Peter Engberg believes Gracie's book was mistaken and that the 'foreign family' Gracie referred to was actually the Kink family.[24]

In short, the notion that Hanne Touma and her two children were definitely saved in Collapsible C is far from proven. It should also be pointed out that the 2012 claim about Mrs Touma's sighting of a man dressed in a woman's coat and wig has come to us second-hand via her relatives and that the passing of many decades often caused survivors (or their relatives) to introduce unintentional inaccuracies (or even enhancements) into their recollections of the *Titanic* disaster. Of course, we cannot disregard Mrs Touma's alleged memory of a man dressed in women's clothing who was saved in her lifeboat, but – in light of our listed *caveats* – there seems to be no way for us to determine whether or not the man in question was saved in Collapsible C or whether or not his name was Daniel Buckley.

Even though there are no 1912 primary sources supporting the premise that a shawl-wearing man was rescued in Collapsible C, let us assume for a moment that Buckley *was* that man. If that was indeed the case, we have solved one mystery by reopening another: 'Who was the shawl-wearing man encountered by Fifth Officer Lowe in boat #14?'

Boat #4

It's a well-established fact that Madeleine Astor left the *Titanic* in lifeboat #4 at 1.50 a.m., and it's equally well known that Daniel Buckley described the woman who concealed him underneath her shawl by telling the Senate inquiry, 'I believe she was Mrs Astor.' Is there any legitimate evidence that Buckley might have left the ship in lifeboat #4 and had personal contact with Mrs Astor?

Bridget Bradley

In Mary Higgins' booklet describing her mother's experiences on board the *Titanic*, Higgins described Bridget Bradley's parting from Daniel Buckley as follows:

> The last Bridget saw of Daniel was when she called 'Goodbye' and hoped he would follow in another boat. He replied, 'If I don't make it, will you please get in touch with my sister?' 'What is the number of your boat?' Bridget replied. 'Number 4.' It was the last remaining boat on the ship. In this boat was Mrs Astor, wife of John Jacob Astor, who was pregnant.[25]

Higgins' use of punctuation is confusing, since she seems to be saying that Bradley asked Buckley for his lifeboat number and that Buckley answered 'Number 4'. However, it was actually Bradley herself who Higgins believes was lowered in lifeboat #4, since a careful reading of the above paragraph and the one that follows it shows that the paragraph's proper punctuation should be as follows:

> The last Bridget saw of Daniel was when she called 'Goodbye' and hoped he would follow in another boat. He replied, 'If I don't make it, will you please get in touch with my sister? What is the number of your boat?' Bridget replied, 'Number 4.' It was the last remaining boat on the ship. In this boat was Mrs Astor, wife of John Jacob Astor, who was pregnant …
>
> As boat number 4 was lowered, Bridget heard someone from above call 'How many women are there in the boat?' 'Twenty-four' came the answer. 'That's enough. Lower away.' As the boat quickly reached the water, Bridget could see at once how seriously the ship was sinking …[26]

In conjunction with the above quote we should pay special heed to a small disclaimer that Mary Higgins wrote in the introduction to her book. 'Some liberties have been taken with the dialogue,' she wrote, 'but the names of the people in this book are all real people …' It is therefore quite possible that the above-quoted conversation between Bridget Bradley and Daniel Buckley never took place at all.

If Bradley really did leave the ship in lifeboat #4 at 1.50 a.m. as Mary Higgins believes, her scenario might support our earlier (unproven) premise that Buckley left the ship shortly afterwards in Collapsible C at 2 a.m. To repeat, though, no 1912 primary sources support the premise that a shawl-wearing male stowaway was saved in Collapsible C.

The Encyclopedia Titanica website claims that, instead of entering lifeboat #4, Bradley left the *Titanic* in boat #13 at 1.40 a.m., but – typically – the website provides no documentation for its claim. In 1912 Bradley herself said only that her lifeboat left the *Titanic* sometime after 1 a.m.,[27] so trying to assign her to a specific lifeboat at this late date seems to be a futile exercise based solely on conjecture.

In any case, it is clear that Mary Higgins' book cannot be used to determine which lifeboat Daniel Buckley entered when he left the *Titanic* and that it almost certainly was not lifeboat #4 (a conclusion strengthened by the fact that not one occupant of boat #4 mentioned seeing a young man wearing a shawl). Besides, despite the fact that Buckley thought it was Mrs Astor who put a shawl over him, storekeeper John Foley said Mrs Astor gave her shawl to a 'Swedish' woman who had a little girl and spoke 'some foreign lingo'.[28]

Boat #10

Mary Fortune

After the *Carpathia* reached New York, an article about survivor Mary Fortune appeared in the *New York Times*:

> Through her son-in-law, H. C. Hutton of Winnipeg, Manitoba, Mrs Mark Fortune told how she and her three daughters, Lucille, Mabel and Alice, now stopping at the Hotel Belmont, were rescued from the *Titanic* and after being separated from her husband and son Charles, were placed in a boat with a Chinaman, an Italian stoker, and a man dressed in woman's clothing. Of all the occupants of this lifeboat, only one, the stoker, could row. Mrs Fortune's daughters took turns at the oars ... Mrs Fortune and her three daughters were placed in the tenth boat that was lowered away ... There was consternation among the passengers on their boat, most of whom were women, when it was ascertained that four of the crew would have to be taken off to man another boat. That left but one member of the crew to navigate. The stoker knew how to handle an oar, but the Chinaman was of little use. The man dressed in woman's clothing did his best to row, but did not seem familiar with an oar. This man wore a woman's bonnet and a veil, in addition to a skirt and blouse, which he had evidently picked up in a hurry as he ran through the ship.[29]

The next day, a seemingly corroborative article containing additional details appeared in the *St Louis Globe Democrat*:

> The mother and daughters were placed in lifeboat No. 10. It was terribly overcrowded, Mrs Fortune told her brother-in-law, and with the exception of a Chinaman, a stoker and four men who were to man the boat, all in it were supposed to be women.
>
> It became necessary to transfer these four men to another boat, which was without a crew. This left only the Chinaman to row. About this time the discovery was made that a veiled person in woman's clothes was a man. He made no explanation as to why he was so dressed and none was asked of him, but that he donned the clothes to escape with the women when men were

being held back to die there was no question. Nor did anyone ask his name or learn it later. The only request made of him was that he take an oar. This he did reluctantly. The Chinaman and stoker knew almost nothing about rowing and the man in woman's clothing knew less.[30]

On 22 April the *Washington Times* chimed in with extra details:

> A man in women's clothes was among the survivors in lifeboat 10, according to Mrs Mark Fortune, Winnipeg, who was rescued with her three daughters on the boat … Mrs Fortune and her daughters were quoted to this effect by H. C. Hutton, Mrs Fortune's brother-in-law …
>
> The lifeboat, said Mrs Fortune, was greatly overcrowded. Four of the survivors were in the boat and the rest were supposed to be women, with the exception of one stoker and a Chinaman. There was a figure forward dressed in a brown mackintosh with a shawl like that of a steerage passenger over its head. The face was completely hidden. Miss Alice Fortune sat directly beside the supposed woman.
>
> Soon after the boat had left the ship the four sailors were transferred to another boat and at this time it was discovered that the figure was that of a man. When somebody asked who he was he refused to say.[31]

Regarding the last article's reference to the disguised man wearing a 'brown mackintosh', it should be noted that Edward Ryan admitted to wearing a 'waterproof overcoat' as part of his own attempt to pass himself off as a woman. Initially, the present author entertained the notion that Ryan might have been the veiled figure who allegedly sat beside Alice Fortune in lifeboat #10, but – as will be seen – additional research has quashed that notion pretty decisively.

When the *Carpathia* arrived in New York, Charles H. Allen, the fiancé of Miss Ethel Fortune, was waiting for the family and acted as their intermediary during their trip home to Winnipeg in his private railway car. On 26 April Mr Allen was interviewed by the local newspaper:

> Mr Allen is indignant at the reports crediting certain 'interviews' sent out from New York to Mrs Fortune and her daughters …
>
> 'Another story has gained currency that a man escaped into a boat dressed as a woman. This may be so, but certainly the Fortune ladies did not say it. They do not know whether it was so or not. They never discussed the matter with a New York reporter; this is certain. I was the channel of communication between them and the world, and I never thought of the thing.'[32]

On 27 April an article was published in the *Minneapolis Journal*:

> Mrs Mark Fortune, whose husband was drowned on the *Titanic*, denies the interviews credited to her and says she never saw a reporter from the time the *Titanic* sank until yesterday. She says that neither her nor her daughter saw anyone shot on board. She denies that she saw Ismay crawling into one of the boats and laughs at the story that a man secured a seat in the boat by dressing as a woman. Her daughters, she says, rowed at times for exercise and to keep warm.

Two days later, a follow-up article appeared in the *Montreal Star*:

> Charles H. Allen, fiancé of Ethel Fortune, who met the Winnipeg survivors of the *Titanic* at New York, characterizes as 'unadulterated fakes' the statements attributed to Mrs Fortune by a New York reporter who he claims never saw her.
>
> These statements were to the effect that Mrs Fortune saw J. Bruce Ismay climb into the boat before the three Fortune ladies and that she saw a man climb into that boat disguised as a woman and that she asserted first class passengers should have been saved before the women.[33]

Charles Allen's statements make it clear that the Fortune ladies never spoke with any newspaper reporters until after they arrived home in Winnipeg. This seems to be true, because at least two of our three newspaper mentions linking the Fortunes with a man dressed in woman's clothing originated with Heber C. Hutton, Mrs Fortune's son-in-law. In any case, it appears that these claims that the Fortunes saw a veiled man wearing a brown mackintosh and shawl in lifeboat #10 were just figments of someone's imagination.

But there are complications, because another survivor (who some researchers believe was saved in lifeboat #10) gave an interview pertaining to this very subject.

Katherine Gilnagh

In 1957 Katherine Gilnagh Manning gave a recorded interview to the BBC in which she said the following:

> Oh yes, there was women [in our lifeboat] and one man; he had jumped with a raincoat and a towel on his head, and he used to help us row the boat ...[34]

We should point out that if Miss Gilnagh was seated in lifeboat #10, the presence of the disguised man in her lifeboat could be explained by the fact that

Fifth Officer Lowe had earlier transferred a disguised man from lifeboat #14 into lifeboat #10, where the man might have been seen by Miss Gilnagh. Just to complicate matters, though, Miss Gilnagh's description of a towel-wearing, raincoat-clad man is identical to the descriptions of a towel-wearing, raincoat-clad man who was seen by other eyewitnesses in lifeboat #13. Since Edward Ryan is the only man we know of who was disguised in a raincoat with a towel wrapped around his forehead, there is a distinct possibility that Miss Gilnagh and the disguised man in her lifeboat were both saved in lifeboat #13 and that the man in question was actually Mr Ryan.

Boat #12

Elias Nicola Yarred

In 1981 a nephew of Lebanese survivor Elias Nicola Yarred (saved in boat #12) wrote an account of his uncle's *Titanic* experiences that included the following information:

> There was one young couple with a baby who 'put one over' on the crew. The wife was very shrewd; she dressed her young husband as a woman, covered his head with a shawl and gave him the baby. He was in one lifeboat and she was in ours. Both were rescued by the *Carpathia*.[35]

This story presents a mystery, since no husband (whether disguised or not) comes to mind who was rescued along with his child in one lifeboat while his wife was rescued in another boat. Perhaps Elias Nicola Yarred's memory of this incident became hazy over the years, or perhaps some sort of misunderstanding occurred between the time Yarred related his experiences to his nephew and the time the nephew recalled those experiences and wrote his recollections of them down for publication.

Collapsible C

Unnamed Passenger

After arriving in New York, Mauritz Björnström-Steffansson told a reporter how he and Hugh Woolner helped counter a rush on Collapsible C by ejecting an unknown man from that boat:

> The second class and the steerage passengers had congregated on the boat deck and things got a little more panicky. Some of the men struggled to get into the boats, and some we had to pull bodily out by the legs. One man I noticed had a blanket over his head and tried to pass himself as a woman, and we flung him back among the crowd.[36]

Since this passenger was ejected from Collapsible C, the only remaining unlaunched boat he might have entered was Collapsible D.

Collapsible D

Borak Hannah

In 2012 a journalist named William Kashatus wrote an online article containing the claim that surviving passenger Borak Hannah (Bert Johns) used deception in order to gain a place in one of the *Titanic*'s lifeboats:

> Borak Hannah tried to stow away on a lifeboat but was recognized by a senior officer. Threatened at gunpoint, he agreed to re-board the ill-fated ship. Later, Hannah, disguised as a woman, managed to get into the last lifeboat which was loaded and lowered at 2:05 a.m. [i.e. Collapsible D].[37]

Unfortunately, the account as it was written by Kashatus does not jibe with the only published (and sometimes rather sensational) accounts describing how Bert Johns left the *Titanic*. According to his 1912 newspaper interviews, Mr Johns leapt down into a lowering lifeboat after being turned away from the boat by the officer in charge.[38] (Johns sometimes claimed he was shot at by the officer and even showed alleged bullet holes in his coat to prove it.)[39] In any case, Mr Johns said nothing about which lifeboat he entered or whether or not he dressed as a woman in order to do so, and it is unknown where William Kashatus obtained his undocumented information.[40] Barring further information, Kashatus's claim cannot be given any credence.

Were Disguised Chinese Passengers in Collapsible C?

One additional alleged incident regarding disguised men in Collapsible C involved the Chinese passengers who were saved in that lifeboat.

Evidence Regarding Their Actual Presence in the Boat

J. Bruce Ismay
Mr Ismay testified about this subject at the Senate *Titanic* inquiry:

> We found four Chinamen stowed away under the thwarts after we got away. I think they were Filipinos, perhaps. There were four of them.[41]

George Rowe
Quartermaster Rowe testified at the Senate *Titanic* inquiry:

> When daylight broke, we found four men, Chinamen, I think they were, or Filipino.

When asked if these men were hidden underneath the seats, Rowe replied:

> Not under the seats then, sir. They came up between the seats.[42]

August Weikman
The evidence surrounding the actual entry of the four Chinese men into Collapsible C is contradictory. According to Weikman's newspaper interview:

> They put the women and the children in the lifeboats and then they started to put in the crew with them. One man to every five women. When no women were near the boats they took the men, whether they were passengers or crew, anybody who stood nearest, and this accounts for the three Chinamen who were taken off.[43]

Emily Goldsmith
Mrs Goldsmith's memories of the Chinese passengers were in stark contrast to August Weikman's description of their sedate entry into Collapsible C:

> The members of the crew tried in vain to get the four Chinese out of the boat, but they refused to budge and they had to let them stay. Just before the men above began to let the lifeboat down a number of Italians tried to get in, and it was only by firing revolvers in the air and threatening to kill them that they were kept out.[44]

Hugh Woolner

Mr Woolner confirmed Mrs Goldsmith's description of the attempt that was made to roust unwilling passengers from Collapsible C:

> There was a sort of scramble on the starboard side [of the ship], and I looked around and I saw two flashes of a pistol in the air ... they were up in the air, at that sort of an angle. I heard Mr Murdoch shouting out, 'Get out of this, clear out of this,' and that sort of thing, to a lot of men who were swarming into a boat on that side ... We went across there because we heard a certain kind of shouting going on, and just as we got around the corner I saw these two flashes of the pistol, and Steffanson and I went up to help to clear that boat of the men who were climbing in, because there was a bunch of women – I think Italians and foreigners – who were standing on the outside of the crowd, unable to make their way toward the side of the boat ... So we helped the officer to pull these men out, by their legs and anything we could get hold of ... I should think five or six [men]. But they were really flying before Mr Murdoch from inside of the boat at the time.[45]

Allegations of Chinese Passengers Wearing Disguises

We've seen from the Goldsmith and Woolner accounts that four Chinese passengers refused to get out of Collapsible C when ordered to do so, but our main focus here is to determine how these men managed to enter the lifeboat in the first place. Although the four Chinese men might have forced their way into the boat with other unruly male passengers and then refused to leave, a number of newspaper survivor interviews suggest that their entry into Collapsible C might possibly have involved disguises.

Edward Dorkings

Mr Dorkings was saved on the overturned Collapsible B, and in May 1912 he relayed the following information while giving a speech at the Star Theatre:

> The rule of 'women first' was rigidly enforced. Two stewards hustled into a lifeboat that was being launched. They were commanded to get out by the officers and on refusing to obey the command, were shot down and thrown into the sea. A Chinaman was also shot for the same cause. Afterwards, aboard the *Carpathia*, I saw six Chinamen who had escaped in the life-boats, disguised as women.[46]

During a theatre presentation the following month Dorkings repeated his claim that 'some Chinamen made their escape by dressing as women'.[47]

Elizabeth Dowdell

Miss Dowdell was saved in lifeboat #13 but had this to say about the rescued Chinese men in Collapsible C:

> Several Chinamen were clever in wrapping themselves snugly into blankets and thereby escaping and joined the women and children who had been saved …[48]

Percival Keen

After returning to the United Kingdom, Steward Keen spoke with a reporter:

> At Southampton we had taken on board ten Chinamen, part of the crew of a ship, some of whom came up dressed as women with shawls over their heads, and managed to smuggle themselves into the boats before we discovered the fraud.[49]

Nellie O'Dwyer

Miss O'Dwyer, who was saved in boat #10, was quoted in the newspapers as saying the following:

> Five or six Chinamen were found at the bottom of one boat. The way they were saved was by fixing their hair down their backs, and putting their blankets about them. They were taken for women when the boats were leaving the ship.[50]

The Daily Telegraph

On 20 April, the *Daily Telegraph* reported the following:

> Among the rescued from the sinking *Titanic* were six Chinese, who stowed themselves away in one of the vessel's boats before she left England.* When the crash came the Chinese did not become excited. They knew the lifeboat would be lowered if there was any danger of the *Titanic* going down. All had shawls, and when they heard the shouts of those on board, 'Women to

* The Chinese seamen did not hide themselves in the lifeboats before the *Titanic* left Southampton but were booked as regular third-class passengers.

> be saved first' they covered themselves with the shawls, leading the crew to believe that they were women. In the darkness they escaped detection. It was not known that they were Chinese until they were taken on board the *Carpathia*. Then some of the *Carpathia*'s crew wanted to toss them into the sea, it was said, but the officers of the Cunard vessel put them in irons instead. How the Chinese escaped being discovered by the crew of the *Titanic* or some of her passengers puzzled those on board the *Carpathia*.[51]

The Denver Post

On 19 April, *The Denver Post* reported the following:

> In one of the last lifeboats launched, two Chinamen, employed in the galley, had hidden themselves. They were stretched in the bottom of the boat, faced downward, and made no sound. So excited were the women that they did not notice the presence of the Chinese until the boat had put off the liner. The Chinamen were found. The officer in charge of the boat drew his revolver and in the presence of the already horror-stricken women shot both to death. The bodies were thrown overboard.[52]

Analysis: Although there is no question that four Chinese passengers saved their own lives by huddling beneath the seats of Collapsible C, it should be noted that no occupants of that lifeboat ever claimed that the men in question were disguised as women. Survivors who relayed those stories to newspaper reporters were all talking about events that supposedly occurred in lifeboats other than their own, and the two newspaper sources did not name the eyewitnesses from whom they supposedly received their information. It should also be noted that all kinds of wild rumours were circulating on board the *Carpathia* after the rescue, and it's possible that the casual racism of 1912 might explain the unsavoury rumours that *Titanic*'s Chinese survivors saved themselves by disguising themselves as women.*

In truth, it seems pretty unlikely that four shawl-wearing men disguised as women could have trooped unhindered into Collapsible C without any

* An example of such racism was experienced by Japanese survivor Masabumi Hosono on the *Carpathia*, after which he wrote, 'While in the smoking room I had been made fun of by everyone and had felt embarrassed and miserable. After all, sailors and others were foulmouthed rascals and I just turned a deaf ear to whatever they said.' *Voyage* #27, winter 1998, pp. 122–9.

bystanders questioning their appearance and pointing them out to First Officer Murdoch.

A Skirt-Wearing Man on Board the Carpathia

Arpad Lengyel
In May 1912 Dr Lengyel, a *Carpathia* passenger, wrote an account of his vessel's rescue of the *Titanic*'s survivors that contained the following passages:

> Many people have asked me to talk about some of the rumours such as were any of the survivors men who wore women's clothes? I remember a young man who had a skirt on; naturally, I didn't think that he did this deliberately; there was nothing else available that he could put on quickly.[53]

Dr Lengyel's use of the phrase '… nothing else available that he could put on quickly' suggests he believed the young man in question donned his skirt during the actual evacuation of the *Titanic*. However, the skirt might actually have been provided to the young man by a generous *Carpathia* passenger who saw he had nothing else to wear. At this late date, it's unlikely we'll ever know the truth of the matter or be able to determine the survivor's identity.

A Man Who was Offered the Chance to Dress as a Woman

Shawneene Abi-Saab
On 12 April 2012 Dr Josyann Abisaab wrote about the *Titanic* experience of his great-grandfather's cousin, Gerios Yousseff Abi-Saab, who was lost in the sinking:

> My father recalls the story told by his uncles, Gerios' sons. One of the surviving women, presumed to be Shawneene [Abi-Saab] since Banoura [Ayoub] never returned to Lebanon, came back after the *Titanic* disaster to the village of Thoum, where Gerios' wife, lived with her children. The survivor revealed that she offered to disguise Gerios with women's clothing in the hope of getting him into one of the few lifeboats but that he declined the offer by solemnly declaring: 'I was born a man and I will die as a man.' As he tried to steer his cousins Shawneene and Banoura to the safety of a

lifeboat, Gerios handed his relative a lock of his hair asking her to deliver it to his wife back in Lebanon. 'Tell her I love her', were Gerios' last words to his cousin.[54]

Did Surviving Men Wear Other Disguises as Well?

Aside from men disguising themselves as women in order to escape the sinking *Titanic*, there are a number of allegations that other men donned different kinds of disguises in order to achieve that same end, all made by Thomas Cardeza. The present writer does not regard our first example to be very credible, but it's not beyond the realm of possibility that the second account has a basis in fact.

Boat #3

Thomas Cardeza
Thomas Cardeza was saved in boat #3 along with his mother, his mother's maid and his valet. On 25 April a Chicago newspaper ran the following story:

> The story of how two men passengers were saved from the sinking *Titanic* by bribing a sailor to disguise them as sailors and get them places in a lifeboat was told in a letter received here to-day by Mme Cardeza from her husband. M. Cardeza said that through bribery of a sailor he obtained two uniforms, one of which he donned, while he gave the other to his secretary. Posing as members of the crew, the men got into a lifeboat and were later picked up by the *Carpathia*. M. Cardeza's mother and woman companion also were saved.[55]

Needless to say, it seems pretty unlikely that a well-known society man would admit (in writing) to his wife that he survived the sinking of the *Titanic* by resorting to underhand means. This is underscored by the fact that two days later Mr Cardeza granted an interview to the *New York Sun* in which he described the way he actually left the sinking vessel:

> We joined the crowd that was pressing about one of the boats forward when I heard the officer in charge of that part of the deck shout: 'What is everybody crowding about here for? There is a much better chance at the

> stern.' I started with my mother to walk back toward the stern and there we came across such a crowd there wasn't any chance apparently of getting my mother near the boat. Then we went back to the forward part of the starboard side and found a boat that was being loaded and they were calling for women to get in. My mother got in with her maid. The officer called for other women, but there were none thereabout. Then he called for men passengers. There were only about six just there, of whom I was one, and we got in. The boat was still not filled, so the officer put in some of the crew. There were in the boat, as near as I could judge, between forty-three and forty-five persons. I know I counted thirty-eight heads and there were some lying in the bottom of the boat. I should not say she was overcrowded. In fact I believe a few more might have been put in safely, but she was sent away as she was. While we were on the boat nothing special happened.

The manner in which Mr Cardeza actually left the *Titanic* was considerably less dramatic than the departure supposedly described in the alleged letter to his wife. This makes sense, too, since Cardeza left the ship in boat #3 (the third boat launched) at around 12.55 a.m. – a long time before any sense of urgency became evident during the ship's evacuation. Indeed, there was little need for Cardeza to don a disguise in order to gain access to boat #3, since First Officer Murdoch was freely allowing men to enter the starboard lifeboats as long as there was sufficient room.

'There's never been any verification of the [disguise] story, that the letter from Mr Cardeza ever existed,' researcher George Jacub has written. 'The only hint of confirmation of the story is a comment by an unidentified stewardess of a passenger dressed as a sailor in her equally unidentified boat. For the time being, the Cardeza file must remain unsolved.'[56]

Men Accused Later of Disguising Themselves as Women

Robert Daniel

In 1997 an article about Robert Daniel appeared in a Virginia newspaper and contained the following paragraphs:

> The Daniel family struggled with the conflicting reports about Robert Sr's conduct and the difficulty in believing he could have survived in frigid waters so long.

'There were some snide things said about him around Richmond by some people. I wanted to think of him as a hero, but I could never be sure,' said nephew William V Daniel, now 68, a former Richmond city councilman and retired banker.

Dinner table gossip sent Helen Rodman on a research mission a few years ago to clear her uncle's reputation.

'In my mind, he is an absolute hero,' she said from her Charlottesville home. 'But it is a sad story. He was a man who I think lived out his life feeling the stigma of being a survivor and it was hard to escape …'

The *Titanic*, though, seemed to float out of Daniel's public life forever. It was something Daniel simply did not talk about.

'Not even his closest friends seemed to know the whole story,' said R W Daniels Jr. 'But my mother told me that it was his wish while he was alive, that the hymn *Nearer My God to Thee* never be played at Brandon Episcopal Church, the family place of worship.'[57]

In conjunction with this article, a local Virginia researcher named Kathleen once contacted me privately and offered some comments pertaining to her own findings about Robert Daniel:

> Hope you enjoyed the article. Gossip still about Daniel in Richmond kind of says that it is believed that he escaped wearing women's clothing in one of the boats. Never substantiated of course, but I personally found it quite odd that someone who at the beginning didn't mind one bit to be interviewed over and over by reporters, to simply clam up and never talk of it again.

Bert Johns

It has already been mentioned that in 2012 a journalist named William Kashatus wrote an online article claiming without evidence that passenger Borak Hannah (Bert Johns) disguised himself as a woman in order to gain entry to a lifeboat:

> Borak Hannah tried to stow away on a lifeboat but was recognized by a senior officer. Threatened at gunpoint, he agreed to re-board the ill-fated ship. Later, Hannah, disguised as a woman, managed to get into the last lifeboat which was loaded and lowered at 2:05 a.m. [i.e. Collapsible D].[58]

Neshan Krekorian

A few days after the *Carpathia* arrived in New York, the *Toronto Star* published a brief article that was headlined 'Used Woman's Clothing to Escape from *Titanic*':

> Ashan Kricorian [*sic*], an Armenian, who was mentioned by Major Peuchen in his evidence at the *Titanic* inquiry at Washington yesterday, as crouching in the bow of the boat in which the major's party escaped, with woman's clothing over him, and a broken arm, arrived in Hamilton this morning and told a thrilling story of the panic in the steerage when the boat hit. The foreigner said the shock as felt in the steerage made the boat quiver. Kricorian admitted that he used women's clothing to escape.[59]

However, on that same date, another newspaper published an actual interview with Krekorian that made no mention of the allegation made against him. Krekorian described how he and several friends hid in a lifeboat before it was prepared for launching and how all the stowaways except for himself were discovered and ejected from the boat before it was lowered to the sea:

> When we had reached the water I was numbed through from lying in the cold water in the bottom of the boat, and I knew I would soon have to crawl out and expose myself. I did so, and one of the men at the end of the boat called to me and told me to take an oar. I was injured in the crush in the steerage and hurt my arm, and found that I was unable to use it. He swore at me and told me to sit down and keep quiet ...[60]

In 2001 a Canadian newspaper published an article about Krekorian that contained the following passages:

> For most of his life, St. Catharines' Neshan Krekorian bottled up awful memories about a doomed ocean liner. A very reserved man, he preferred not to speak or be reminded about the night of April 14 and 15, 1912. Only rarely would he let his guard down ...
>
> How Krekorian got into a raft isn't totally clear. One story, disputed by the family, suggested he stowed away on one of the boats. According to *Titanic* historians, testimony from surviving upper-class passengers and crew were often suspect and racially motivated. A stigma of being a male survivor also often followed those men who lived. A Brantford paper, for instance, propagated a myth Krekorian dressed like a woman to escape the *Titanic*. (Armenian village men often wore kerchiefs and baggy trousers in cold weather).

The headline in a post-disaster story read 'Armenian Who Dressed in Women's Clothes to Get Off *Titanic*.' In that interview, Krekorian denied he'd worn ladies clothes to save his skin. According to family members and reliable accounts,* he used a rope to leap into lifeboat No. 10, which was being lowered portside just before 1:10 a.m. 'Nobody noticed him in there, he was very lucky,' said daughter Alice Solomonian, 75. 'He didn't say anything.'[61]

Alfred Nourney

In 1962 Richard Williams wrote a lengthy memoir of his *Titanic* experience in which he alleged that an unnamed man (Alfred Nourney) disguised himself as a woman (in lifeboat #7).

> For mass bravery, there have been few situations to equal it. There were one or two exceptions. I heard a couple of shots and found out later that one of the officers had fired into the air to keep some men from rushing a lifeboat. One passenger dressed in women's clothes and thus got a place in a lifeboat …
>
> At some place in this narrative I mentioned that one man dressed himself in women's clothes in order to get a place in the lifeboats. This fact might not have been generally known except for his extraordinary action on the *Carpathia*. Each man passenger quartered in the smoke room had been given one blanket apiece. There were no more to go around but it was ample under the circumstances. The upholstered benches were reasonably comfortable but were not long enough to stretch out on. The result was that during the night you would sleep but for a short time and then get up to stretch your legs before lying down again. However this was not to the liking of our friend. On the second evening before we had 'retired' he proceeded to gather all the blankets, whose occupants were not in the immediate vicinity, and make himself a most comfortable bed. By actual count, he had nine blankets as a foundation, one rolled up as a pillow and two to cover him. Unfortunately we had lost our sense of humor for we could have had a lot of fun with him. Someone reported him to the Captain and after he had been taken away it was said that he had been put in irons, at any rate we did not see him again and his immediate past was discussed, and if I am not mistaken, his future abode was predicted. But the poor fellow should no doubt have

* It seems likely that Krekorian's family obtained its information about 'lifeboat No. 10' from the Encyclopedia Titanica website, which has 'assigned' Krekorian to that lifeboat with little or no supporting evidence to document that claim.

been pitied rather than censored; the whole thing was too much for him and he had lost his senses.[62]

Emilio Portaluppi

In the late 1990s researcher Paul Quinn shared the following information with the *Titanic* discussion group:

> I just did some research on Emilio as he lived right nearby … A couple of older members of the local Italian chapter in his town holds the belief that Emilio escaped by wearing a woman's shawl over his head. It's not clear how that got started, but supposedly Emilio was shamed by his community because of this, causing him to become a recluse before ultimately moving back to Italy.[63]

William Sloper

In 1937 a New York newspaper published the following interview with Mr Sloper:

> A survivor of the *Titanic*, which sank twenty-five years ago tonight with a loss of 1,513 lives, branded as a 'brutal injustice' today an accusation which has pursued some of the rescued men – the charge that they gained the safety of the lifeboats by wearing women's clothing.
>
> 'The brutal injustice of this accusation, along with further misconceptions and distortions of fact concerning the wreck, stands out even more strongly in my mind than the actual horror of the disaster,' said William T. Sloper, a wealthy broker.
>
> 'I know of one man whose wife divorced him, whose children left him, and who lost his friends, because he was accused of leaving the boat in woman's clothes. I saw him ten years after. He was broken in spirit, alone in the world, all his interest in his fellow-beings and activities around him gone – dejected to a state of melancholy.
>
> 'And that man was innocent.
>
> 'The lifeboat he was in came alongside ours, and this man, mustached and wearing only his dinner suit – who had left the ship without even bothering to pick up a heavier coat – was blue in the face from the cold. I threw him my overcoat.
>
> 'I know of another survivor, also accused but innocent of the same charge, who was unable to continue under its merciless pursuit, and some years after shot himself to death.

'I, too, have been accused of the cowardly act, both in a newspaper account and by word of mouth, but I am thick-skinned, and it does not bother me any. My innocence has helped to fortify me against worrying.

'Immediately after it was realized that the ship was in danger of sinking a call was issued to board the lifeboats.

'Since most of the passengers held back, because the idea of leaving a brightly lighted vessel to embark on a dark, watery expanse in a small boat seemed even more precarious at the time, men were allowed and even asked to leave at the start. Officers with megaphones shouted to the passengers to leave in the lifeboats, pointing out that the sea was perfectly calm and adding, 'If we do not sink, we will pick you up later.'

'All the lifeboats were marked for sixty-six occupants. Yet ours was lowered and sent away with three sailors and sixteen passengers, because the people were so hesitant about getting in. I saw another lifeboat with only twelve people in it.

'So you can readily see that from the start it was not necessary for us to dress in women's clothes or to camouflage ourselves in any other way, as we were free to leave as we were.

'Later, when it was definitely known that the ship was sinking, I understand that only women and children were allowed to leave, but even then I can't see how any man could have got away in women's clothes, because the deck was as bright as day with the floodlights blazing away, and it would have been easy to discover such a deception.'[64]

Gilbert Tucker

In 2013 an article was written about Mr Tucker that contained the following information:

> Gilbert M. Tucker Jr. climbed into lifeboat No. 7 of the RMS *Titanic* with three female companions and a Pomeranian dog wrapped in a blanket. The lifeboat was loaded with 12 women, 13 men and three crew members, and it was the first lifeboat lowered as the disabled British passenger liner took on water and slowly sank after colliding with an iceberg. It was about half-full.
>
> The decision to take a seat in lifeboat No. 7 saved Tucker's life and gave him notoriety as a *Titanic* survivor. Tucker was one of 325 men who survived the April 15, 1912, catastrophe, while 1,509 people died, including 56 children and 114 women.
>
> He spent the rest of his life carrying a heavy burden, trying to rationalize his survival while rebuffing rumors that he disguised himself as a woman to secure his spot in the lifeboat.

Back home in Albany, Tucker heard mocking whispers of 'women and children first' as he walked the streets, which sometimes led to scuffles with tormentors …

'I never heard him say one word about the *Titanic*,' said Norman Rice, 88, a longtime trustee of Albany Rural Cemetery and emeritus director of the Albany Institute of History & Art. Rice dined regularly with the Tuckers, took dance lessons with them, vacationed together in Cape Cod and visited them in California. 'I didn't know anything about him surviving the *Titanic* until after he died.'[65]

Unnamed Male Survivor

In 1999 Margaret Graham Moore's daughter Clucas wrote a letter describing an unexpected event that traumatised her mother and caused her to recall the *Titanic* disaster. A newspaper reporter described the incident:

> It happened during a family trip to Edgartown, Mass., sometime in the 1970s.
>
> 'We were all in Edgartown, lunching on the porch of our Inn, when mother suddenly blanched,' Clucas wrote. 'She pointed to a man sitting alone at a table – she told us not to speak to him.'
>
> Graham Moore identified the man – who the family never saw again – as a passenger on the *Titanic*.
>
> In that brief moment, the sheer scope of the tragedy came into focus. There sat a mysterious man, who, the group would soon learn, served as a stark reminder of just how dire the circumstances aboard the *Titanic* were.
>
> 'He had jumped into a lifeboat on *Titanic*,' Clucas wrote, 'dressed as a woman.'[66]

Oddly enough, a case is on record where a man who never even set foot on the *Titanic* was accused of having survived her sinking by disguising himself as a woman. The man in question was a professional gambler.

W.J. 'Doc' Owens

In 1922 a newspaper article made the following allegation:

> News reached New York today of the death at Havana on January 14 of W. J. (Doc.) Owens, a notorious old time gambler, considered one of the most expert card men of his time. He fell down stairs at a hotel and died soon afterwards … He broke into the headlines at the time of the *Titanic* disaster when it was reported in the press on both sides of the ocean that he

had escaped in a life boat by disguising himself as a woman. He denied the report and said he would bring suit for libel, but he never did.[67]

Summary of the Author's Conclusions

Boat #13: It's this writer's opinion that Edward Ryan, the young towel-wearing Irishman, was probably the same young, towel-wearing Irishman who was seen in lifeboat #13.

Boat #14/Collapsible C: It's this writer's opinion that shawl-wearing Daniel Buckley was probably the same shawl-wearing man who was encountered by Fifth Officer Lowe in lifeboat #14.

A case can also be made that Buckley might have been saved in Collapsible C. (Buckley's Senate testimony stated that Bridget Bradley was in his lifeboat, and Bradley said in the 20 April 1912 issue of the *Glen Falls Daily Times* that she was in Bruce Ismay's lifeboat.) If we suppose that Buckley *was* saved in Collapsible C, though that of course reopens the mystery of the identity of the shawl-wearing man who was *definitely* in boat #14. If he wasn't Daniel Buckley, *who was he*? The evidence (such as it is) pertaining to this proposition is very sketchy and unreliable, but it boils down to the following two accounts – one of which was recorded second-hand and the other reported third-hand.

Thamine Tannous (Thelma Thomas) might *possibly* have been saved in boat #14 (according to the often-unreliable website Encyclopedia Titanica). Tannous sat next to a Lebanese man who was wearing a woman's coat and babushka, and she pulled the babushka off his head and urged him to help row when the other men called for assistance. The man replied that he was afraid of being thrown overboard if he did as she asked, but he nevertheless answered the call to help with the rowing.[68]

Borak Hannah (Bert Johns) is alleged by journalist William Kashatus to have disguised himself as a woman and entered 'the last lifeboat', which was loaded and lowered at 2.05 a.m. (a reference to Collapsible D, not Collapsible C).[69]* Hannah's interviews regarding his own survival are contradictory but do not claim he was in either Collapsible D or C or that he dressed like a woman in order to enter one of those boats.

* On the other hand, historian Don Lynch feels that Mrs Touma was not in boat #14. 'It's more likely that Thelma Thomas was in boat 13,' Lynch says. 'She is the only woman who comes close to being the lady Ruth Becker described as being next to her in that boat.'

However, there *is* one striking correlation between the undocumented claim about Bert Johns and the separate recollections of Thamine Tannous: Mrs Tannous (who was from Lebanon) said that the babushka-wearing man in her lifeboat was also from Lebanon – and Borak Hannah was Lebanese. If Mrs Tannous was in boat #14, and if the shawl-wearing Daniel Buckley was not the same shawl-wearing man who was saved in boat #14, might that disguised man have been a babushka-wearing Borak Hannah (Bert Johns)? We may never know.

Boat #4: The only reason this boat has come under our scrutiny is because Daniel Buckley believed Mrs Astor was the woman who covered him with her shawl. Since nobody ever reported seeing a shawl-wearing man in boat #4, and since we have evidence that Mrs Astor actually gave her shawl to a foreign woman and her child, the premise that Daniel Buckley was in boat #4 seems to be untenable.

Boat #6: Neshan Krekorian was apparently saved in this boat along with Major Peuchen, but the accusation that he wore women's clothing seems to be without foundation. Krekorian was from Turkish-occupied Armenia and reportedly had an injured arm that prevented him from rowing, so he couldn't have been the disguised 'Lebanese' survivor who allegedly sat beside Thamine Tannous and helped to row (possibly) boat #14.

Boat #7: Alfred Nourney was mistakenly accused of disguising himself as a woman to enter this lifeboat.

Boat #10: The Fortune family disavowed newspaper 'interviews' in which they supposedly described seeing a man dressed in woman's clothing in boat #10.

Boat #12: Elias Yarred claimed that a married woman disguised her husband in woman's clothing and that he and their child were saved in one boat while she was saved in another. This description fits no known couple on board the *Titanic* and probably was based on a 1912 rumour or else was due to the failing memory of an aging survivor who told his story many decades after the sinking.

Collapsible C: Mauritz Björnström-Steffansson reported that a man wearing a blanket around his head was ejected from Collapsible C, so this man – whoever he was – was not saved in that lifeboat.

Despite melodramatic claims that *Titanic*'s Chinese survivors let down their long hair and covered themselves with blankets in order to be mistaken for women, these reports were second-hand and were never attributed to a specific survivor, which therefore means they cannot be given any weight in our present discussion.

Collapsible D: A journalist made the undocumented claim that Borak Hannah was saved in Collapsible D and that he dressed as a woman in order to do so, but at the present time no known evidence supports either of these allegations.

In conclusion – and despite the fact that many of our survivor newspaper interviews are at opposite ends on the scale of reliability – the fact remains that at least two *Titanic* survivors (Edward Ryan and Daniel Buckley) unquestionably resorted to the ruse of utilising women's clothing in order to enter (or remain unnoticed) in their respective lifeboats. The so-called 'legend' of the man who disguised himself as a woman in order to escape the *Titanic* is based solidly on fact.

19

Voices from the Grave?

After the *Titanic* disaster a number of messages purportedly written by lost *Titanic* passengers washed ashore in various parts of the world. Only the first communication in our following discussion proved to be authentic.

Jeremiah Burke

Jeremiah Burke boarded the *Titanic* at Queenstown on 11 April 1912, and no more was heard from him until the early summer 1913 when a postman was walking his dog on a beach at Dunkettle near Cork Harbour. The man spotted a small glass bottle washed up on the shore and discovered the following pencilled note inside:

> 10/4/1912
> from Titanic,
> Goodbye all:
> Burke of Glanmire, Cork

The bottle and its handwritten message were brought to the local police station and were subsequently delivered to the Burke family. Burke's grandniece, Brid O'Flynn, believes Burke's mother had given him a small bottle of Lourdes holy water as a good luck gift before he left home to board the *Titanic* on 11 April, but historian Don Lynch says the bottle was actually part of a fitted toiletries case that Burke had been given before his sailing date. In any case, 'This is unmistakably the bottle that had left thirteen months previously and unmistakably her son's handwriting,' Brid O'Flynn told a reporter.[1]

The date scrawled at the top of Burke's handwritten note is difficult to read with certainty. Some people think it says '10/4/1912' while others believe the zero in the numeral '10' was struck through and replaced with a '2,' '3' or '5', meaning the note might have been written on either 12, 13 or 15 April. (Brid O'Flynn seems to subscribe to the latter date. 'A bottle of holy water in those days that your mother gave you was a reverent thing,' she insists. 'It wasn't something you threw out the side as you left Ireland. To me it senses of panic.')[2]

Although Jeramiah Burke's note in a bottle was legitimate, the 'last messages' allegedly written by several other *Titanic* victims were not.

John Jacob Astor

Early in 1913 a floating message was retrieved that was allegedly written by Mr Astor during his last hours of life, and the following newspaper account described the circumstances of that discovery:

> **ASTOR MESSAGE PICKED UP**
>
> By telegraph to *The Tribune*. Gulfport, Miss., Jan. 4 – A fragment of a deck chair from the *Titanic* on which was said to be scrawled, apparently with a knife, the last message of Colonel John Jacob Astor, was picked up by the steward of the steamer *Longscar*, according to a story told by the captain of that vessel to Captain Mallet of the British steamer *Florentia*, now at this port. The *Florentia* was in communication with the *Longscar* at Montevideo, where the latter craft was undergoing repairs.
>
> The steward was trolling with a line off the stern for deep sea fish, it is said, when he drew up the fragment of the deck chair which bore the tidings from Colonel Astor. The message was a farewell, with love for all, and the last impulse that of faith: 'We will meet in heaven.' A reward was mentioned in the writing for its delivery to his relatives.
>
> The relic will be forwarded from England, when the steamer arrives there, to the Astor family in the United States.[3]

The following day, another newspaper gave a fuller description of the message that was carved on the fragment of deck chair:

> Love to all. Will meet you in heaven. Finder will receive $1,000 for delivering this message. John Jacob Astor.[4]

Three months later the *Longscar* finally arrived at the port city of Boston, and once again her captain's story about the alleged Astor message was published in American newspapers:

> **FLOATING NEAR *TITANIC*'s GRAVE**
> Special to The New York Times
> Boston, April 18th – A small board, which he says bears a message scratched into the wood and signed 'John J. Astor,' was brought to this park today by Captain J. Willis of the British tramp steamer *Longscar*.
> Capt. Willis says he saw this board floating on the Atlantic as his steamship was driving through the waters at about the latitude and longitude where the *Titanic* sank. According to his statement, he has telegraphed Mrs Madeleine Force Astor, widow of the colonel, informing her of the alleged message, the nature of which he does not disclose.[5]
>
> **FINDS ASTOR MESSAGE ON GRAVE OF *TITANIC***
> Skipper Brings Board on Which
> Name of Colonel is Scratched.
> BOSTON, April 19 – A small board bearing a pathetic message scratched in the wood as though with the point of a nail and signed 'John J. Astor,' was brought to this port by Captain J. Willis of the British tramp freighter *Longscar*. This scratched message is, as far as known, the very last farewell from the wreck of the White Star liner *Titanic*, which sank April 13 [*sic*], 1912. Colonel Astor, it is believed, sent this final message when he realized the *Titanic* was sinking. Captain Willis spied the board in the latitude and longitude in which the *Titanic* went down.[6]

Nothing more was heard in the press regarding this alleged farewell message from Mr Astor. Since no survivors ever reported seeing Astor carving a lengthy message into a piece of wood that night, we can pretty safely assume that the message in question was a fake. (The present author finds it curious that Captain Willis would stop his vessel in mid-ocean merely to retrieve a floating board whose appearance must have been unremarkable to observers standing at the ship's railing.)

Archibald Butt
Three months after the *Titanic* went down, a bottle containing a handwritten message was picked up on a Rhode Island beach, and the incident was duly reported in the newspapers:

> **FIND MESSAGE IN A BOTTLE WITH MAJ. BUTT'S SIGNATURE**
> Two Men Pick Up Note in Long Island Sound Purporting to Come from Victim of *Titanic*
> Providence, R. I., July 31 – [Special] – Much interest is being manifested here in the message purporting to have been written by Maj. Archibald Butt, aid to President Taft and a victim of the Titanic disaster, which was picked up in a bottle off Block island on Friday [July 26] by A. J. Loran of New York City and W. H. L. Jones of Paterson, N. J., who showed it to Joseph S. Aiken of North Attleboro, Mass.
>
> The fact that it was written on the official wireless blanks of the *Titanic* leads those who have seen it to believe it may have been written by Maj. Butt. The message was dated April 16, two [*sic*] days after the steamer went down, and reads:
>
> 'Mid-ocean. Help. On a raft. *Titanic* sinking. No water or food.'
>
> It is signed 'Maj. A. Butt.' It was found where six bodies from the wreck of the steamer *Larchmont* were picked up by Capt. Littlefield. The message is now in the possession of Jones.[7]

On that same date a lengthier report about the same incident was published in another New York newspaper:

> **LAST WORD FROM MAJOR BUTT**
> **LOST ON THE *TITANIC***
> Message in a Bottle Picked Up on the Shore of Block Island
> — An Urgent Appeal for Help.
> Pawtucket, R. L. Aug. 1—(Bulletin)—A message purporting to be the last Word from Major Archibald Butt, aide to President Taft was picked up in a bottle off Block Island today and read as follows:
> 'April 16—Mid ocean—Help—On a raft—*Titanic* sinking;—no water or food—Major Butt.'
> The message was written on a wireless blank bearing the official imprint of the *Titanic*.
>
> The message bearing the date of Tuesday, following the Monday morning when the *Titanic* went down, was brought here by Joseph Aiken of North

Attleboro: A J. Loran of New York, and W. H. Jones, of 1044 Madison Avenue, Paterson, N.J. They said they found the bottle while out sailing. At first they said they were inclined to believe it as a ghastly joke but on second thought decided to report it.

Numerous witnesses testified that Major Butt stood on the deck of the sinking ship, and that probably in the whirl that marked the ship's disappearance, Major Butt, might have caught hold of a raft and might have been carried away from the wreckage.

The fact, however, that so many bodies and boats remained right on the scene of the wreck and later were picked up seemed to make this theory extremely improbable.

It was also pointed out that it would have been very unusual for the President's aide to have signed his name 'Major Butt.'

Opinion was strongly divided as to the possibility of the message being authentic and an effort will be made to have the handwriting identified.

News of the finding of the note was brought here from North Attleboro, Mass. where Joseph Aiken runs a barber shop. Except that the note was declared to have been written on the *Titanic* wireless paper and that it was enclosed in a bottle with a metal cork, no other details were given out by the men. The note was taken by W. H. Jones to his home in Paterson. He said he would forward it to President Taft or some other friend of Major Butt to be identified.[8]

Boston. July 31 – Joseph Aikin a barber of North Attleboro, Mass., today confirmed the report of the finding of a note, supposed to have been written by Major Butt who went down with the *Titanic* in an interview over the long distance phone.

'A. J. Loran, of Manhattan, New York, director of the Cathedral orchestra and W. H. Jones, of No. 1014 Madison avenue. Patterson, N. J., picked up the bottle containing the note while walking along the beach on Block Island,' said Aiken to a United Press reporter today.

'We were hurrying back to Copelan cottage, where we were stopping with Captain Charlie Littlefield. The note was written in pencil in a firm round hand. There were three lines of writing. The bottle, had a metal screw top and was of the kind in which pickles are sold.'

Jones took the note to Patterson.[9]

Aside from the fact that Major Archibald Butt customarily signed his name as 'A. W. Butt' without including his military rank, another objection to the note's authenticity was registered by one of the men named in these newspaper articles.

BUTT 'MESSAGE' BRANDED HOAX

New London, Conn., Aug. 1 – Capt. Littlefield, formerly navigator for the Carnegie non-magnetic yacht on its globe-circling tour, declared today that the 'message' of the late Maj. Butt who perished in the Titanic disaster must have been a hoax.

The 'message' in a bottle, was picked up off Block Island. Capt. Littlefield says it could not possibly have drifted there from the scene of the disaster as any flotsam would necessarily have drifted in the direction of Europe.[10]

Another newspaper article presented additional reasons for believing that this message was a hoax:

NOTE IN BOTTLE SIGNED 'BUTT' DECLARED HOAX

Newspaper dispatches from Providence yesterday told of the finding of a bottle off Block Island last Friday containing what purported to be a message from Major Archibald W. Butt, aide to President Taft, who lost his life in the *Titanic* disaster. The bottle was picked up by A. J. Loran of New York and W. H. Jones of Paterson, who showed it to Joseph A. Aiken of North Attleboro. The message was dated April 16, the day after the *Titanic* disaster, and reads:

'Midocean—help—on a raft—*Titanic* sinking—no water or food.
'Major A. Butt.'

The bottle was found at the spot where six bodies from the wreck of the steamer *Larchmont* were picked up by Capt. Littlefield. Mr Aiken was boarding at Capt. Littlefield's house, where Mr Jones also was staying. Mr Jones has started back to his home at 1044 Madison Avenue, Paterson, taking the bottle and message with him.

The dispatches from Providence state that the message was written on one of the official wireless blanks of the *Titanic*.

The White Star officials heard nothing concerning the reported find. They said the story sounded improbable for several reasons. In the first place, the information given by various passengers of the *Titanic* regarding Major Butt was that the President's aide was standing on the deck of the *Titanic* just before the ship sank, and that he was not taken off by any of the small craft by which the survivors were saved. The probabilities therefore seem to be that Major Butt went down with the ship.

The White Star officials also pointed out that the *Titanic* carried no rafts. She had collapsible lifeboats and these, as well as the wooden lifeboats, were accounted for after the wreck. They said also that although the *Titanic* was never in this port and the officials of the line here never saw the wireless telegraph blanks she carried, in the case of all other ships entering New York, including the *Olympic*, the name of the ship does not appear on the Marconi blanks. They are furnished by the Marconi Company and are the same on all ships just as land telegraph blanks of the same company are similar all over the country.[11]

John Grimes

In September 1912 an Irish newspaper correspondent wrote a letter describing his discovery of another bottle containing a handwritten note of farewell from the *Titanic*. His letter was published in the newspaper:

> A bottle destined for Liverpool has been washed ashore on the Murvagh Islands, Donegal Harbour, Donegal Bay, north-west coast of Ireland (Lat. North 54 degrees 38 minutes: Long. West 8 degrees 10 minutes), which has found its way from the sinking *Titanic* over 2,000 miles of water, avoiding St John's Point and the rocks on this coast, and which contained a scrap of paper with the following message to the wife of a stoker:- 'Our ship *Titanic* sinking. All hope of being saved abandoned. Forward this to my dear Wife at No 26, Stanley Road, Liverpool – John Grimes stoker.'
> I am, Sir, your obedient servant, SIMS WILLIAMS, Murvagh, Ballintra, Co. Donegal, Sept 12.[12]

Since no 'John Grimes' was listed on the *Titanic*'s crew roster, there's no doubt this farewell note was a fabrication. (One can't help but wonder if occasional seamen might have resorted to post-disaster subterfuges like this in order to escape unhappy marriages or other problems.) In any case, the spuriousness of the note in question was recognised even in 1912.

> **PRACTICAL JOKERS**
> Are Often Silly and Amuse Themselves With Human Imitations of Cruelties of Chance

> (From *The London Times*.) It is clear that the message in a bottle found on the Irish coast and professing to be written by a stoker of the *Titanic* was a practical joke; and it is one of the silliest that ever was practiced. But practical jokes of this kind are still common, and it is worthwhile to inquire what is the motive of them …[13]

John Stewart

Steward John Stewart survived the *Titanic* disaster, but a note-in-bottle supposedly written by him was illustrated in the book *Beyond Reach*, by William Hoffman and Jack Grimm. The note read:

> Our ship is lost all hope of being saved is abandoned. Jack Stewart. Ill Fated *Titanic*

Aside from the fact that the signature on this note doesn't match John Stewart's actual signature on *Titanic*'s crew roster, referring to a ship as being 'ill-fated' is something usually done with the benefit of hindsight instead of during its actual evacuation. No documentation was provided about where and when this note was supposedly recovered, but it's pretty clearly a fake.

Unknown Passenger

In November 1928 a bottle washed ashore in South Wales containing a note purportedly written by a *Titanic* passenger:

> Message from *Titanic*
>
> While walking along the Swansea seafront recently, a man found a bottle, which had been washed up by the sea. In it was a note, a scarf pin with the stone missing and a photograph of two men. He threw away the photo as being too defaced to be of any use. The note read:
>
> 'This, the last moment the great ship *Titanic* sank. I am left here with my brother in law, John Williams, wife and little child, Jean, having left the doomed ship on the last boat. The band are still playing, the officers are running here and there, although their tasks are hopeless; men are going mad while … (passage indecipherable), a group of men are gathering around a clergymen [*sic*] who is in a fit upon the promenade deck.'
>
> For over sixteen years the bottle, with its pitiful story inside it, has bobbed around in the waves of the Atlantic. More than half of the Titanic's 3150 [*sic*] passengers found watery graves that day.[14]

Unfortunately, no 'John Williams' was on board the *Titanic*, nor was there a related family group consisting of a husband, wife and daughter Jean.

Harry Wilson

In October 1912 an American newspaper mentioned a message in a bottle that washed up on the coast of Iceland:

> **ECHO OF TITANIC DISASTER**
> CHRISTIANIA, Oct. 19 – A report from Reykjavik, Iceland, says a bottle was picked up on Oct. 4 near Skogarnes on the Vaxa fjord, which contained a note reading:
>
> I am one of those wrecked on the *Titanic*.
> Harry Wilson[15]

Needless to say, no 'Harry Wilson' was on board the *Titanic*.

Unknown

On 22 April 1912 another message from an alleged (and anonymous) *Titanic* passenger was retrieved off the coast of England:

> Mr J. Cloke, owner of the boat *Harmony*, of Mevagissey, picked up a bottle on the fishing grounds off the Dodman on Monday night. Inside was a strip of paper, on which was written:- '15 April, 1912. s.s. *Titanic* Struck iceberg. No hope of many being saved.'
>
> The idea of the message having come from the *Titanic* has been ridiculed by seafaring men.[16]

The present author agrees that it is unlikely that a genuine message from the *Titanic* would have been retrieved from the ocean so soon after the disaster.

Mathilde Lefebvre

Our final case is at the opposite end of extremes timewise, because the following bottle is said to have been found on a Canadian beach 105 years after the *Titanic* went down. The note was written in French, and its text was translated as follows:

> I threw this bottle into the sea in the middle of the Atlantic. We should arrive in New York in a few days. If anyone finds this, tell the Lefebvre

[family] in Liévin.
[signed] Mathilde Lefebvre[17]

The bottle is said to have been discovered in June 2017 by a local inhabitant who was walking on a beach in the Bay of Fundy. The note inside the bottle was supposedly written by Mathilde Lefebvre, a 13-year-old girl from Liévin, France, who lost her life along with her mother and three younger siblings when the *Titanic* went down in 1912.

The present author does not know what to make of this note. Judging from photos, it appears to be in superb condition except for the fact that it has been torn into two halves from top to bottom. The note shows no sign of damage caused by mould or condensation inside the bottle, and one observer has noted that the handwriting on the note is 'beautiful' for a 13-year-old.

One suspects that the only conclusive way of confirming the authenticity of this note would be to compare it with another document *known* to have been written by Mathilde Lefebvre before her untimely death in 1912. Unfortunately, the likelihood of finding another such document written by a 13-year-old girl more than a century ago would seem to be pretty remote, so for the time being the reader must make up his/her own mind whether this note is genuine or whether it is yet another example of the hoaxer's art.

Notes

The essays in *The Titanic Files* have been written and collected over nearly fifty years and due to the changing nature of the internet, some of the references cited no longer exist. We have done our best to update these where we can, but have chosen to preserve the dead links for posterity.

CHAPTER 1

1 *Death of a Purser*, Frankie McElroy, Author House, 2011, p. 26. Also 'Hugh Walter McElroy, Chief Purser R.M.S. TITANIC, 1874–1912, Frankie McElroy, uk.geocities.com/frankiemcelroy/purser_mcelroy.html

2 www.encyclopedia-titanica.org/community/threads/unknown-animals-aboard-titanic.4865/

3 'From Deep in Atlantic, *Titanic* Relics Sail Toward Auction Block', Eliza Ronalds-Hannon, 19 May 2017, www.bloomberg.com/news/articles/2017-05-19/titanic-relics-hardly-used-setting-course-for-auction-block

4 *Titanic* contract ticket list, National Archives, New York Branch, Military Ocean Terminal, Bayonne, New Jersey.

5 *Ibid*.

6 'Elizabeth Nye – *Titanic* Survivor', Dave Bryceson. Streets Publishers, 2009, p. 54. Quoted from *The War Cry*.

7 See 'On Board RMS *Titanic*: Memories of the Maiden Voyage', George Behe.

8 *Sunday Independent*, 15 April 1962, contained in *The Irish Aboard Titanic*, Senan Molony. Wolfhound Press, 2000 p. 232.

9 'Nose for a Story', Anne Hailes, *Irish News* – Global Edition. I accessed the article online on 21 March 1998.

10 *Titanic Voices*, Donald Hyslop et. al., p. 98, Southampton City Council, 1994, courtesy Bruno Piola.

11 *Lost at Sea*, Michael Goss and George Behe. Prometheus Books, 1994.

12 *Titanic Survivor*, Violet Jessop and John Maxtone Graham, Sheridan House 2004.

13 Museums Victoria (Australia), museumsvictoria.com.au/discoverycentre/discovery-centre-news/2010-archive/titanic-animals/

14 *Titanic: Destination Disaster*, Jack Eaton and Charles Haas, p. 122. A posting containing no documentation by 'Joseph' (31 March 2012) in the Encyclopedia Titanica bulletin board thread 'Unknown Animals on the *Titanic*' says the claim was for $250.87, www.encyclopedia-titanica.org/community/threads/unknown-animals-aboard-titanic.4865/page-2#post-79490
15 *National Magazine*, October 1912.
16 *East Kent Gazette*, 4 May 1912.
17 *Not My Time to Die*, Lilly Setterdahl, pp. 199–203. From *Nordstjernan*, New York, 23 April 1912.
18 *The Titanic Files: A Paranormal Sourcebook*, George Behe. Lulu.com Press, 2015. Also, *The Independent* (Plymouth), 26 May 1968, courtesy Don Lynch. (Note: *The Irish Aboard Titanic* claims that Nellie Hocking shared a cabin with Edwina Troutt and Nora Keane and that she told an unnerving story about hearing a cock crowing at dusk to the pair; however, Hocking never shared a cabin with Troutt and Keane, and Don Lynch (a close friend of Edwina's, who questioned her many times over the years about her *Titanic* experience) never heard her mention Keane having any kind of contact with Hocking or hearing a story about a cock crowing.)
19 www.geni.com/people/Ellen-Mary-Mockler/6000000016207934655
20 Sister Mary Patricia interview, *Worcester Telegram* (Massachusetts), 15 April 1982.
21 Courtesy Don Lynch.
22 Don Lynch, personal communication with the author, 12 July 2017.
23 *Soldier of Fortune*, Joyce Sharpey-Schafer. Utica, N.Y. 1984.
24 *Portland Evening Express and Daily Advertiser* (Maine), 27 April 1912.
25 *The Evening Journal* (Ottawa), 22 April 1912.
26 After the disaster Anderson put in a $50 claim for his lost Chow. The National Archives (UK), courtesy Don Lynch.
27 *New York Evening Telegram*, 22 April 1912, courtesy Bruno Piola.
28 Edith Rosenbaum account, *Irish Independent*, 16–20 April 1956, courtesy Mike Poirier.
29 *New York Herald*, 22 April 1912.
30 *New York Evening Telegram*, 22 April 1912.
31 *New York Daily Graphic*, 24 April 1912, courtesy Bruno Piola.
32 *Brooklyn Daily Eagle*, 19 April 1912.
33 *New York American*, 20 April 1912. Also *The Sinking of the Titanic*, Jay Mobray, 1912.
34 *Titanic: Destination Disaster*, Jack Eaton and Charles Haas. Patrick Stephens Inc., 1987, p. 23.
35 'Animals' (an unpublished essay about *Titanic*'s animals by Bruno Piola.)
36 *Dowagiac News*, 20 April 1912.
37 *Detroit News Times*, 21 April 1912, courtesy Bruno Piola.
38 *Carlinville Daily Enquirer*, 11 July 1913, courtesy Don Lynch.
39 William Carter, claim of losses against the White Star Line.
40 *Whitby Gazette*, 30 April 1912, courtesy Bruno Piola.
41 *London Daily Mirror*, 30 April 1912.
42 *Carlinville Daily Enquirer*, *c.* 11 July 1913. Note: a short article in the *New York Sun* of 13 July 1913 says the replacement dog's name was 'Mee Too' instead of Hee Too, so one wonders if the name Mee Too was an acknowledgement that the Carter's second Pekingese was a replacement or if the spelling 'Hee Too' might have been

a newspaper's typographical error and perhaps the first dog was named Mee Too as well.

43 Lucile Carter diary, Bonhams Auction, 19 June 2012, www.bonhams.com/auction/20009/lot/3190/
44 *Richmond Dispatch*, 20 April 1912.
45 Michael Findlay posting, *Titanic*-Discuss forum, 5 September 2001.
46 Michael Findlay posting, 22 August 1998. Forum: alt.history.ocean-liners.titanic.
47 Michael Findlay posting, *Titanic*-Discuss forum, 7 September 2001.
48 Washington Dodge account, 16 April 1912. From the Frank Blackmarr Collection, transcribed by Jim Harper.
49 After the dog's death, Mr Daniel filed a $750 claim for its loss with the White Star Line.
50 frenchbulldogclub.org/about/our-clubs-history/frenchies-and-the-titanic
51 *Shadow of the Titanic*, Eva Hart & Ronald Denney, Greenwich University Press, 1994.
52 Eva Hart interview, courtesy Paul Lee, paullee.com/titanic/EHart.php
53 Edith Rosenbaum account, *Cassell's Magazine*, June 1913, courtesy Paul Lee.
54 Edith Rosenbaum account, *Irish Independent*, 16–20 April 1956, courtesy Mike Poirier.
55 Edith Russell, 1966 interview for the Associated Press, courtesy Randy Bigham. In support of this account, Robert Daniel's son once told Philip Gowan that it had always been his understanding that Gamin de Pycombe was in the cabin with his father – not in the ship's kennels. (Phil Gowan posting on *Titanic*-Discuss Group, 11 May 2002, 3.52 a.m.)
56 'C.Q.D.', Richard Williams, 1962. Historical Society of Pennsylvania.
57 Courtesy Phil Gowan, who on 27 August 2005 told the present author, 'But Daniel also told his daughter that he "tried to save all the dogs". I got that little titbit from Sen. Daniel's son, who is still living. He was only four when his father died and doesn't remember anything his father might have said concerning *Titanic* but his sister is older and brought that subject up on numerous occasions – as a little girl proud of her daddy for doing something to help the dogs.'
58 *Shadow of the Titanic*, Eva Hart & Ronald Denney, Greenwich University Press, 1994.
59 *Titanic* contract ticket list, National Archives, New York Branch, Military Ocean Terminal, Bayonne, New Jersey.
60 In the *Titanic*'s ticket manifest the cross-Channel passengers have entries beside their names that none of the other passengers do. Mr Dulles and his dog are listed there, as is Mrs Meanwell, who brought a canary on to the ship. Neither Dulles nor Meanwell were cross-Channel passengers, however, and the reason they were listed as such is a mystery.
61 *American Kennel Club Stud Book Register*, Vol. 27 (January–December 1910), p. 316.
62 *New York Daily Tribune*, 12 February 1912, courtesy Bruno Piola.
63 *New York Herald*, 24 February 1910, courtesy Bruno Piola.
64 *American Kennel Club Stud Book Register*, Vol. 28 (January–December 1911).
65 *Ibid*., Vol. 34 (January–December 1917), p. 513.
66 *Auburn Citizen*, 16 April 1912.
67 *New York Sun*, 20 July 1913.
68 *Titanic* contract ticket list, National Archives, New York Branch, Military Ocean Terminal, Bayonne, New Jersey.
69 *Titanic Survivor*, Violet Jessop. Sheridan House, 1997.
70 *Harper's Weekly*, 27 April 1912.

71 *New York Herald*, 15 December 1912.
72 *Ibid.*, 26 January 1913.
73 *New York Sun*, 22 June 1913.
74 *Ibid.*, 21 September 1913.
75 *New York Herald*, 22 May 1913, courtesy Bruno Piola.
76 *New York Sun*, 20 July 1913, courtesy Don Lynch.
77 *Ibid.*, 22 November 1914.
78 *Riverside Daily Press*, 1 July 1914, courtesy Don Lynch. Also *St Louis Post-Dispatch*, 20 April 1912.
79 *Riverside Daily Press*, 1 July 1914, courtesy Don Lynch.
80 *Ibid.*
81 'The Potters and the *Titanic*', Michael Findlay. *Voyage*, No. 27, *c.*1998–99.
82 *A Night to Remember*, Walter Lord. Holt, Rinehart & Winston, 1976. (Note: Lord does not name the girl who was carrying her Pomeranian, but she was almost certainly Miss Hays.)
83 *Riverside Daily Press*, 1 July 1914, courtesy Don Lynch.
84 'The Potters and the *Titanic*', Michael Findlay, *Voyage*, No. 27, *c.*1998–99.
85 (Pitman testified, 'I transferred two men and a woman and child from my boat to No. 7 to even them up a bit.') *The Truth About the Titanic*, Archibald Gracie. Mitchell Kennerly, 1913.
86 Washington Dodge letter to Ed Kamuda, 1960s, *Commutator*, Issue No. 29, December 1970, pp. 23–24.
87 *Western Star*, 13 July 1912.
88 *Riverside Daily Press*, 1 July 1914, courtesy Don Lynch.
89 *Gazette Times*, 21 April 1912.
90 *The Sinking of the Titanic and Great Sea Disasters*, Logan Marshall. 1912.
91 *Riverside Daily Press*, 1 July 1914, courtesy Don Lynch.
92 *Ibid.*
93 'Margaret Hays' Journey to Southern California,' Don Lynch. *Commutator*, Vol. 34, No. 189, 2010.
94 *New York Evening Telegram*, June 1917, courtesy Don Lynch.
95 Don Lynch, personal correspondence with the author.
96 'Children of the *Titanic*: Their story – Their words', www.adamslib.org/titanic/Children%20of%20the%20Titanic.pdf
97 *New York Evening World*, 22 April 1912.
98 'Animals', Bruno Piola (unpublished manuscript).
99 *New York Sun*, 19 April 1912. The steward must have been referring to Miss Hays when he referred to the 'earlier lifeboat', since Elizabeth Rothschild and her Pomeranian were in boat #6, which was one of the last boats to be picked up by the *Carpathia*.
100 'Animals', Bruno Piola (unpublished manuscript).
101 *Ibid.*
102 *Dayton Herald*, 13 June 1912, courtesy Mike Poirier.
103 *Niles Daily News*, 25 April 1912.
104 *Geelong Advertiser* (Vic.: 1859–1929), 1 June 1912, p. 9, courtesy Dr Paul Lee.
105 *Mt Vernon Daily Argus*, 19 April 1912.

106 Information about the dog's death comes from Mrs Rothschild's nephew, courtesy Phil Gowan. Confirmation comes from Helen Barrett (86), niece-in-law of 'Aunt Lizzie' Rothschild, courtesy Marty Crisp, 11 September 1998.
107 Ron Vertone, posting in Facebook's *Titanic* Passenger and Crew Research Group, 14 August 2017.
108 'Animals', Bruno Piola (unpublished manuscript).
109 'Through the Windows of St. Mary's of the Lake: A 150 Year Reflection', Jean Argetsinger & Patricia Suits Ellison (1995). Mentioned on the Encyclopedia Titanica website.
110 'Animals', Bruno Piola (unpublished manuscript).
111 *Tramps and Ladies*, James Bisset. Criterion, 1959.
112 'Animals', Bruno Piola (unpublished manuscript).
113 Vera Dick account, *Washington Post*, 19 April 1912.
114 *The Sinking of the Titanic and Great Sea Disasters*, Logan Marshall. 1912.
115 *Charlevoix County Herald*, 6 July 1912, courtesy Don Lynch.
116 Imanita Shelley account, *Powell County Post* (Deer Lodge, Montana), courtesy Mike Poirier.
117 *St Paul Dispatch*, 18 April 1912.
118 *New York Press*, 18 April 1912.
119 *New York Herald*, 21 April 1912.
120 *Ibid.*, 21 February 1918.
121 *New York Sun*, 19 April 1912.
122 *Geelong Advertiser* (Victoria, Australia), 1 June 1912, p. 9, courtesy Bruno Piola.
123 *Daily Sketch*, 6 May 1912.
124 *Montour Falls Free Press*, 1 May 1912, courtesy Bruno Piola.
125 *The Sinking of the Titanic and Great Sea Disasters*, Logan Marshall. 1912.
126 *Albany Times-Union*, 19 April 1912.
127 *Ibid.*
128 Howard Chapin's written account, *Providence Evening News*, 19 April 1912.
129 Geoffrey Whitfield, email to the author, 31 May 2018.
130 *Chicago Daily Tribune*, 19 April 1912.
131 *New York Herald*, 19 April 1912.
132 *Cincinnati Enquirer*, 21 April 1912.
133 *New York Herald*, 19 April 1912.
134 Southampton City Council, 11 November 1985, www.paullee.com/titanic/EHaisman.php
135 *Providence Evening News*, 19 April 1912.
136 *Seattle Daily Times*, 22 & 23 April 1912.
137 *The Irish Aboard Titanic*, Senan Molony. Wolfhound Press, 2000, p. 86.
138 'William Greenfield's Account', courtesy Nell Greenfield and Grant Woollacott, www.encyclopedia-titanica.org/william-greenfields-account.html
139 *New York American*, 19 April 1912.
140 Charles Pellegrino posting in the '*Titanic*: Secrets of the Lost Liner' Facebook group, 17 May 2015 at 11 a.m.
141 Edith Rosenbaum account, *Irish Independent*, 16–20 April 1956, courtesy Mike Poirier.
142 Lord-Macquitty Collection, National Maritime Museum and Paul Lee website, www.paullee.com/titanic/mslocombe.html

143 An issue of the *Northern Constitution*, May 1912. Reprinted in the *White Star Journal* of the Irish Titanic Historical Society, September 2002.
144 *New York Tribune*, 19 April 1912.
145 *New York Herald*, 21 April 1912. Also, *The Sinking of the Titanic*, Logan Marshall, 1912.
146 For instance, see 'The Bark', thebark.com/content/dogs-titanic
147 'Animals', Bruno Piola (unpublished manuscript).
148 *I'll See You in New York*, David Haisman. Boolarong Press, 1999. Don Lynch points out that earlier in her life, Edith spoke of encountering First Officer Murdoch but that later in life she said it was Captain Smith.
149 *The Irish Aboard Titanic*, Senan Molony. Wolfhound Press, 2000, p. 174.
150 *Daily Mirror*, 29 April 1912.
151 *Southampton Evening Echo*, 27 May 1968.
152 Lord-Macquitty Collection, National Maritime Museum, courtesy Paul Lee, www.paullee.com/titanic/kgilnagh.html.
153 *Daily Sketch*, 13 May 1912.
154 www.motherjones.com/politics/2008/08/polar-bears-found-swimming-60-miles-offshore/
155 Michael Findlay posting, 9 May 1999, alt.history.ocean-liners.titanic
156 *Tavistock Gazette*, 19 April 1912.
157 *The Titanic Files*, George Behe. Lulu.com Press, 2015. Information came from a posting from 'Glenravel Online' on Mark Taylor's *Titanic*-Discuss Bulletin Board. The Irish publisher was promoting its 1996 book *Titanic: The Unknown Story* by Joseph Baker and Michael Liggett.
158 Sarah Freeman posting on Encyclopedia Titanica forum, 15 April 2005.
159 'My Maiden Voyage', Roberta Maioni, *London Daily Express*, 1926, www.encyclopedia-titanica.org/roberta-maioni-titanic-account.html
160 *The Loss of the SS Titanic*, Lawrence Beesley. Houghton, Miflin, 1912.
161 Johan Cervin Svensson memoir in *Not My Time to Die*, Lilly Setterdahl, pp. 187–9. Nordstjernan, 2012.
162 *Bournemouth Daily Echo*, 30 April 1912.
163 Paris Museum of Letters and Manuscripts, courtesy John Lamoreau.
164 'Sealed Orders', Helen Candee, *Collier's Weekly*, 4 May 1912.
165 *Ibid.*
166 National Maritime Museum.
167 Don Lynch, personal communication with the author.
168 Paris Museum of Letters and Manuscripts, courtesy John Lamoreau.
169 'Sealed Orders', Helen Candee, *Collier's Weekly*, 4 May 1912.
170 *Daily Sketch*, 13 May 1912.
171 'The Middle Watch – April 15th, 1912', Charles Victor Groves. Published in *The Atlantic Daily Bulletin*, March 1998.
172 *New York Herald*, 26 April 1912.
173 *Plattsburgh Daily Press*, 18 April 1912 (under 'Ice Reports').
174 *Auburn Daily Advertiser*, 23 April 1912.
175 *Syracuse Post-Standard*, 24 April 1912.
176 *The Irish Aboard Titanic*, Senan Molony. Wolfhound Press, 2000, p. 86.
177 *World Telegram*, 14 April 1952.
178 *Washington Post*, 28 April 1912.

179 *Mitchell Daily Republic*, 14 April 2012, www.mitchellrepublic.com/content/titanic-victim-was-headed-ethan
180 *Minneapolis Star & Tribune*, 16 April 1982, courtesy Don Lynch. Interestingly, Don believes it was Mrs Snyder who once told him about sighting polar bears from her lifeboat; he apparently didn't record that fact in his notes, though, so we must go with what the reporter said in the present article and couple it with our own knowledge about the relative sizes of walruses and seals.
181 *The Evening Record* (Greenville, Pennsylvania), 22 April 1912, courtesy Mike Poirier.
182 *The Sinking of the Titanic and Great Sea Disasters*, Logan Marshall, 1912. Miss Birkhead is not named in the book, but the account is identical to the one she wrote for publication (with the exception of this and several other paragraphs that a few newspapers edited out of their own versions of the account.) See my book *Voices from the Carpathia* (The History Press, 2015) for a slightly edited version of her account.
183 *The Sinking of the Titanic*, Jay Mobray. 1912.
184 *The Irish Aboard Titanic*, Senan Molony. Wolfhound Press, 2000, p. 86.
185 *Voyage* 27, Winter 1998, pp. 122–9.
186 Courtesy Don Lynch.
187 *Atlantic City Daily Press*, 5 May 1912.
188 *Bath Chronicle*, 5 May 1912.
189 Pony Horton, personal communication with the author.
190 Don Lynch, personal communication with the author.
191 *The Sinking of the Titanic and Great Sea Disasters*, Logan Marshall. 1912.

CHAPTER 2

1 Courtesy Bill Sauder.
2 *Ibid*.
3 Information about the Lehrer deck plan courtesy Tim Trower.
4 Courtesy the late Roy Mengot.
5 'C.Q.D.', Richard Williams, 1962. Historical Society of Pennsylvania.
6 Eva Hart interview, courtesy Paul Lee, paullee.com/titanic/EHart.php
7 *I'll See You in New York*, David Haisman. Boolarong Press, 1999.
8 *Titanic: The Ship Magnificent*, Bruce Beveridge et. al., Vol. 2, p. 222. History Press, 2008.
9 Bill Sauder, personal communication with the author.
10 *Ibid*.
11 *Titanic: Triumph and Tragedy*, Jack Eaton and Charles Haas, W.W. Norton, 1986.
12 Bill Sauder, private communication with the author.
13 'London Statutes from 1750 to 1907', G.L. Gomme, Vol. II, 1889 to 1907, p. 41, books.google.co.uk/books?id=KLhHAQAAMAAJ
14 'Reports from the Commissioners, Inspectors and Others', Parliamentary Papers Vol. XXXVII, 1914 (Addendum B – Regulations, 1912). books.google.co.uk/books?id=nbwOAQAAIAAJ
15 The author would like to thank Bill Sauder for graciously allowing me to make use of his research and photographs and for offering his crucial observations regarding the true location of *Titanic*'s kennels.

CHAPTER 3

1 Maurice Parkhouse turned out to be an able-bodied seaman who served on board the *Olympic*.

CHAPTER 4

1 The content from this chapter is developed from this author's other works on this topic. Archie Butt's letters and personal papers are held at the Georgia Archive, in Atlanta, Georgia.
2 Archibald Willingham Butt's transport diary, courtesy of the Georgia Archive.
3 Robert Heinl, 'A Famous Presidential Aide', *Leslie's Weekly* (c. 1910), page 108 of the Butt scrapbooks, courtesy of the Georgia Archive.

CHAPTER 5

1 For instance, see *Unsinkable: The Full Story of RMS Titanic*, Daniel Butler. Stackpole Books, 1998, p. 136.
2 *Philadelphia Evening Bulletin*, 2 May 1912.
3 *Ibid*.
4 *Buffalo Morning Express*, 1 May 1912.

CHAPTER 6

1 Text of the postcard comes from 'Gilded Lives, Fatal Voyage', Hugh Brewster (Crown Publishers, 2012).
2 This is according to the Cave passenger list. However, in his Senate testimony, Major Peuchen thought Ross was in A-12 and that Beattie and McCaffry were in 'A-8 and numbers similar to that close by'.
3 Peuchen interview, *Toronto World*, 20 April 1912.
4 Jason Tiller, 'Peuchen and the *Titanic*', unpublished manuscript.
5 William Sloper, 'My Eyewitness Story of the *Titanic* Disaster Rewritten from My Original *New Britain Herald* Report of April 19, 1912'.
6 Arthur Peuchen Senate testimony.
7 *Manitoba Free Press*, 20 April 1912.
8 *Hamilton Spectator*, 24 April 1912. The account was given by Charles Allen, the fiancé of either Alice or Ethel Fortune. Also *New York Times*, 23 April 1912.

CHAPTER 7

1 'Stead, the Man', Estelle Stead; Stanley May letter, 10 April 1912.
2 *London Globe and Traveller*, 16 April 1912.
3 Jay Roches, Encyclopedia Titanica Facebook forum, 4 June 2018.
4 *Titanic Voices*, Donald Hyslop et. al., p. 95.
5 Stanley May letter, 10 April 1912. Henry Aldridge auction catalogue, 14 September 2002.

6 Sidney Collett, unknown newspaper, posted by Mike Poirier in the Encyclopedia Titanica Facebook forum, 4 June 2018.
7 *Hudson Dispatch*, 20 April 1912.
8 Thomas Byles letter written on board the *Titanic*, 10 April 1912.
9 Courtesy Carolyn Bailey (Parson's great-granddaughter), www.brunel.ac.uk/~cssrcab

CHAPTER 8

1 *The Daily Herald* (London), 29 April 1912.
2 *Daily Sketch*, 29 April 1912, courtesy Paul Lee.
3 *Western Independent*, 5 May 1912, courtesy Paul Lee.
4 1954 Texas newspaper article, courtesy Darren Honeycutt.
5 *Port Huron Times Herald*, 14 April 1938.
6 *The Dayton Herald*, 13 June 1912.

CHAPTER 9

1 *William McMaster Murdoch: A Career at Sea*, Susanne Störmer, p. 322. Also footnote 45 on p. 427.

CHAPTER 10

1 *New York Sun*, 20 April 1912.
2 *The Sinking of the Titanic and Great Sea Disasters*, Logan Marshall, p. 52.
3 *The Sinking of the Titanic*, Jay Henry Mobray, 1912.
4 *Indianapolis Star*, 19 April 1912.
5 *New York Herald*, 20 April 1912.
6 *Brooklyn Daily Eagle*, 21 April 1912.
7 *Philadelphia Evening Bulletin*, 20 April 1912.
8 'Shots in the Dark', Bill Wormstedt and Tad Fitch, wormstedt.com/Titanic/shots/shots.htm
9 *Washington Post*, 19 April 1912.
10 *The Sinking of the Titanic*, Jay Henry Mobray, 1912.
11 Vera Dick memoir written for the *Washington Post*, 19 April 1912.
12 *The Sinking of the Titanic*, Jay Henry Mobray, 1912.
13 *Bureau County Republican*, 2 May 1912.
14 *New York Herald*, 19 April 1912.
15 *Cedar Rapids Evening Gazette*, 24 June 1912.
16 *Brooklyn Daily Eagle*, 19 April 1912.
17 *New York Herald*, 19 April 1912.
18 *New York Times*, 19 April 1912.
19 *New York Sun*, 19 April 1912.
20 *The Weekly Telegraph*, 10 May 1912 (quoted in *Titanic: Waiting for Orders*, Philip Littlejohn).
21 *Boston Globe*, 20 April 1912.
22 *The Sinking of the Titanic*, Jay Henry Mobray, 1912.

23 *The Toronto World*, 20 April 1912.
24 *The Evening Journal* (Wilmington), 20 April 1912.
25 *New York Tribune*, 19 April 1912.
26 *New York American*, 26 April 1912.
27 *New York Press*, 22 April 1912.
28 *Providence Evening Bulletin*, 22 April 1912.
29 *Chicago Daily Tribune*, 20 April 1912.
30 *New York World*, 19 April 1912.
31 *Daily Sketch*, 30 April 1912, courtesy Paul Lee.
32 *Western Daily Mercury*, 29 April 1912, courtesy Paul Lee.
33 *Hampshire Independent*, 4 May 1912, courtesy Paul Lee.
34 *London Daily News*, 29 April 1912, courtesy Paul Lee.
35 *London Daily Chronicle*, 29 April 1912.
36 *New York Sun*, 23 April 1912.
37 J.O. McGiffin letter to Diana Bristow, facsimile published in *Titanic R.I.P.*, Diana Bristow. Harlo Press, 1989, p. 172.
38 *London Daily Telegraph*, 29 April 1912, courtesy Paul Lee.
39 *Western Daily Mercury*, 29 April 1912. Quoted in *The Mammoth Book of the Titanic*, Geoff Tibballs. Carroll & Graf, 2002, p. 336.
40 *London Daily Chronicle*, 29 April 1912.
41 *Chicago Daily Tribune*, 20 April 1912.
42 *The Night Lives On*, Walter Lord. William Morrow & Co., 1986.
43 *Washington Post*, 21 April 1912.
44 *The New York Times*, 26 June 1915.
45 *The Night Lives On*, Walter Lord. William Morrow & Co., 1986.
46 *New York Herald*, 20 April 1912.
47 'C.Q.D.', Richard Williams, 1962. Historical Society of Pennsylvania.
48 *Dumfries & Galloway Standard and Advertiser*, 11 May 1912.
49 Susanne Störmer email to Tad Fitch, 22 May 1999, courtesy Tad Fitch.
50 'The Loss of the *Titanic*', Washington Dodge. (Address given at the Commonwealth Club in San Francisco, 11 May 1912.)
51 *New Haven Evening Register*, 22 April 1912.
52 *Scranton Times*, 19 April 1912.
53 *Daily Sketch*, May 1912. Quoted in 'Shots in the Dark', Bill Wormstedt and Tad Fitch, wormstedt.com/Titanic/shots/shots.htm
54 *London Daily Chronicle*, 30 April 1912.
55 *Ilford Graphic*, 10 May 1912.
56 Thomas Whiteley interview, *Louisville Courier-Journal*, 21 April 1912.
57 *Western Daily Mercury*, 29 April 1912.
58 *Ibid*.
59 *Daily Chronicle*, 29 April 1912. This unnamed steward supplied his name and address to the newspaper reporter and was perfectly willing to vouch for the truth of his statements.

CHAPTER 11

1 *New York World*, 17 April 1912.
2 *Daily Sketch*, 18 April 1912.
3 *Buffalo Morning Express*, 16 April 1912.
4 Senate *Titanic* Inquiry, p. 1070.
5 *New York Herald*, 16 April 1912.
6 Mark Rowe, 'Race to find £200m treasure inside crumbling *Titanic*', *Independent* on Sunday, UK, 23 July 2000, p. 12, www.independent.co.uk/news/science/race-to-find-pound-200m-treasure-inside-crumbling-titanic-706274.html
7 According to historian Don Lynch, 'Kevin Jones, who is researching the couture on the ship, says the *Times* list is full of inaccuracies.'
8 '*Titanic*'s hidden treasures dismissed as myth by expert; Historian John Eaton gives opinion on sunken liner', *The Times*, UK, 12 September 1985, link.galegroup.com/apps/doc/A117959912/STND?u=lom_kentdl&sid=STND&xid=05274cbf
9 DocsTeach, www.docsteach.org/documents/document/claim-of-laura-moore-as-assignee-of-the-owners-of-certain-cargo
10 *Titanic* Claims 8183, Limitation of Liability papers, The National Archives (UK).
11 *Richmond Times-Dispatch*, 16 April 1912.
12 *Fogerty's Jewelers' Directory*, 1917–1918, archive.org/stream/fogertysdirector00mrsj/fogertysdirector00mrsj_djvu.txt
13 *Huntington Herald Dispatch*, 17 April 1912.
14 *Fond du Lac Daily Reporter*, 19 April 1912.
15 *Syracuse Post Standard*, 16 April 1912 for information about the registered post.
16 *New York Herald*, 16 April 1912.
17 *New York Times*, 16 April 1912.
18 *Arkansas Gazette*, 21 April 1912.
19 *Bismarck Daily Tribune*, 30 April 1912.
20 *New York Evening Telegram*, 22 April 1912.
21 *Lexington Leader*, 27 April 1912.
22 *New York Herald*, 23 April 1912.
23 *On Board RMS Titanic: Memories of the Maiden Voyage*, George Behe. The History Press, 2012. Original Birnbaum letter courtesy the Alford family.
24 *Waterbury American*, 30 April 1912.
25 *Denver Post*, 26 April 1912.
26 *Oakland Tribune*, 7 May 1912.
27 Limitation of Liability records, National Archives, Bayonne, New Jersey. (While examining these records I made a handwritten notation of the Birnbaum information but did not record the specific document in which it appeared.)
28 'Connecting to the *Titanic* in Montclair', 14 March 2015, www.northjersey.com/community-news/connecting-local-history-and-the-titanic-1.1289265
29 Limitation of Liability document filed Mrs Cardeza.
30 'Daughters of Rescued *Titanic* Passenger Killed in Chicago Holocaust', *New York Times*, 17 April 1912.
31 *New York Times*, 15 April 1913.
32 '*Titanic* Victim's Descendants Hope for Lost Jewels', 18 April 2012, www.jckonline.com/editorial-article/titanic-victims-descendants-hope-for-lost-jewels

33 www.encyclopedia-titanica.org/community/threads/how-many-died-on-the-carpathia-after-being-rescued.1210/#post-8794, 26 July 2001.
34 www.encyclopedia-titanica.org/community/threads/how-many-died-on-the-carpathia-after-being-rescued.1210/#post-8794, 27 July 2001.
35 Milton J. Long, letter to the Titanic Historical Society, 22 February 1999, courtesy Don Lynch.
36 'Titanic People', Craig Stringer.
37 'A Night to Remember, a Survivor Forgotten: Historian uncovers *Titanic* survivor's path to Napa', *Napa Valley Register*, 15 April 2012, napavalleyregister.com/news/local/historian-uncovers-titanic-survivors-path-to-napa/article_b34ee7ec-868d-11e1-9445-001a4bcf887a.html
38 Phillip Gowan email to Laura Myhre, 26 April 1998.
39 Phillip Gowan email to 'Rebecca', 1 September 1998.
40 Frances Reynolds, 13 September 2017, www.encyclopedia-titanica.org/community/threads/samuel-beard-risien-who-was-he-really.21173/#post-389710
41 Laura Myhre email to George Behe, 22 April 1998.
42 Samuel Beard Risien: 'From the CSS *Alabama* to the *Titanic*', Terry Foenander, July 2001, home.ozconnect.net/tfoen/risien.htm
43 'Echoes from the *Titanic*: Chance puts Texas couple on ill-fated voyage', Bob Belcher, *Corsicana Daily Sun*, 9 April 2012, www.corsicanadailysun.com/news/local_news/echoes-from-the-titanic-chance-puts-texas-couple-on-ill/article_c618d289-52fa-5ed3-a85b-1fcbcb582f0c.html. Fran Reynolds was the Risiens' great-granddaughter.
44 *St Louis Post Dispatch*, 1 May 1912.
45 *New York World*, 23 April 1912.
46 *Philadelphia Evening Bulletin*, 22 April 1912.
47 *The Daily Home News*, 23 April 1912.
48 *The New York Times*, 22 April 1912.
49 'Titanic People', Craig Stringer.
50 '*Titanic* Sinking Hit Home' by Dick Shearer, Lansdale Historical Society. (Information for this story was compiled from issues of the *Lansdale Reporter*, the *Montgomeryville Spirit* and numerous *Titanic*-related websites. In truth, it is unknown whether or not *Titanic*'s steerage passengers were permitted to consign valuables to the ship's purser.)
51 Robert Bell (one of Maud van Billiard's grandchildren), courtesy North Wales Historic Commission. '*Titanic* Sinking Hit Home', Dick Shearer. Lansdale Historical Society. (Information for this story was compiled from issues of the *Lansdale Reporter*, the *Montgomeryville Spirit* and numerous *Titanic*-related websites.)
52 List of recovered bodies and effects.
53 Limitation of Liability records, National Archives, Bayonne, New Jersey. (While examining these records I made a handwritten notation of the van Billiard information but did not record the specific document in which it appeared.)
54 Courtesy Linda Greaves, who examined and transcribed the original documents for me.
55 *On a Sea of Glass*, Tad Fitch, Kent Layton and Bill Wormstedt. From the typed notes of August Wennerström used in his talks about the disaster, preserved by the Wennerström family. Courtesy Jerry Wennerström and Mike Herbold.
56 Francis Dyke letter (27 April 1912), courtesy Dartmouth Heritage Museum.

57 Arminias Wiseman 1953 account, *Commutator*, Vol. 20, No. 2, August–October 1996, pp. 18–19.
58 *The Sinking of the Titanic*, Jay Henry Mobray, 1912.
59 *Newark Star*, 2 May 1912.

CHAPTER 12

1 Douglas affidavit to the Senate *Titanic* Inquiry, 2 May 1912.
2 *When We Went First Class*, Ellen Williamson, p. 112.
3 *Discretions and Indiscretions*, Lady Duff Gordon (Jarrolds, 1932).
4 *Seattle Daily Times*, 22 & 23 April 1912.
5 *Liberty Magazine*, 23 April 1932.
6 Minahan, 11 May 1912 letter to Senator William Alden Smith, Senate *Titanic* Inquiry.
7 Smith deposition to the Senate *Titanic* Inquiry, 20 May 1912.
8 Thayer affidavit quoted in *Titanic*: *The Full Story of a Tragedy*, Michael Davie.
9 'Sealed Orders', Helen Candee, *Collier's Weekly*, 4 May 1912.
10 *The Truth About the Titanic*, Archibald Gracie.
11 *New York Tribune*, 25 November 1912.
12 *Titanic Survivor*, Violet Jessop.
13 *Rhode Island Sunday Magazine*, 15 April 1962.
14 Peuchen, Senate *Titanic* Inquiry.
15 Rosenbaum memoir, 1 April 1934, www.charlespellegrino.com/passengers/edith-russell/
16 *A Night to Remember*, Walter Lord, 1976 Edition, p. 203.
17 *The Truth About the Titanic*, Archibald Gracie.
18 Margaretta Spedden diary, *Commutator*, Vol. 16, No. 3 (November 1992–January 1993).
19 Martha Stephenson and Elizabeth Eustis, *The Titanic – Our Story*, courtesy Christina Gorch and Jacque Gorch.
20 Thayer letter to Judge Charles Long, 23 April 1912.
21 *Portland Oregonian*, 27 April 1912, courtesy John Lamoreau.
22 *New York World*, 21 April 1912.
23 *Minneapolis Tribune*, 21 April 1912.

CHAPTER 13

1 *The Truth About the Titanic*, Archibald Gracie. Mitchell Kennerley, 1913, p. 31.
2 This imaginative claim about the 'soot-blackened' body seems to have originated in the 1998 book *Unsinkable*, Daniel Butler.
3 *The Sinking of the Titanic and Great Sea Disasters*, Logan Marshall, 1912.
4 'C.Q.D.', Richard Williams, 1962. Historical Society of Pennsylvania.
5 *Wilmington Evening Journal*, 20 April 1912.
6 *Commutator*, Vol. 23, No. 147, 1999, p. 166. Transcribed by Jim Harper.
7 *The Outlook*, 27 April 1912, courtesy Randy Bigham.
8 *I'm Going to See What Has Happened*, Gerald Nummi and Janet White.

9 *Western Daily Mercury*, 29 April 1912. Quoted in *The Mammoth Book of the Titanic*, Geoff Tibbals. Carroll & Graf, 2002, p. 336.
10 www.paullee.com/titanic/BBC1956.php
11 Lord-Macquitty Collection, National Maritime Museum, Paul Lee website, www.paullee.com/titanic/whurst.html
12 *Titanic Survivor*, Violet Jessop.
13 Charles Lightoller, British *Titanic* Inquiry.
14 Charles Lightoller, *Christian Science Journal*, October 1912.
15 *Titanic and Other Ships*, Charles Lightoller. Ivor, Nicholson & Watson, 1935.
16 'On Board the Titanic', Commander C.H. Lightoller, *The Listener*, 4 November 1936, Vol. XVI, No. 408.
17 *Western Daily Mercury*, 29 April 1912, courtesy Paul Lee.
18 *Belfast Newsletter*, 29 April 1912.
19 *Manchester Guardian*, 29 April 1912.
20 Photocopy of deposition sold by Henry Aldridge & Son Auction House, September 2002.
21 *Arkansas Gazette* (Little Rock), 20 April 1912.
22 *New York Herald*, 20 April 1912.
23 *Manchester Guardian*, 20 April 1912.
24 *Western Daily Mercury*, 29 April 1912, courtesy Paul Lee.
25 *Manchester Guardian*, 29 April 1912.
26 *Boston Herald*, 21 April 1912.
27 *Evening Telegraph* (Dundee), 29 April 1912, courtesy Dr Paul Lee.
28 *London Daily Telegraph*, 30 April 1912.
29 *Syracuse Post-Standard*, 27 April 1930. Courtesy Mike Poirier.
30 *Atlantic Daily Bulletin*, No. 2, 2002, pp. 20–21. *Commutator*, issue No. 26, April 1970, pp. 4–15.
31 Emily Ryerson, Senate *Titanic* Inquiry.
32 *The Sinking of the S.S. Titanic*, John B. Thayer, 1940.
33 *Philadelphia Evening Bulletin*, 14 April 1932.
34 *Western Daily Mercury*, 29 April 1912. Quoted in *The Mammoth Book of the Titanic*, Geoff Tibbals. Carroll & Graf, 2002, p. 336.
35 *Washington Post Semi-Monthly Magazine*, 26 May 1912.
36 *Sphere*, 25 May 1912.
37 *St Louis Star*, 28 April 1912.
38 Patrick Dillon, British *Titanic* Inquiry.
39 *Illinois State Register*, 21 April 1912.
40 *The Sinking of the S.S. Titanic*, John B. Thayer, 1940.

CHAPTER 14

1 *Detroit News*, 21 April 1912.

CHAPTER 15

1 *Niagara Falls Gazette*, 19 April 1912.
2 *New York Press*, 20 April 1912.

3 *New York Daily Star*, 20 April 1912.
4 *New York Herald*, 20 April 1912.
5 *Chicago Tribune*, 21 April 1912.
6 *Brooklyn Daily Eagle*, 21 April 1912.
7 Mahala Douglas affidavit, Senate *Titanic* Inquiry.
8 *Berkshire Evening Eagle*, 22 April 1912.
9 *Lost Voices from the Titanic*, Nick Barratt, pp. 234–35.
10 Emily Ryerson testimony, Limitation of Liability hearings.
11 Grace Bowen, Limitation of Liability hearings.
12 Bruce Ismay testimony, Limitation of Liability hearings.
13 *New York Times*, 25 June 1915.
14 Bruce Ismay, Limitation of Liability hearings; also *Titanic: an Illustrated History*, Don Lynch & Ken Marschall.
15 *New York American*, 22 April 1912. A later article in the *Philadelphia Inquirer* of 23 April 1912 says that 'two sources' gave 'emphatic denials' that Mrs Widener had asked her brother-in-law Joseph Widener to place the substance of this conversation before the Senate *Titanic* Inquiry, but it is unclear whether these 'two sources' were denying the existence of the conversation itself or if they were simply denying that Mrs Widener instructed her brother-in-law to send the information to Washington.
16 Alfred Shiers testimony, 1913 Limitation of Liability hearings.
17 Copy of Amended Answer of Frederick K. Seward and Others, Box 19, A55-279, Folder 2A, Amended Answers, The National Archives (UK).
18 www.encyclopedia-titanica.org/ryan-v-osnc.html

CHAPTER 16

1 Sources for this chapter include *Los Angeles Herald*, 17 April 1912; *Rockford Republic*, 18 & 19 April 1912; *Chicago Record Herald*, 26 April 1912; *Aurora Beacon-News*, 17, 18, 19, 22 & 25 April 1912; *Joliet News*, 25 April 1912; and a personal interview with Eleanor Johnson Shuman (Mrs. Johnson's daughter, who was one year old in 1912.).

CHAPTER 18

1 Logan Marshall, *The Sinking of the Titanic and Great Sea Disasters*, 1912.
2 *The Daily Herald*, 15 April 1984.
3 *On Board RMS Titanic: Memories of the Maiden Voyage*, George Behe.
4 *Ibid*.
5 Daniel Buckley, Senate *Titanic* Inquiry, p. 1020.
6 *Ogdensburg Journal*, 4 May 1912.
7 *Washington Herald*, 22 April 1912.
8 *Southern Evening Echo*, 16 April 1962, courtesy Brian Ticehurst. Also *The Irish Aboard Titanic*, Senan Molony.
9 Pre-1973 letter from 'Leit' to Ed Kamuda in which he translated Mrs Sandström's account.
10 *Des Moines Register*, 26 March 1972.
11 Harold Lowe, Senate *Titanic* Inquiry, pp. 407–8.
12 *Ibid*., p. 1100.

13 E.g. Hugh Woolner, *New York Sun*, 19 April 1912.
14 'My Great-Grandfather Died on the *Titanic*', Dr Josyann Abisaab, abisaab.wordpress.com/stories/my-great-grandfather-died-on-the-titanic
15 *The Charleroi Mail*, 23 April 1912.
16 *Michigan City News Dispatch*, January 1980.
17 *Gary Evening Post*, 24 April 1912.
18 'Survivor of *Titanic* Tells of Coward in Woman's Garb', *Philadelphia Inquirer*, 15 April 1962.
19 *Washington Evening Star*, 17 February 1959. Also *Sunday Independent* (Wilkes-Barre, PA), 10 April 1960.
20 'True *Titanic* love story remembered by surviving family members in Burton', www.mlive.com/entertainment/flint/index.ssf/2012/04/titanic_love_story_recounted_b.html
21 A footnote on the often-unreliable Encyclopedia Titanica website says, 'It is not clear which collapsible boats were involved but Michael thought his boat was Collapsible D and that his mother and sister were in C.'
22 *Detroit Free Press*, 20 April 1912.
23 *Grandma Survived the Titanic*, Joseph L. Thomas. Trafford Publishing, 2002.
24 Personal communication with the author.
25 *Unsinkable Bridget: Reflections of a Titanic Survivor*, Mary Higgins, self-published, 1985.
26 *Ibid.*
27 *Daily Times*, quoted in *The Irish Aboard Titanic*, Senan Molony, p. 6.
28 Jay Henry Mobray, *The Sinking of the Titanic.*
29 *New York Times*, 20 April 1912.
30 *St Louis Globe Democrat*, 21 April 1912.
31 *Washington Times*, 22 April 1912.
32 *Winnipeg Tribune*, 26 April 1912.
33 *Montreal Star*, 29 April 1912.
34 Gilnagh interview recorded in 1957 by BBC News.
35 www.encyclopedia-titanica.org/i-survived-the-sinking-of-the-titanic.html
36 *New York American*, 28 April 1912.
37 '*Titanic* Odyssey', William Kashatus, 18 April 2012, www.citizensvoice.com/2012/04/07/titanic-odyssey
38 'Manitowoc man had eleven relatives on *Titanic*, only one survived', 14 April 2012, www.htrnews.com/article/20120415/MAN0101/107100004/-1/7daysarchives/Manitowoc-man-had-11-relatives-Titanic-only-1-survived
39 'Man Shot At 6 Times On Titanic Is Finally Saved', *Chicago American*, Tuesday, 22 April 1912, p. 2, c. 5.
40 Kashatus credited Mae Thomas (daughter of survivor Thelma Thomas) with helping him with his article, but it is unknown if this relative had anything to do with the reporter's undocumented claim that Bert Johns dressed as a woman. The present author's email query to Kashatus yielded no response.
41 Bruce Ismay, Senate *Titanic* Inquiry.
42 George Rowe, Senate *Titanic* Inquiry.
43 *Daily Enterprise* (Burlington, New Jersey), 20 April 1912.
44 *Detroit News*, 24 April 1912.
45 Hugh Woolner, Senate *Titanic* Inquiry, pp. 886–7.

46 *Bureau County Republican*, 2 May 1912
47 *Cedar Rapids Evening Gazette*, 25 June 1912.
48 *Hudson Dispatch*, 20 April 1912.
49 *Bournemouth Daily Echo*, 30 April 1912.
50 *Limerick Echo*, 7 May 1912.
51 *Daily Telegraph*, 20 April 1912.
52 *Denver Post*, 19 April 1912.
53 *Magyarorszag* (1980), courtesy Kalman Tanito.
54 'My Great-Grandfather Died on the *Titanic*', Dr Josyann Abisaab, abisaab.wordpress.com/stories/my-great-grandfather-died-on-the-titanic
55 *Chicago American*, 25 April 1912.
56 'EXCLUSIVE. THE MAN WHO ESCAPED THE TITANIC DRESSED AS A WOMAN---IDENTIFIED', *Titanic*'s Secrets Unfold, titanicsecrets.blogspot.com/2012/04/exclusive.html
57 'A *Titanic* Love Story – Difficult Lives of Survivors Make Fitting Sequels to Sea Mystery', *Richmond Times-Dispatch*, 15 April 1997.
58 '*Titanic* Odyssey', William Kashatus, 18 April 2012, www.citizensvoice.com/2012/04/07/titanic-odyssey
59 *Toronto Star*, 25 April 1912.
60 *Hamilton Spectator*, 25 April 1912.
61 'Neshan Krekorian and the *Titanic*', *The Standard* (St Catharines, Ontario, Canada), article by Don Fraser, 10 April 2001.
62 'C.Q.D.', Richard Williams, 1962. Historical Society of Pennsylvania.
63 Transcription in the author's collection.
64 'Tells *Titanic*'s Tragic Sequel', *New York Sun*, 14 April 1937.
65 'Gilbert M. Tucker Jr (1880–1968): *Titanic* survivor', Paul Grondahl, 5 December 2013, www.timesunion.com/local/article/Gilbert-M-Tucker-Jr-1880-1968-Titanic-4983854.php
66 www.stamfordadvocate.com/news/article/greenwich-women-forever-changed-by-titanic-ordeal-3482752.php
67 *Fairmont West Virginian*, 11 February 1922.
68 'Survivor of *Titanic* Tells of Coward in Woman's Garb', *Philadelphia Inquirer*, 15 April 1962.
69 '*Titanic* Odyssey', William Kashatus, 18 April 2012.

CHAPTER 19

1 *The Irish Echo*, 25 January 1998; *Nationwide*, RTE-1, 2 February 1998, www.derryjournal.com/news/local/from-titanic-good-bye-all-a-message-that-still-resounds-for-therese-a-century-on-1-3717830
2 *The Irish Echo*, 25 January 1998; *Nationwide*, RTE-1, 2 February 1998.
3 *New York Tribune*, 5 January 1913.
4 *Buffalo Courier*, 6 January 1913.
5 *New York Times*, 13 April 1913.
6 *Syracuse Daily Journal*, 19 April 1913.
7 *Chicago Tribune*, 1 August 1912, p. 1, c. 5.
8 *The Niagara Falls Gazette*, 1 August 1912

9 *Ibid.*
10 *Buffalo Courier*, 2 August 1912.
11 *New York Sun*, 1 August 1912.
12 *The Times*, 13 September 1912.
13 *Troy Times*, 5 December 1912.
14 *Canberra Times*, 29 November 1928, courtesy Steve Hall.
15 *Chicago Tribune*, 20 October 1912, p. 1, c. 6.
16 *Western Daily Mercury*, 25 April 1912.
17 Information supplied by Jacques Lefebvre, great-nephew of Marie Lefebvre (Mathilde Lefebvre's mother) on Facebook's RMS *Titanic* Official page on 29 November 2020. The only press account (with a photo of the note) that I've been able to find is located at www.acadienouvelle.com/actualites/2017/11/27/lettre-dune-jeune-victime-titanic-aurait-ete-retrouvee-famille-de-dieppe

Bibliography

Books

American Kennel Club Stud Book, Vol. 29. Published by the American Kennel Club, 1912.
British *Titanic* Inquiry, 1912.
'C.Q.D.', Richard Williams, 1962. Manuscript at the Historical Society of Pennsylvania.
Death of a Purser, Frankie McElroy. Author House, 2011.
Discretions and Indiscretions, Lady Duff Gordon. Jarrolds, 1932.
Elizabeth Nye – Titanic Survivor, Dave Bryceson. Streets Publishers, 2009.
Grandma Survived the Titanic, Joseph L. Thomas, Trafford Publishing, 2002.
I'll See You in New York, David Haisman. Boolarong Press, 1999.
I'm Going to See What Has Happened, Gerald Nummi and Janet White. J.A. White, 1996.
The Irish Aboard Titanic, Senan Molony. Wolfhound Press, 2000.
The Life and Times of Andrew Jackson Sloper, William Sloper. Privately published, 1949.
London Statutes from 1750 to 1907, G.L. Gomme, Vol. II, 1889 to 1907. London City Council, 1907.
The Loss of the SS Titanic, Lawrence Beesley. Houghton, Miflin, 1912.
'The Loss of the *Titanic*', Washington Dodge. (Address given at the Commonwealth Club in San Francisco, 11 May 1912.)
Lost at Sea: Ghost Ships and Other Mysteries, Michael Goss and George Behe. Prometheus Books, 1994.
The Mammoth Book of the Titanic, Geoff Tibbals. Carroll & Graf, 2002.
The Night Lives On, Walter Lord. William Morrow & Co., 1986.
A Night to Remember, Walter Lord. Henry Holt & Co., 1955.
Not My Time to Die, Lilly Setterdahl. Nordstjernan Forlag, New York, 2012.
On a Sea of Glass, Tad Fitch, Kent Layton and Bill Wormstedt. Amberley, 2012.
On Board RMS Titanic: Memories of the Maiden Voyage, George Behe. The History Press, 2012.
'Reports from the Commissioners, Inspectors and Others', Vol. XXXVII, 1914 (Addendum B – Regulations, 1912).
Shadow of the Titanic, Eva Hart & Ronald Denney, Greenwich University Press, 1994.
The Sinking of the S.S. Titanic, John B. Thayer. Privately published, 1940.
The Sinking of the Titanic, Jay Mobray. The Minter Company, 1912.

The Sinking of the Titanic and Great Sea Disasters, Logan Marshall. L.T. Myers, 1912.
Soldier of Fortune, Joyce Sharpey-Schafer. Privately published in Utica, N.Y., 1984.
Stead, the Man, Estelle Stead. William Rider & Sons, 1918.
Titanic and Other Ships, Charles Lightoller. Ivor, Nicholson & Watson, 1935.
Titanic: Destination Disaster, Jack Eaton and Charles Haas. Patrick Stephens Inc., 1987.
Titanic: The Full Story of a Tragedy, Michael Davie. The Bodley Head, 1986.
The Titanic: Our Story, Martha Stephenson and Elizabeth Eustis. Privately published, 1912.
Titanic: The Ship Magnificent, Bruce Beveridge et. al. The History Press, 2008.
Titanic: Triumph and Tragedy, Jack Eaton and Charles Haas. W.W. Norton, 1986.
'Titanic Disaster: Hearings Before a Subcommittee of the Committee on Commerce', United States Senate, Sixty-Second Congress, Second Session, 1912.
The Titanic Files: A Paranormal Sourcebook, George Behe. Lulu.com Press, 2015.
'Titanic People', Craig Stringer. (CD-ROM). Family History Indexes, 2003.
Titanic R.I.P., Diana Bristow, Harlo Press, 1989.
Titanic Survivor, Violet Jessop and John Maxtone-Graham. Sheridan House 1997.
Titanic Voices, Donald Hyslop et. al. Southampton City Council, 1994.
Tramps and Ladies, James Bisset. Criterion, 1959.
The Truth About the Titanic, Archibald Gracie. Mitchell Kennerly, 1913.
Unsinkable: The Full Story of RMS Titanic, Daniel Butler. Stackpole Books, 1998.
Unsinkable Bridget: Reflections of a Titanic Survivor, Mary Higgins. Self-published, 1985.
When We Went First Class, Ellen Williamson. Doubleday & Co., 1977.
William McMaster Murdoch: A Career at Sea, Susanne Störmer. Stormbreakers Verlag, 2002.

Periodicals

Albany Times-Union
Arkansas Gazette (Little Rock, Arkansas)
Atlantic City Daily Press
Auburn Citizen
Auburn Daily Advertiser
Auburn Semi-Weekly Journal
Aurora Beacon-News (Illinois)
Bath Chronicle
Belfast Newsletter
Berkshire Evening Eagle
Bismarck Daily Tribune
Boston Globe
Boston Herald
Bournemouth Daily Echo
Brooklyn Daily Eagle
Buffalo Courier
Buffalo Morning Express
Bureau County Republican
Canberra Times
Carlinville Daily Enquirer (Illinois)
Cassell's Magazine
Cedar Rapids Evening Gazette
The Charleroi Mail
Charlevoix County Herald (Michigan)
Chicago American
Chicago Record Herald
Chicago Tribune
Cincinnati Enquirer
Collier's Weekly
Corsicana Daily Sun (Texas)
Daily Chronicle
Daily Enterprise (Burlington, New Jersey)
The Daily Herald (London)
The Daily Home News
Daily Mirror
Daily Sketch
Daily Times
Dayton Herald
Denver Post
Des Moines Register
Detroit News
Detroit News Times
Dowagiac News (Michigan)
Dumfries & Galloway Standard and Advertiser

East Kent Gazette
The Evening Record (Greenville, Pennsylvania)
Evening Telegraph (Dundee)
The Evening Journal (Ottawa)
The Evening Journal (Wilmington, Delaware)
Fairmont West Virginian
Fond du Lac Daily Reporter (Wisconsin)
Gary Evening Post (Indiana)
Gazette Times
Geelong Advertiser
Hamilton Spectator (Ontario)
Hampshire Independent
Harper's Weekly
Hudson Dispatch
Huntington Herald Dispatch (West Virginia)
Ilford Graphic
Illinois State Register (Chicago)
Independent on Sunday (London)
Indianapolis Star
The Irish Echo
Irish Independent
Irish News – Global Edition
Joliet News (Illinois)
Lexington Leader (Kentucky)
Liberty Magazine
Limerick Echo
London Daily Chronicle
London Daily Express
London Daily Mirror
London Daily News
London Daily Telegraph
London Globe and Traveller
Los Angeles Herald
Louisville Courier-Journal
Manchester Guardian
Manitoba Free Press
Michigan City News Dispatch
Minneapolis Star & Tribune
Minneapolis Tribune
Mitchell Daily Republic
Montour Falls Free Press
Montreal Star
Mt Vernon Daily Argus
National Magazine
Newark Star
New Britain Herald
New Haven Evening Register
New York American
New York Daily Star
New York Daily Graphic
New York Daily Tribune
New York Evening Telegram
New York Evening World
New York Herald
New York Press
New York Sun
New York Times
New York Tribune
Niagara Falls Gazette
Niles Daily News
Northern Constitution
Oakland Tribune
Ogdensburg Journal (New York)
The Outlook
Philadelphia Evening Bulletin
Philadelphia Inquirer
Port Huron Times Herald
Portland Evening Express and Daily Advertiser (Maine)
Portland Oregonian
Powell County Post (Deer Lodge, Montana)
Providence Evening Bulletin (Rhode Island)
Providence Evening News
Rhode Island Sunday Magazine
Richmond Dispatch
Richmond Times-Dispatch
Riverside Daily Press
Rockford Republic (Illinois)
St Louis Globe Democrat
St Louis Post Dispatch
St Louis Star
St Paul Dispatch
Scranton Times
Seattle Daily Times
Southampton Evening Echo
Southern Evening Echo
Sphere
The Standard (St Catharines, Ontario)
Sunday Independent
Syracuse Daily Journal
Syracuse Post Standard (New York)
Tavistock Gazette
The Times (London)
Toronto World
Troy Times (New York)
Washington Evening Star

Washington Herald
Washington Post
Washington Post Semi-Monthly Magazine
Washington Times
Waterbury American (Connecticut)
The Weekly Telegraph
Western Daily Mercury
Western Independent
Western Star
Whitby Gazette
Winnipeg Tribune
Worcester Telegram
World Telegram

Historical Journals

The Atlantic Daily Bulletin (British Titanic Society)
The Commutator (Titanic Historical Society)
Voyage (Titanic International Society)
White Star Journal (Irish Titanic Historical Society)

Archives

Dartmouth Heritage Museum
National Maritime Museum: Lord-Macquitty Collection (Greenwich, UK)
National Archives (New York Branch, Bayonne, New Jersey)
Paris Museum of Letters and Manuscripts
Public Record Office (now The National Archives of the UK)
Southampton City Council

Online Resources

Bill Wormstedt's website: wormstedt.com/Titanic/shots/shots.htm
Dr Paul Lee's website: paullee.com/titanic/mslocombe.html
Dr Charles Pellegrino's website: charlespellegrino.com
Encyclopedia Titanica: encyclopedia-titanica.org
Titanic-Discuss forum: alt.history.ocean-liners.titanic
Titanic Passenger and Crew Study Group of Facebook

Online Articles

'Children of the *Titanic*: Their story – Their words', www.adamslib.org/titanic/Children%20of%20the%20Titanic.pdf

'Connecting to the *Titanic* in Montclair', 14 March 2015, www.northjersey.com/community-news/connecting-local-history-and- the-titanic-1.1289265

'Frenchies and the *Titanic*', frenchbulldogclub.org/about/our-clubs-history/frenchies-and-the-titanic

'Gilbert M. Tucker Jr. (1880–1968): *Titanic* survivor', Paul Grondahl. www.timesunion.com/local/article/Gilbert-M-Tucker-Jr-1880-1968-Titanic-4983854.php

'Greenwich Woman Forever Changed by *Titanic* Ordeal', stamfordadvocate.com/news/article/Greenwich-women-forever-changed-by-Titanic-ordeal-3482752.php

'Manitowoc man had 11 relatives on *Titanic*, only 1 survived', David Hennessey, 14 April 2012, www.htrnews.com/article/20120415/MAN0101/107100004/-1/7daysarchives/Manitowoc-man-had-11-relatives-Titanic-only-1-survived

'My Great-Grandfather Died on the *Titanic*', Dr Josyann Abisaab, abisaab.wordpress.com/stories/my-great-grandfather-died-on-the-titanic

'*Titanic* Odyssey', William Kashatus, www.citizensvoice.com/arts-living/titanic-odyssey-1.1295760

'*Titanic*'s Secrets Unfold', George Jacub, titanicsecrets.blogspot.com/2012/04/07/titanic-odyssey/

Businesses

Henry Aldridge & Son Auction House

Index

The History Press
The destination for history
www.thehistorypress.co.uk